Running from Home

A Memoir

Rita B. Ross

Hamilton Books
A member of
The Rowman & Littlefield Publishing Group
Lanham • Boulder • New York • Toronto • Plymouth, UK

Copyright © 2008 by
Hamilton Books
4501 Forbes Boulevard
Suite 200
Lanham, Maryland 20706
Hamilton Books Acquisitions Department (301) 459-3366

Estover Road
Plymouth PL6 7PY
United Kingdom

Library of Congress Control Number: 2009924798
ISBN: 978-0-7618-4562-1 (paperback : alk. paper)
eISBN: 978-0-7618-4563-8

To my family members: aunts, uncles, cousins, grandparents, and friends
who were murdered by the Nazis,
while the "good people" stood by and did nothing.

To the righteous Gentiles who helped to save countless persons
at the risk of losing their own lives.

To the courageous and outspoken few who are fighting
genocide, ignorance, prejudice even today,
because so many have not learned the futility of war.

Contents

Acknowledgments

I am deeply indebted to many people who helped and encouraged me in this endeavor. My husband, Dan, the love of my life urged me on, researched and corroborated my memories, checked for historical accuracy, took me on a trip to Poland to validate my early impressions, made all the computer adjustments, suggested a title, resurrected old documents and photographs, and stood by me encouragingly while I went back to explore my painful past.

My editor, shrink, teacher and mentor, Melinda Blau who was relentless in getting me to do the best I was capable of, forced me to go back to my past and dig further than I wanted to, kept me focused, was always available for consultations. She empowered and encouraged me by saying "I know you can do better than that." In the process, she helped me tackle the destructive roots lodged in my heart, bring them to light and give up my ongoing chronic bouts with depression.

To my agent Anne Devlin who encouraged me to stick with the task, made loads of helpful suggestions and held my hand when I felt lost. To my loyal readers, I thank you from the bottom of my heart. Your eager willingness to read through this manuscript helped, encouraged and validated my effort: Leora Chalow Blumenthal, who read through the manuscript several times, making suggestions, telling me what was confusing and needed to be addressed to make my characters more sympathetic, was a sounding board for me via the telephone, Bridie Powers, my friend, who encouraged me and told me what was missing for her, made suggestions as to what needed amplification, and to Rosalie Shaw, a role model, friend and ally for her enthusiasm, her corrections and suggestions.

Prologue

I am sitting on a cold train surrounded by a pack of growling wolves, scratching at the windows, salivating, and howling. Their sharp, jagged teeth, glistening tongues and gums are dripping blood. They pant loudly. The only barriers between me and the wolves are the shards of broken glass left in the windows of the train. I try to scream, but I can't get a sound out of my throat.

By the age of nine I had spent most of my life fleeing from the Nazis, but well into adulthood I tried to convince myself that I'd had a normal childhood. My blond, blue-eyed Aryan-looking (but Jewish) mother, wanting to spare my brother and me from the horrifying truth, told us that our flight was all part of an adventure. None of it mattered, not the loss of our home and everything we owned, not the hiding, freezing and hunger, not the horrors of the Krakow ghetto. I was cautioned not to complain, because all we endured was part of the adventure bringing us closer to America to see the father I barely remembered. Each new terrifying situation demanded that I become someone else—a Nazi girl in Vienna, a Catholic in Poland, and a Jew in our last stop a POW camp in Germany.

The hoped for "new life" in America did not end as promised. I had to continue being someone else, trying to fit in with my peers, but always feeling like an outsider. My beautiful, once strong, and courageous, mother subjugated herself to my domineering and bitter father, a man utterly unlike the Prince Charming I had conjured in my fantasies. When I voiced a fear, a hurt or a desire, I was told to be grateful, count my blessings and think of our unfortunate relatives who perished during the war. Any expressions of sadness and pain were dismissed as exaggeration or lack of gratitude. To gain approval and love from my mother, I had to silence any emotion that did not serve her denial.

Even as an adult, I did not consider myself a "Holocaust survivor." Certainly, I had been hungry, scared, and freezing cold, but I never experienced starvation, beatings, mutilation, and didn't even have a number tattooed on my forearm. When the German government began offering monetary reparation to victims of the Holocaust, I refused to pursue it, claiming that I'd had a normal childhood and was not going to revisit it in order to claim something I wasn't entitled to. More recently I was videotaped by Steven Spielberg's SHOAH Foundation repeating over and over again what a wonderful childhood I'd had.

Incredible as it seems now, I didn't link my depression or sense or defeat to the atrocities I witnessed as a young child. Of course I wondered about the nightmares that to this day invade my sleep regularly and leave me with the sense of impending danger.

Neither I nor several therapists I worked with were able to penetrate the armor of denial I had polished over the years. I was so committed to my version of my childhood, that at one point, after reading *Many Lives, Many Masters*, I became convinced that the bouts of depression that began to plague me in early adolescence were rooted in a former existence, maybe a hundred or even a thousand years ago I consulted a past life regression therapist.

The dimly lit office, with new age tape playing in the background and the scent of incense, were welcoming and safe. I told him my story stressing, as I always did, that I was one of the lucky ones, alive and able to leave that chapter of my life behind. I was a high- functioning adult—a good mother, an esteemed teacher, an active member of my Temple, a volunteer in many worthy organizations. Whenever I was asked to lecture young people about that time of my life, I entitled my talk, "A Happy Childhood in Spite of the Holocaust."

The therapist listened intently, jotting notes on a yellow pad. When I finished, I thought he'd offer to put me in a trance so that I could revisit earlier lives. Instead, he sat up straight in his chair, shaking his head.

"Bullshit!" The word shot out his mouth like a spit ball. "Unless you're some kind of a zombie you had to be affected by your early years. Do you really think you had a *normal* childhood? Go home. If you decide to work with me, be prepared to examine your present life before going off on some past life expedition."

I was taken aback, but as Buddhists say, "When the student is ready, the teacher appears." His observations forced me to strip away the layers of denial I had swaddled myself in for over fifty years. Rather than work with yet another therapist, I decided to *write* about my past. I struggled with many drafts putting on paper the same well-rehearsed story. It didn't ring true. The persistent anxieties didn't abate, and the whole exercise left me feeling incomplete. Eventually, I forced myself to face the truth and to see that my hardships did not magically end when I came to America. Reluctantly I began to look beneath my abiding sense of doom and deprivation. The fears, sense of abandonment, and resentments at having been lied to as a child by my mother, the person I loved and trusted more than any other surfaced.

I gained a new—wider—appreciation of the word *survivor*. I have come to accept that most of us are survivors of one thing or another, but in order for us to proceed with our lives we have to acknowledge our past. In coming to this awareness, I dredged up memories that, up until recently were buried in my unconscious, but have haunted me for most of my life. The fruit of that recent and emotionally costly journey is this book.

Photo of my mother, brother and myself
taken at the Liebenau Internment Camp during October 1943.

Part I

RUNNING

Chapter One

Good-Bye

The windshield wipers are rhythmic, repetitive and reassuring. I am just three years old, in a dark, warm car traveling from our home in Vienna to visit my father's parents, my beloved "Omma" and "Oppa" They live in Bartdfeld, about twenty kilometers from us. I am with my father- a special treat because I am seldom alone with him. My little brother is too young to come along and so he stays home with *Mutti* (Mommy) and Liselle, the nanny. I know it is unusual for us to be out late at night. I feel very special and grown up. The sound of humming tires, swishing windshield wipers and sense of quiet companionship fill me with joyful anticipation. Little do I know that this will be the last time we will see Omma and Oppa.

We stop at an intersection. A uniformed officer motions us to open the window. Droplets of rain are hanging from the visor of his officer's cap, waiting to splash onto his dripping nose. He pokes a high beam flashlight into the open window.

"Gutten abend. Ist alles im ordnung?" my father asks.

The officer peers into the car for a few minutes and, seeing me asks for no further identification. He waves us on. Later, when we get home, I will hear my papa tell everyone that he took me along as protection. I am too young to understand that a curfew has been imposed on the Jews in 1939 and cars are stopped at random and searched, and that a blond, blue eyed child is like an insurance policy.

"Maidi!" (My nickname, meaning little girl) Omma and Oppa exclaim, and I look up to see them greeting us from the top of the dark stairs railed with a shiny wooden banister. They live one flight up in a simple, small apartment that has a large dining room table in the parlor and a small bedroom in the back. They are dressed in dull, shapeless clothing. Oppa is wearing a black

velvet *kippa* (skullcap) on his head and Omma's head is covered with an ill-fitting, brown everyday *sheytl*, a wig that all pious Jewish women wear.

We are delighted to see each other. They are without a doubt my favorite people, and I feel like I am theirs. They each take one of my hands and counting to three, swing me inside. The apartment smells delicious, full of chocolates and cookies, especially baked for our visit. Oppa and I play our usual game, a pony ride. He sits on a chair and crosses his legs, while I straddle his shoe and bounce up and down, shouting *schneller, schneller* (faster, faster.) I am happy that my little brother, Moschel, whose nickname is *Bubbi* (little boy), isn't with us. I hate to share the spotlight with him. He can't even talk yet. I know that I am the most adored grandchild from the youngest child in my mother's family and the first grandchild in my father's family, so I am used to everyone vying for my attention. I learn to sing before I talk and love being with doting relatives.

I go into their bedroom— there are two beds separated by a night table and a large black dresser where two wooden dummy heads stand next to each other; twins with no faces. My grandmother uses them for her *sheytls*. I love looking at the heads, especially when they are bare. Bereft of their wigs, their baldness gleams at me, and I reach up to pat them. I wonder if my Omma removes her own head every night when she goes to sleep and places it on the dresser next to the wig stands. The imagined ritual has a magical quality to it. Perhaps, I reason that this is what all women do when they get older.

It is a loving reunion with no hint of what is to come. I eat Omma's cookies, generously offering to take one home for Bubbi and make silver balls and shiny rings out of the tinfoil wrappers used to package the chocolate. I sing my repertoire of German songs, to lots of applause and encouragement. They give me a gift of two red hats, call me "*Rothöpchen*" (Red Riding Hood) and wave goodbye from the top of the steps. This good-bye must have been painful for them, yet they never betray any hint of impending danger.

Shortly after our visit Omma and Oppa will disappear.

Chapter Two

Heil Hitler

It is 1938 and I am parading around our apartment on Josef-gall-gasse. It is a sunny and large apartment, with polished parquet floors and oriental rugs strewn about. Tall windows overlook a courtyard and I am wearing my mother's high heeled shoes, marching around the apartment and singing at the top of my lungs, the SS anthem, *"Haute gehert uns Deutschland, morgen die ganse velt....Sig heil, Sig heil."* I raise my pudgy arm straight into the air as I have seen soldiers doing on the streets. My mother does not try to stop me. A long time from now I will wonder whether she was amused at her little girl's innocence or she believed that sometime in the future my affinity for things German might be useful.

The trees are budding, the earth has the warm, moist smell of the approaching springtime, and Hitler is coming to Austria. We hear him ranting on the radio, his voice echoes through the loudspeakers on the streets and into our open windows. *"Warum ist der mann so bose?* (Why is the man so angry?)" I ask my mother.

The German Werhmacht has crossed the border and on the next day, Hitler announces the *Anshluss* (annexation) of Austria into the Third Reich. The Austrians are ecstatic. Celebrations take place all over Vienna. Colorful paper flags wave frantically, welcoming the soldiers of the Third Reich. The green and beige uniforms, with scarlet, black and white swastika armbands encircle the upper arms of the SS. They are marching like toy soldiers, unsmiling, unbending, ramrod straight in highly polished black leather boots that go up to their stiff knees. Drama and festivity reign in the streets as the marchers keep pace with the patriotic songs.

They extend their right arms and shout "Heil Hitler," never missing a beat. The crowd of civilians lining the streets goes wild, their faces streaked with tears of joy. They respond by raising their right arms in the air, shouting in unison, "*Sig heil.*" Strangers hug each other like family members and children are lifted onto shoulders by excited fathers. Everyone is celebrating, welcoming the strangers into their midst with open arms and grateful hearts.

We go for a walk to the park. I raise my arm to greet everyone on the street, loudly imitating what I have heard so many times; "Heil Hitler," I say to a man with a big, bushy white moustache and a gnarled walking stick.

"Heil Hitler," he responds enthusiastically, and then turns to my mother, "What a sweet little girl." He hands me lollypop and I curtsy and thank him.

I get warm smiles of encouragement from strangers and soldiers alike. They seem delighted by my spirit, with my blue eyes and blond hair— a child so representative of the master race and I am delighted by their attention. Later, when I am an adult and can discuss this time with my mother, I will understand the she cringed at such moments and wondered how long our appearance would protect us.

My father comes into our apartment in tears. I have never seen him so distraught. He sobs loudly. I feel a shock go through my body. I have discovered where my heart is. I am scared.

"They're coming after all the old and helpless people," he tells us. "It won't be much longer before no Jew will be safe here."

He continues between sobs, "I was walking on the street; it was early in the morning when I saw several Chassidim walking back from *shul* (Synagogue) carrying their *tallis* bags. Out of nowhere, young hoodlums came running out and started pulling them by their earlocks and their beards. They knocked the old men to the ground," he went on, "and started kicking them and shouting insults. They pulled out handfuls of hair, knocked out several teeth; blood was running all over the street, while the cultured, civilized Austrians stood by watching and doing nothing." My father looks helpless and frightened. He too has earlocks, although they are safely tucked behind his ears.

"I watched the whole attack and I stood by like a puppet. I knew that there was nothing I could do to protect them without unleashing their violence towards myself. When the hooligans left, I tried to help them up. They were so broken. These dignified old men, humiliated, covered in blood and dirt, with their clothing torn. What is going to happen to us?" He rocks back and forth, clutching his elbows as if to safeguard his body.

"We can't stay here any longer," he tells my mother. "We have to find a way to get out of Austria before we're all victims of this new regime."

Chapter Three

Alex

The lash of anti-Semitism was not new to my father. Born in Czechoslovakia in May of 1906 near a border that was constantly shifting, he attended public elementary school in his home town which was designated as a part of Austria. Long before Hitler came, hatred toward Jews was widespread in the region, even in the little school he attended. Every day when attendance was taken, little Alex Schmelkes was forced to state his religion. While most students answered *Romish Catolish,* Alex and the other Jewish boys answered *Hebraish.*

"Hey Jew boy, what you got under your little hat?" one of the boys would taunt him whenever the teacher was not looking or listening.

"Probably chicken fat and a piece of that dried cardboard that the Jews eat on Easter!" another would respond. They roared at their own joke.

Sometimes, their ridicule took on a more menacing turn. A group of boys would follow Alex home and threaten to get him. One day, when he was walking home from school by himself, he spotted them waiting in a doorway.

"Here he comes, the little Jew," one shouted.

"Get him, get him," said another. Suddenly, one of the bullies grabbed him from behind while his buddy rubbed pork into Alex's face.

"Here's a little treat for you, Christ killer!"

Alex spat and rubbed his arm across his mouth to rid himself of the putrid smell and taste. He could do little more. Telling the authorities would only enrage the offenders, and since none of them would get punished for beating up a Jew boy, they were likely to do it again. They hated him for being smart, for being Jewish and for being alive. He made a decision right there that he was never ever going to tolerate being ridiculed and humiliated again. He was going to fight back, if not with his body, then with his brains.

7

My father's family did not have material wealth. Alex and his eight years younger sister grew up with their parents in a modest Jewish neighborhood in Bartfeldt, an outskirt of Vienna. However, Alex came from a long line of learned and respected Talmudic scholars. Dark and intensely serious, he was an excellent student, studying mathematics, art and science in public school and Judaic studies at home. The rabbis who tutored him predicted that he would follow in the family tradition and become a Torah scholar. He loved his Judaic studies but he dreamed of becoming a doctor or a professor of languages. Torah study was a noble calling, but he was a practical person. Even as a boy, he knew that he could never make a living wage as a scholar.

After elementary school, my father became eligible for "gymnasium," the equivalent of secondary school. Motivated and curious, he yearned for a universal education in addition to his study of ancient Jewish texts. Although he qualified academically Saturday attendance was mandatory. Some of his Jewish friends attended class, but they did not write or take notes. However, Alex's father did not permit him to break the tradition of observing the Sabbath and going to the Synagogue. "No one in our family ever took the easy way out," my grandfather said to him. "Besides, all the boys who go to gymnasium and university come out of there behaving and living like *"goyim."*

My father tried to console himself by remembering the Jewish martyrs of earlier times who had accepted torture and death rather than renounce their religious beliefs. Forgoing higher education was a small price to pay for not defiling his religion, he told himself. But for all his rationalization, he still felt conflicted. And so, on his own, he began to study music, history and the arts. He taught himself French and English and went to concerts in Vienna before Hitler prohibited Jews from attending them. He read extensively, went to museums, and was knowledgeable about cultural and political events. For all his hard work the lack of secondary education closed the door to the formal study he craved. He would never gain entry to the University or to the professional world he so desperately wanted. Even though his self-education ultimately made it possible for him to journey to America and bring his family over, until the day he died, he never got over the disappointment of making do with less.

Chapter Four

Freda

My mother Freda Perlberger was born to a wealthy, business family in Wieliczka, Poland, a small village famous for its salt mines. My grandfather owned a successful leather tannery that supplied the Polish army with leather for coats, boots and saddles. Although her family was concerned with music, the arts, literature and travel, the Perlbergers had deep reverence and respect for religion and had produced great Torah scholars as well. Few Jewish families had the money, the leisure, the creativity and interest in the arts that the Perlbergers had. One of my mother's first cousins, Artur Schnabel, became a world famous concert pianist. Freda, the youngest of eleven children was the beautiful, adored baby of many doting relatives. Two of her brothers and one sister were already married when she was born and she was an aunt as soon as she arrived, with nephews and nieces who were older than she was. In fact, out of deference and respect to age, she couldn't bring herself to call her oldest brother by his given name, and referred to him as "Uncle Moshe."

My mother had the education of all well- bred girls, taking piano, embroidery, and painting lessons to augment her formal education. Her parents were elderly by the time she reached adolescence and it was Freda who was the primary nurse when her father became ill and disabled with arteriosclerosis. She often talked about her father, whom she adored, and how very privileged she felt when he called for her upon awakening. He had a beautiful voice according to my mother and he often sang in order to distract himself from his pain. He died in 1925 long before anyone heard of Hitler.

Freda was in her mid-twenties when she met Alex. She was a tall, slender, graceful, blue-eyed, fun-loving young woman who played the piano, and appreciated art. My father was introduced to her by her sister, who was already living in Vienna. At twenty-eight, he was a dark and handsome man, spoke perfect German, French and English, was self taught and could speak about any current topic. His seriousness was offset by her sense of humor. They got married in August of 1934 and moved to the fairy tale city of Vienna, where the boots of Hitler's soldiers were already rumbling and echoing underground, overhead and throughout the neighborhoods.

My mother loved Vienna, which was an enchanting city; a dream come true especially to a small town girl. The excitement of living in a large apartment building, with neighbors across the hall, and above, and below were a huge novelty for her. These people were nothing like the superstitious peasants, her neighbors in Wieliczka.

The first years of their marriage were idyllic. They had many friends, and my mother had family living close by. Alex and Freda went to concerts every Sunday, and out to coffee houses with friends. She was able to go to museums without having to get on a train and leave the city. Although she had traveled with her family throughout Europe, she enjoyed the many cultural attractions right there on her doorstep. She had become a bona-fide Viennese hausfrau. A large ebony baby grand piano, a Bechstein, dominated the living room. It was the wedding gift my father gave to her, proof of his love for her and the music.

Chapter Five

Vienna

In May of 1935, my mother becomes pregnant. She and my father are thrilled. She does not know what to do to prepare for this event since buying things or even decorating a nursery is not done before the baby is actually born. Superstition, which she never got rid of entirely, forbids it. She enrolls in a *mutter schule*, a school for expectant mothers run by the government. She finds the classes very informative; the modern techniques are so different from the way things were done in Wieliczka. She learns how to diaper a baby, how and why to burp it, what kind of behavior warrants punishment and what needs to be rewarded.

She is determined to be the best mother in Vienna. I finally arrive on a snowy day, February 2, 1936. Later my mother tells me that initially she was disappointed in having given birth to a girl. She so badly wanted a son whom she could name after her beloved father. They do name me Rita, after my grandfather, Reuven, a man I would later think of as my guardian angel, because although dead for many years, the use of his name in a fake birth certificate will save our lives.

My mother quickly gets over her disappointment and loves me like she has never loved before. Liselle, a young woman who my parents hire to be my nanny, has two long blond braids, broad shoulders, strong hands, an easy forthcoming smile which reveals a huge space between her teeth, causing her to lisp. She is an experienced nanny and helps my mother by changing diapers, pureeing food for me, and staying at home with me while my parents go out. Liselle lives with us and between her and my mother, I get lots of loving attention, am taught many German songs, and am played with like a doll which belongs to my mother, but whom she is willing to share with Liselle.

Two years later my brother Moschel, arrives. His nick name is Bubbi and I am not particularly thrilled with him. My mother tells of the time she came into the nursery to hear him screaming while I was forcing a knife into his mouth.

"*Was machs du den?* What are you doing?" she asks me in a frightened and angry voice.

"*Das kint weil doch buter haben.* The child wants to have some butter," I calmly respond.

Chapter Six

Parting

Although most of the Jewish people in Austria feel that the rest of the world will come to its senses, my father does not believe this. He has experienced anti-Semitism all his life and knows its appetite for Jewish scapegoats. He is determined to leave the hotbed of Europe and save whomever he can. Years before meeting my mother, years before Hitler was a threat, my father had thought of visiting America. He taught himself English, was completely fluent, and read many English and American classics. He dreamed big, despite the many opportunities denied him. If he ever had the time and the money, he reasoned, he might go on a tour of America. He acquired a visa and a permit for himself and his younger sister to visit the United States. Sari, his sister went on her eighteenth birthday and remained there. His own visa and permit are tucked in a drawer.

My father has only one visa, however, that will allow only one person to escape. If he stays in Vienna, he fears, he is convinced that the whole family will perish. If he leaves, he at least has a chance of sending for us once he arrives in the United States. He makes up his mind to leave.

I understand nothing of this, of course, as I am only three, but I remember the good-bye visit to Omma and Oppa, and the packing up of wicker baskets. When I question the packing, my mother tells me that we are going to America, not explaining that only my father is going. I dance around the baskets singing, "*Wir fahren nach America,* (We are going to America, we are going to America)." No one tries to disabuse me of my conviction.

A few days later, my father comes into the living room. He is dressed to go out, wearing his long overcoat and brown fedora. He hugs Bubbi and me, holding onto us for a long time in an embrace so tight that I am having trouble breathing.

"I'm going away for a little while, but soon we will all be together and happier than you ever imagined." I don't understand. "Where is he going?" I ask. My Mutti talks to me but does not answer my question, "We'll be together soon," she promises. He stands up and I see the tears in his eyes. He walks to the front door, swallows hard and turns around to look at us, sighs deeply and picks up his valise. Mutti goes out with him leaving us with Liselle while she accompanies him to the train that will take him to the ship. When I am a grown woman my mother tells me that as the train was pulling out of the station, and she was running after it, she heard two German soldiers comment to one another, "The poor woman is saying good-bye to her husband who is going to the front."

I am much too young to understand what is happening around me or why it is occurring. But I do realize that our lives are changing. The house feels cold and empty. The rugs are gone from the shiny parquet floors, the paintings and photographs have been removed from the walls, a few blankets are rolled up in a basket and some our clothing is packed up. Bubbi and I stomp around the rooms making loud echoing noise on the bare floors.

"Ven fahren wir nach America? When are we going to America?" I ask my mother again and again.

As always, she's vague in her response. Today she seems especially distracted and distant. *"Ich weiss nicht,* I don't know." She doesn't sound very sure of herself. There is a knock on the door. It is our upstairs neighbor, Frau Yaeger. She does not answer my friendly *"Heil Hitler,"* but looks at me through small, red rimmed eyes. She is accompanied by two miniature, white poodles, yapping and sliding all over our uncarpeted floor. She is tall, skinny like a broomstick, wearing a long, brown satin dressing gown that hangs from her as if it is on a hanger. Her matted blond hair lies flat on her head and looks like left over scrambled eggs. Her thin lips are compressed, an invisible line.

She shuffles over to my mother's china closet and opens it without permission. *"Das gafehlt mir,* I like this,* she says to no one, as she picks up our good china serving platter, turns it over and examines the stamp on the back. She takes all the dinner plates, soup bowls, cups and saucers belonging to the set and places them on the table.

She never takes her gaze away from the china as she says to my mother,

"The Germans are already here, practically on our doorstep. They will take all of your precious possessions," she continues, holding a large dinner plate up to the light, and keeping her eyes focused on the china, "I might as well take them. If I don't, they will. You can have your things when times are better," she adds as an afterthought. "My maid will be picking these up in a few minutes. Please don't let anyone else take them," she says as she leaves.

My mother sighs. She examines her hands as if she has never seen them before, turning them over and over again in her lap. Soon the other neighbors come to our apartment, fighting over our silver, linens, crystal as if we are already dead and they were crows picking the carcasses.

I can't stand watching this. I shout at them. *"Heraus, heraus,* (get out, get out!)" I scream. "Get out of our house, you stealers!"

One of the women looks at me sadly, shaking her head. She gets on her knees to achieve eye contact. *"Leibchen,* darling, I promise you that when all this is over, your Mama and Papa will have their things back. At least your family knows where their things are. If we don't take them, the Nazis will come here and break what they do not take. They are safe with us."

My mother overhears her. "Yes, yes," she agrees. "Our things are safe here in Vienna with you." Then I hear her whisper to herself, "but what will become us?"

After they leave, our apartment is emptier and colder than ever. The china cabinet is empty; my mother's pretty things are all gone. It becomes clear, even to me that we are leaving Vienna. Naturally, I assume that we will be going to meet my father and go off to America, just like that.

In a matter of days we are packed and a taxi is waiting for us downstairs. Our few possessions, clothing and some books and toys are being piled into the trunk. Liselle is standing there. She is sobbing loudly, shaking her head from side to side. She comes to say good-by to us and she and my mother hug, burying their heads on each other's shoulders as if they will never let go. Then they step apart and the two look at each other for a long time as if to memorize each other's faces. We speed off in the taxi. I am convinced that we are going to America. Palpable joy fills my chest so that I have trouble breathing. "Are we finally going to America?" I ask my mother?

Again she's vague, "Well sort of. First we are going to Wieliczka, the town where I was born and lived when I was a little girl like you. We'll stay there for a while with all your aunts, uncles and cousins, and then we will go to America." I persist with my questions and finally she breaks down.

"Papa is on his way to America. He has taken a train to the ship and then we will join him there soon."

"What?" I demand, outraged. "He went to America without me?"

"Yes, but you'll see. We will be going there soon ourselves."

"Papa promised to take me," I cry.

"He never promised to take you. He said we would all be going there soon, and we will," she tries to reason with me.

"Why, why, why didn't he take me along?" I wail. "He made a promise. He made a promise and now he broke it. That's like telling a lie. Papa lied to me. Papa made a sin." I start sobbing, big, wet tears.

"Stop it," my mother says harshly. "Stop sniveling and don't you ever accuse your father of lying to you," she warned me. "Your Papa is a truthful man. He never told a lie."

I let out a long grief stricken wail, "Papa lied to me."

My sobbing gets louder and louder and my mother becomes embarrassed and impatient. We are in the taxi cab and people on the street look at us every time the taxi stops. My mother is afraid of the attention.

A new fear grips me. Where are we going without our Papa? What if he comes back and sees that we are not at home? How will he find us? What if our mother leaves us just as Papa did? Will Bubbi and I be just like Hansel and Gretel? Orphans? I surrender my anguish over America and permit a new terror to plant itself in my subconscious. What if we end up all alone in the world?

Chapter Seven

Poland

My mother has many reasons for going back to Poland. It is the middle of February and Poland is not yet under German rule. Moreover, my mother has a large and prosperous family and we can buy some time until my father is ready to send for us.

We travel by airplane from Vienna to Krakow, a large city that is only about fifteen kilometers from Wieliczka. When we land in Krakow the three of us get on a train that takes us to the center of the city. The train station is noisy, filled with people carrying packages and suitcases. Everyone is rushing to be somewhere else.

My mother looks around and she spots him! An old man, wearing a dirty sheepskin coat rushes towards her.

"*Pani Freda, yak przyjemny* (Miss Freda, how good to see you.) We are so happy to have you home at last." My mother clasps his arms warmly. She turns to me. "Stanislav," she says, "is our faithful friend. He takes care of all the horses and cows on the farm. He is going to take us to my old home- your new home." I don't know what to say, so I curtsy to Stanislav. After all, he is my mother's friend. Stanislav smiles at us; his face creased like crepe paper, his blue eyes twinkling at us under white, bushy brows. "So *Pani* Freda, these are the famous Maidi and Bubbi we've all been hearing so much about."

We follow Stanislav out to the street. Two chestnut horses, harnessed to a beautiful sled await us. I have never seen anything like this. Stanislav lifts me and Bubbi and helps my mother onto the soft leather seats. We snuggle under the warm fur blankets while he tosses our luggage in the back and mounts the high seat in front. He clicks his tongue and the horses respond toward an unknown destination.

The horses plod along, their heads bobbing up and down in time with their feet, while the little silver bells strung around their necks tinkle. The bright, snow covers the countryside. It begins looking like a picture in a fairy tale. The few houses we pass are small, nestled under thatched roofs piled high with snow. They look like a Viennese dessert, giant chocolate cakes topped with mountains of whipped cream. The scenery is captivating. Being a child who loves fairy tales, I expect to see a little, old, hunch-backed witch emerge from her cottage, leaning on her cane, her head covered by a black scarf and a long apron protecting her dress.

This is not so bad, I tell myself. I have never ridden on a giant sled, nor have I ever been pulled along by horses. My mother looks all around. "Nothing has changed here on the road from Krakow to Wieliczka," she shouts up to Stanislav. "I've been gone for quite a while and it feels as if time has stood still." Slow tears collect in the corners of her eyes. "So much has happened since," she says to herself, nodding her head, rocking, her whole body agreeing with her words.

Stanislav shakes his head, but remains silent. We start climbing a big slippery hill. The horses begin to lose their footing under the heavy load of luggage and passengers. I am scared and excited. We are slipping backwards, down the snow-covered hill. But Stanislav is persistent. He's done this before and he halts the horses, giving them time to catch their breath. After a few minutes he tightens the reins, clicks his tongue three times and the horses once again resume their ascent. We slow down in front of the iron gates that are left open in anticipation of our arrival. There are several houses behind the gates. A door opens and a noisy throng of people come flooding out. I know many of them because they have come to see us in Vienna, but some of them are new to me.

"Freda is here with the children!" I am being passed around, hugged and kissed by so many people who are speaking Polish, a strange language to my ears, that I feel frightened and start to scream. *Nein, nein. Horin sei auf. Wo ist meine Mutti?, Sie hat verschwindt!* ("No, no. Stop. Where is my mommy? She's disappeared!") My mother rushes over to me, scoops me up in her arms and comforts me. She dries my tears with her pink embroidered handkerchief, smoothes my damp hair off my worried forehead. She holds me tightly, stroking my back, "You're fine, and it's alright. I will never leave you. We are with my brothers, sisters, all your uncles, aunts and cousins. They are all so happy to see you. Don't be frightened Maidi. We are safe here."

My mother's birthplace in Wieliczka was a farm/estate/factory. Many of my aunts, uncles and cousins live there. They run the leather tanning factory, fill orders for the Polish army and other customers, overseeing the farm and reside in the various living quarters. Each family has its own apartment on the estate grounds, and we are immediately ushered into ours. It has always been there for my mother and father as though waiting for our return. It is a large, beautiful, bright suite of rooms. Tall windows, framed in white lace curtains overlook the gates we had to pass through. In the corner of the bedroom, two large closets one containing men's clothing, the other one empty await our arrival. Since we all eat our meals together in the main house, the apartment contains no kitchen.

Bubbi and I are the youngest children on the estate and everyone tries hard to please us. A rocking horse made of real horse hide; stuffed animals, coloring books and crayons are waiting for us in our room.

Chapter Eight

The Farm

When we first get there, life in Wieliczka is pleasant and peaceful. I am encouraged to be myself, to explore and to learn. My aunts and uncles never pass by me without giving me a loving tap or if they have time, they bend down to plant a kiss on my head.

The farm is certainly the most exciting place for Bubbi and me. We have never had so much freedom. We are allowed to explore as we wish since there are always people around to supervise us if we get into trouble. The barn yard is full of noisy chickens and one angry rooster.

"Shoo, shoo," I say, my arms flapping, frightening the poor chickens into a frenzy of activity.

Large, snorting horses and fat, lazy cows who are constantly chewing live in the stable. The horses frighten me. They appear like monsters. They are noisy and restless, pawing the ground and neighing. The cows, on the other hand, though big, are quiet and look bored. They stand around, munching, not making a sound and hardly ever moving, except to swing their tails at an annoying fly. I am intimidated and challenged by their size and bulk. But on the other hand, they are so serene and content. I want to conquer my fear of them. I love to stand near them, and occasionally pat their black hides.

The young stable boy, wearing knee length pants, a white shirt and a black cap comes into the barn carrying a short stool. He claps the stool down, sits at the rear of a cow, chewing nonchalantly on a blade of grass and starts pulling on the cow's udders. He pulls the udders rhythmically and each yank produces a squirt of milk. I watch, fascinated. "Want some fresh milk?" he asks me, grinning.

"Sure," I respond eagerly.

"Come here then." He positions my head below the cow's udders. "Open you mouth wide." I do as I am told and feel a shot of warm milk enter my mouth. "It's hot," I exclaim.

"Of course, what did you expect, refrigerated milk straight from the cow?" He laughs with me. He moves on to another cow and repeats the process. I would love to try it but am too shy to ask.

It is a warm day in April, the sun is shining and the sky is full of puffy, cotton ball clouds. I am three years old, sitting on a stone stoop in front of our house, my chin is resting on my knees. I am wearing a navy blue pinafore over my yellow dress to keep it clean. Today I have a mission; I am going to learn to speak proper Polish. The patriotic Poles, whose love of their country is almost as great as their hatred for Germany and Austria, encourage me to speak only in Polish. I am learning quickly but need to get rid of my rolling Austrian "r" and master the hard Polish "r." I spend days sitting in the sun and practicing, but today, I am determined to get it right.

I practice it over and over again and suddenly I've got it! "Mutti, Mutti," I shout, running to her eagerly, "I can say it. Listen, '*kurrra, Krakow, crrravatka,*'" I feel powerful and Polish, just like everyone around me. The Poles applaud.

Life is good on the farm. It is full of surprises. Nothing is expected of us. All we have to do is play and be happy. There are no loud voices, band music or marching boots. I miss the excitement of Vienna but enjoy the freedom of Wieliczka. Little do I know that this will be the happiest period of my childhood.

Although the world closes in on us, I have good memories of the early time in Wieliczka. Bubbi and I attend a pre-school for Jewish children. We have very few toys but make up for that with much imaginative play in the sandbox, dressing up, telling stories, singing, and putting on shows. In the spring and summer, we pick flowers and replant them in our little sand garden. I love the attention I get when I do something special and am soon bossing everyone around.

Chapter Nine

The Sardines

"A letter, a letter for Freda," my Aunt Angie announces. She comes into the library breathless. "Fredel," she says, trying to catch her breath, "You have a letter from Alex." The whole family trudges in behind my aunt. A letter from my father is always a cause for celebration.

"Open it, open it at once," My Uncle Heshel says. My mother puts down the piece of embroidery she is working on, a large linen tablecloth, wipes her hands on her dress and opens the letter.

She reads it quietly to herself, then clears her throat and reads aloud. "My darling Freda," the letter begins. "I arrived in Genoa and only have to get on board the ship to go to America. The salami we packed up was delicious!" We all applaud.

The salami was a plan for my father to get my mother's diamond engagement ring out of Austria, and Germany. Before leaving for America, my father gently opened a small salami and stuffed the ring deeply inside of it, hoping to keep it from the prying, greedy eyes of the customs officials who scrutinized every Jewish passenger's belongings. No gentile custom's officer would question the reason for a Jew to be carrying kosher salami smelling of garlic.

A few days later, a small package arrives. We excitedly rip the package open. Inside are two, small, flat, rectangular, shiny cans. Bubbi and I are surprised, and delighted.

"What's in there?" I ask my mother, "a toy?"

"No *maidchen*, these are sardines." "Sardines? What are sardines? Do you make things with them?" I stroke the shiny, smooth surface of one of the cans. It is perfectly formed.My mother laughs, again. "No *schatzie*, they are little fish packed in oil."

"What do we do with such flat little fish?"

"We eat them, of course," she answers.

I am eager to try them. I can't believe that a real fish can be shrunken to fit such flat cans. "Open them," I beg," let's at least see them."

"Not now, we have to save them for a special occasion," she insists as she carefully hides them between two tablecloths in the huge linen closet belonging to the estate.

Every day after that I pull a chair over to the closet, climb up and look at the sardine cans. I caress them longingly; hold their shiny cool sides against my face. "Is today the day we open the sardines?" I ask, my mother, hopefully. How can a fish be made so small and flat? My pleading never works. My mother is holding out. She's waiting for a special day to come that warrants a can of sardines. She puts my pleading aside. As it turns out, the special day never arrives.

Chapter Ten

Jew Girl

I am walking with my eight year old cousins, Gizelle and Miriam. We are stopped by several Polish girls, who shout, "Zyidoweczki, (little Jew girls.)" They pull our hair and hit us with sticks. We run home crying, but there is nothing anyone can do to protect us even though our families know who they are. In fact, some of their parents work for our family: the men in the leather factory and as farmhands, the women as cooks, laundresses, and general housekeepers. Jewish children are fair game to bullying Polish kids who make a sport out of taunting us. They hide around corners and in doorways surprising and scaring us with sticks and belts.

A few days later, we are on our way to town to get ice cream. "Hey, Jew girls, let's see what you've got in your pockets," they shout at us. We're scared; there are five of them and only three of us. Moreover, they are bigger than we are and armed with sticks. We do as we are told. We empty our pockets and they take what they find: our ice cream money, a blue eraser, a sugar cube, some green string wrapped around a piece of cardboard, and a small embroidered handkerchief. We run home quickly, crying. My aunts tell us that we are not to leave the farm unless accompanied by an adult. Even the streets of our little village, Wieliczka, are not safe.

It is getting more and more difficult to stay in Poland. The political climate is turning against the Jews. New laws are enacted daily and now all Jewish adults have to wear an armband with the Star of David on it to identify their religion. The war is coming to Poland, and historically few Polish people need encouragement to vent their age old feelings towards the Jews. A sense of approaching doom is suspended like a heavy curtain, hanging between what is and what was.

One evening, in early September, 1939, my mother's older brother, Herzl, comes into the house. He tells us that he was in Krakow and had gone to visit one of his friends who had come out of prison. "It was terrible," he cries, "the guards have dogs and Yaakov was bitten on his arms and legs. He was chained and unable to defend himself from the wild beasts. And why? For speaking out against the Nazis who are occupying Krakow? The Poles hate the Nazis and yet they imprisoned him, a Polish citizen. Krakow isn't safe anymore," he continues, "There are many Polish collaborators. Last week thirty Jews and several professors from Jagiellonian University were executed, right in the town square." I do not understand what he is saying, but his tone and my aunts' and uncles' reaction frightens me. They are wringing their hands, looking desperate. I want to know what they are talking about, but am afraid to ask. "No Jew should remain in Krakow," he declares, shaking his head in disbelief.

My Uncle Moshe claps his hands to his cheeks, while my aunts continue wringing theirs. "How can that be? We thought the Nazis haven't even attacked Krakow. Who is doing the shooting?"

"I thought Krakow would be spared," my aunt wails, "such a beautiful city, so many historic sights!"

A few days later my Uncle Herzl does not come home. We wait for him, and try to communicate with anyone who might know his whereabouts, but no one is able to help. We contact his friend Yaakov in Krakow, but he has also disappeared. My grandmother and all her children and grandchildren stay up all night waiting for his return. He doesn't come home that night, nor does he appear on the following three nights. We mourn his disappearance. Where could he have gone, we ask each other? There are no answers and no one to ask. Every official who has ever done business with my grandfather or uncles shrugs his shoulders when we ask about Herzl. He has vanished.

Where is my Uncle Herzl? I still have a picture of him in my mind. He is tall, slender, wearing a beige suit with a waist coat, his straight brown hair is combed back off his high forehead, and white eyebrows and lashes frame the bluest of eyes. A slow smile spreads across his whole face making his eyes crinkle at the corners whenever he comes into the room. He is the only one of my uncles who does not have a beard. He carries a watch in his vest pocket and squints to read the dial. How can such a real person vanish? All I have to do to see him is close my eyes and imagine he is in the room. I love him. He gives us rides on his broad shoulders and makes the most unbelievable folk and fairy tales ring true by changing his voice and his accent. But most of all I love him for his gentle manner. He never raises his voice, always looks into my eyes when I have something to say to him, he makes me feel as important as a grown up, and he never laughs at my questions. He is a safe person to be around. I feel a paralysis next to my throat that prevents me from taking a deep breath. I am afraid that if I breathe, I'll start crying, and if I cry, I will never be able to stop. If I start crying, I might make his disappearance real. If I can just keep my tears in check, he might come walking in through the door with chocolate for us, telling us he was delayed by the weather. We will have a joyful reunion, if only I don't cry. If only I don't cry it won't be real. But the pain in my chest is pressing against my heart. I can control my tears, but I can't control my fear, my pain, and my paralysis.

My mother has gone to Krakow to buy some medicine for my Aunt Paula and chemicals for the factory. The reason she was sent, I am later told is because she looks totally Aryan and her German is flawless. She will be able to go to a pharmacy, order the medicine in German and no one is likely to question her. She kisses us and promises to bring us a toy when she returns. "I'll be back before supper," she tells Bubbi and me. The morning passes uneventfully. Bubbi and I play in the field with our cousins. Right after lunch, we are told to take a nap and as soon as I get up, without wanting to, or planning, I start *waiting*.

My mother is the only one who can leave our house without wearing the Star of David on her arm. No one stops her on the street, and she is the one dispatched to buy supplies for the farm: chemicals for the operation of the tannery, which is now running twenty-four hours a day. The army needs leather for saddles, boots and belts. I know she has to do this but it does nothing to stop me from waiting and worrying.

When my mother isn't home by late afternoon, the fear takes up a definite space inside of me. The sun sets and, suddenly, to my horror I forget what my mother looks like. I quickly rummage through a night table drawer and find an old photograph of her. I tuck the picture into a window pane in our room and continue waiting. "Good," I say to myself. Now I'll recognize her. I am in an ever swelling state of panic. I can't help myself. I am determined to sit with her picture until I see her coming up the walk. I start to pray, *"Shma Yisroel,* Please God, let my mother come home. I will never ask You for anything again, just let my mother, please come home." I refuse to eat supper. I am waiting, and nothing will move me from my vigil at the window. My ritual takes on a new dimension. "If I stop looking out for her," I tell myself, "I might not see her coming up the walk and then she might not come home." I believe that I am able to draw her home with my prayers, and the power of my eyes. It has gotten dark, and I refuse to budge. Even at the age of four, I have my own ritual of obsessive waiting. I will practice it for the rest of my life. It is always accompanied by catastrophic thinking, as if the thinking will ward off the disaster from occurring. I pace, I sweat and I feel breathless. I cannot be distracted. When I am waiting I am too busy to do anything to pass the time. I press my finger tips hard into my palms. I am alert for the slightest sound or movement. I am prey, waiting for the predator.

"Please Maidi," my aunt Angie implores, "Come and eat your supper. Your *Mutti* will not be happy to see that you haven't eaten." I can see that she too is beginning to look worried. I don't answer her. I'm afraid that if I talk, I might cry, and if I cry, my mother's disappearance will become real. I sit in silence on the window seat. By now, everyone is peering out. Finally at nine P.M., I see her trudging up the walkway to our house.

"Where were you so long?" everyone asks her.

"You know," she replied. "Everything takes longer. First, I had to wait in the pharmacy. Then I had to wait for the train which was late. When it got there, I couldn't get on as it was so crowded. Finally, I went outside and begged a driver with a horse and carriage to take me to Wieliczka, I paid him in advance, of course, but when we got out of Krakow, he told me to get out. He wouldn't take me all the way. I had to walk quite a few kilometers." She collapses on a chair, totally exhausted. It is not safe to be walking in Wieliczka alone, at night. Even I know that.

Now that I see her, it is safe to cry. I am inconsolable. I sob convulsively until I exhaust myself and finally go sleep without having eaten supper.

Chapter Eleven

The Visit

We are sitting in the dining room, eating dinner when insistent pounding at the front door interrupts the adults' conversation. "Open up, open up, before we knock the door down," a loud, threatening voice shouts. Before my uncle has a chance to reach the door, it bursts open. Four Polish army officers storm into our house. They push my uncle aside and proceed directly into the parlor. They are dressed in identical uniforms, with lots of brass buttons, colorful insignias pinned to their chests and shoulders, shiny high boots, and thick leather belts encircling their waists. Their faces gleam menacingly under their peaked military hats tilted upward to add height to their already haughty stance.

"Bring in all the furs," one of them snarls. He is here on behalf of the Polish army. He is fat, with a large scar across his upper lip that gives his face a perpetual smirk, "and don't think you can hide any of them away, you filthy Jews."

"We know your tricks," the younger man hisses, baring his large crooked teeth. He hooks his thumbs into his belt, rocks back on his heels, "we're going to search everywhere before we leave. And heaven help you if we find any fur, even a dead mouse, ha, ha, ha," he turns to his fellow officers laughing, looking for appreciation of his humor.

From behind the china closet I watch, terrified, as my mother, her siblings, and their spouses clear the dining room table. They then throw fur coats, jackets, stoles and hats on the table. The furs slide across the long, shiny table while the soldiers collect them in burlap sacks. One of the younger men, his face covered with red angry acne cysts picks up my grandmother's sable hat and plops it on his head. "How do I look boys?" he asks, swiveling his hips and mincing around the table. "Am I elegant? Would one of you kiss me?" They laugh at him. One of the others spits on the floor.

28

In happier times, transactions between the Polish officers and our family were marked by smiles and handshakes. And when the deal was closed, a toast with a glass of whiskey would bind the agreement. *"Na-zdrowie* (to your health,)" they would say lightheartedly.

"Lchaim," my uncles would respond good-naturedly. Everyone would be laughing and joking.

But this time the very same officers are terrifying. "Filthy Jews," one of them hisses, "You won't be needing furs where you're going!" He and the others stuff the furs into the bulging sacks. There are no smiles, no pats on the back, no handshakes, no whiskey, only our tears as they stomp out of the house.

Within days, strange workmen come to the estate and start building concrete huts. They are not high enough for an adult to stand up in, but to me they look sturdy and protective. They have iron gates that open and shut smoothly and no windows. Although they are bleak and cold looking, they are the perfect sized playhouses for Bubbi and me.

"Are these going to be our new houses?" I ask one of the workmen.

"Naah," he answers. "Not unless you start barking and baring your teeth. They're for the dogs."

"What dogs?" I ask.

"The police dogs. As soon as we're finished building here, the police are bringing their dogs over here to train them."

I shiver, recalling Uncle Hertzl's sad news about the dogs that attacked his friend Yaakov. "Police are training dogs in our fields? Why?" I ask.

He shrugs, "Who knows. Maybe Wieliczka is joining the rest of the world." He and the others laugh, but I will not understand the joke until years later when my adult mind replays the scene.

Chapter Twelve

Trip to Krakow

On a lovely spring day in May, of 1940, my mother takes Bubbi and me to Krakow. We are going to have our pictures taken and we are noisy and excited. It is a great adventure to travel to Krakow by train. The wooden benches and the clickety-clack of the train are promises of a wonderful day. My mother has become quite bold about going to Krakow without her Star of David armband and she knows her way around. She is wearing a tiny, silly looking hat made of two squares of starched, black lace, held together by a large, pink silk rose, with a spider web of a veil, and a black, silk dress. I am wearing a black velvet dress, with a white lace collar. A huge pink, puffy taffeta ribbon is tied in a bow, on my hair. Bubbi, whose hair has not yet been cut in a grown up style, wears black velvet short pants, held up by suspenders, and a white shirt. He looks like a girl. I tease him along the way. My mother has taken her little grandniece, one year old, Halinka, along for the photo session. Halinka who is dark, with curly hair and an olive complexion is dressed in a white knit sweater and matching skirt. We are laughing and joking. It is such a beautiful day, the air is fragrant, and Krakow, to my delight, is filled with German speaking soldiers, not the menacing, angry Polish officers, but good-natured, laughing young men who push each other around and pound each other on the back, pink cheeked, handsome, joking and well fed.

We walk around Krakow, to the famous town square, *Sukiennice,* Clothe Hall, a covered stone structure dating back to the time of Kazimierz, the Great in the thirteenth century. Hundreds of stalls are filled with all kinds of merchandise. Farmers, artists, tailors, shoemakers, and jewelers all bring their wares to sell. On an impulse my mother stops to admire some colorful blankets. She buys two of them. They are dark mustard yellow with bright red lines running horizontally and vertically creating a box pattern.

We leave the market and continue walking around the cobblestone square. Horses with colorful ribbons braided into their tails, and harnesses adorned with matching reigns are hitched to brightly painted wagons. The drivers wear costumes to match their horses and buggies: white shirts and jodhpurs, beaded, embroidered vests and top hats matching the colors of the ribbons entwined in the horses' manes. They are lined up waiting for clients. Musicians play at every corner. We stop to listen to three accordionists. They play sad songs and are so engrossed in their music that they don't even look at the many people who surround them. My mother drops a few *zlotys* on the towel in front of them and we continue walking.

We stop at a tailor shop and walk inside. A little bent over man, wearing a skullcap is standing, facing a dress dummy. His mouth is full of pins as he adjusts a long swath of green silk on the dummy's body. The floor is covered with scraps of material, and the slanting sunlight from the window lights up a shaft of dancing dust particles. I hear the sound of a sewing machine coming from behind a curtain.

The man walks over to us, removes the pins from between his lips. "*Aha, Panna Perlbergeruvna*," he addresses my mother by her maiden name, "Nice to see you again. Are you interested in having something made?"

My mother produces the blankets and tells him that she would like to have coats made for the children.

"Oh yes," he shakes out the blankets, inspecting them. "These will make beautiful winter coats. So colorful, you will never lose sight of the children," he laughs.

We stand still while he takes our measurements. Bubbi, Halinka and I will have identical coats to wear in the winter. When he is finished measuring, he tells her that he's going to rush the coats. "Times are bad," he says, "and I want you to have these coats before the cold weather gets here." My mother agrees and tells him that she is in a hurry to have them. They shake hands, and he assures her that they will be ready before the end of summer, in time for the High Holidays.

We leave and continue on our trip. We stop at the photographer's studio. The studio is in a small, dimly lit, store. Several props are positioned in various places: a table with flowers on it; a tall cardboard column that looks like it's made of marble, a mural of a lake with trees bordering it with a real bench in front of the painted scene, and several articles of clothing hanging on a clothes tree. The photographer is a young woman, dressed in a man's white shirt, with a red scarf underneath her collar and black trousers cuffed at the bottom. She has dark curly hair, pulled back severely from her face bouncing in back of her every time she moves. Her black eyebrows rise and fall with every syllable she utters, and a crimson slash outlines her narrow lips. She poses us in front of the column, standing around my mother who is sitting, with Halinka on her lap. Then she hands me a bouquet of fake flowers and tells me to hold it in front of my chest, underneath my chin. I do as I am told. She puts her head under a black cloth, snaps a picture and comes out. She decides to take yet another picture. This time, she has me sit on a stool in front of my mother and hold Halinka on my lap. She makes small talk with my mother.

"So," she asks casually, "why are you having pictures taken? for a special occasion?"

"No," my mother answers her. "My husband is in the army, on the front, and I want to send him pictures of our family. He hasn't seen the baby yet."

"Hmm," she muses, her eyebrows almost reaching her hairline, "Is this a second marriage for you?"

"No, of course not! Why would you ask such a question?" My mother blushes.

"No. No reason. I was just wondering," she answers.

"Come on now," my mother says to her, "You must have had a reason to ask such a question."

"Look madam," she responds, facing my mother squarely, "this is none of my business. But there is no way that your baby has the same set of parents as your older children." My mother acts shocked.

"Listen, if your husband is fooled into thinking that this is his child, it's alright with me," she continues while adjusting a lens. "But I'm a professional. There is no way that this small boned, dark skinned, black eyed baby has the same parents as your two, big, fair, large boned children. They resemble you, and unless the baby had an Italian, Greek or Spanish father, this child has a different father from your other children."

The photographer has no idea that we are Jewish nor does she suspect that Halinka is a grandniece. Her offhand observation frightens my mother who later tells us that the photographs were being made in order to see if my father could use them to have fake documents forged for us; possibly an American passport. She wants to save Halinka, take her to America and pass her off as her own daughter. She is frightened by the photographer's comment. She sits quietly, thinking and then realizing that she is probably putting the rest of us into a dangerous position, shrugs her shoulders, "You know what?" she says to the photographer. "Why don't you just take one more picture of just my older children and me?" She laughs, and looks at her knowingly, "I'm not looking for trouble. If he asks about the baby, I'll just write and tell him she was sick when we had the pictures taken. There's time for discussion later, when he returns."

The photographer nods agreeing, and winks, "I don't blame you."

Weeks later another letter arrives from my father. "Read it, read it," we all beg her. It is the only news we receive that doesn't include loss and death.

My mother clears her throat and begins, "My darling Freda and my sweet children, I am happy to tell you that I am having some wonderful coats made for you with the material I received from overseas. I will send them to you as soon as they are ready. They should fit you and hopefully protect you from the harsh climate in Poland." Everyone applauds.

"Coats?" What coats? I ask. "Aren't we having coats made in Krakow, by that old man with all those pins in his mouth? Papa had coats made for us in America? Why do we need so many coats?" Everyone laughs at me. Later, I will find that out "coats" is the code word for the papers and documents that we will use to pass for Americans and that the pictures my mother sent him are the "material" used to produce the "coats." Much later, when we get to America, my father will tell Bubbi and me about all the ploys he used in order to secure our safety. First, he tried to enlist in the US army because that would have granted him immediate American citizenship and protected our family by giving us status as civilian American citizens. He was rejected because he had a hernia. He contacted American officials and government workers who, although extremely sympathetic, were powerless to help him. He was desperate. He went to printing shops and requested all kinds of counterfeit documents, with gold insignias, and official looking seals, because the Nazis were impressed by papers bearing many official looking signatures and seals. Later, on a whim, he devised a brilliant scheme that will ultimately save our lives.

He bought an old Jewish Bible in a used book shop, the pages were brittle and yellow with age, and the binding was frayed. He wrote a long list of names in Yiddish, recording next to each name the dates of births and deaths, and cities they took place in. He thus created an imaginary family tree. Before the twentieth century, families recorded these important events in family bibles. He added my grandfather, Reuven Perlberger's name to this list, giving his birth-date as July, 1878 and place of birth as Philadelphia. With this Bible in hand, he went to City Hall in Philadelphia, and approached a clerk in the statistics office.

"My father-in-law needs a birth certificate to put in a claim for Social Security," he told her, "and all he has to prove his birth is this old Bible. Would that suffice to apply for a birth certificate?"

"Sure," said the clerk as she inserted a blank birth certificate into the typewriter. "We get these requests all the time. Now how do you spell his name?"

Just like that! No red tape, no bureaucracy, no questions asked. My father sent this document along with the other notarized official looking papers, bearing our photograph to my mother.

I hear talk among the grown ups. It is time for us to leave Wieliczka. Poland is overrun with Germans who are encouraging enthusiastic Poles not to tolerate the hateful Jews. It doesn't take much prodding to unleash the open anti-Semitism. Wieliczka is becoming a dangerous place for us where everyone can identify us as Jews, and where my mother has to wear the Star of David on her arm every time she leaves the house. The family is talking about retreating to a bunker underneath the factory that has been there since 1914: our family hid in it during World War I. "Fredel, listen" my aunt Angela says, looking sad and worried. "You take the children and go hide in Krakow. No one will mistake you for being Jewish, and if you stay here with us in the bunker, Bubbi may cry and give away our hiding place." My mother agrees that young children can be very dangerous to people who are hiding. She makes plans to leave. She packs only a few things for us in a leather bag; a change of underwear and socks, tooth brushes and pajamas. She forgets about the sardines— and so do I until years later when I allow myself to recall the darkness and disappointments of a childhood spent in fear.

Chapter Thirteen

On the Run

My mother kneels on the floor, in front of Bubbi and me, gathers us into her arms and tells us, "Forget Jewish. You were never Jewish. It was just your imagination. Like Little Red Riding Hood, this is not a true story and it is not true that you were ever Jewish." It is August of 1940, I am four years old. My mother is serious, a crease forms between her eyebrows and she tells us that we will be leaving Wieliczka very soon.

"Now look, Bubbi and Maidi," my mother instructs us. "We are going to live in Krakow and we have to be very sure of who we are. We are not, and never have been Jewish. Do you understand how important it is for you to remember this?" My mother knows that we might betray her and land all of us, who knows where. I nod my head enthusiastically. Who wants to be Jewish? All you get for being Jewish is beat up and stolen from. I don't want to be Jewish. I am happy to finally be like everyone else.

Bubbi is not so compliant. He tells my mother, "*Bylem zhidde, jestem zhiddem e zawsze bendem zhiddem,* I was a Jew, I am a Jew and I will always be a Jew."

"No, no Bubbi, you don't know what you are saying," my mother tells him. He is three and very sure of himself. He loved going to the little *shul* (Synagogue) with my uncles on Friday evenings and every morning. He couldn't wait to wind *t'fillin,* leather straps around his left arm and place the small box, Phylacteries on his forehead. He wants to become a Jewish man. "It was all a game" she presses on, "We were never Jews and we are not Jews now." How could she make him understand the importance of being Catholic? She is in a panic. She must convince him that we are not Jewish.

My mother gives us small crucifixes to wear around our necks. She teaches us how to cross ourselves when we pass a church, how to genuflect. But

35

Bubbi does not relent. My mother crouches down to his eye level saying, "Listen Bubbi, what do you want to be when you grow up?"

Without a moment's hesitation he replies "A blacksmith," *kowal* in Polish.

"Alright Bubbi, your new name is *Tomek Kowalczik,* Tommy the Blacksmith. Now, you know that a blacksmith can't be Jewish" she implores. "Let's just be Catholic so that you can become a blacksmith when you grow up. But for now we are Catholic Then, when you are grown up, you can be anything you want to be. Maybe you can even be Jewish again." He reluctantly gives in as long as he is assured that someday he will again be Jewish.

We go to Krakow with Pan Janowski, who used to bring mail to us in Wieliczka. He is a kind, sympathetic man who recently got married and now has a two year old boy. He tells my mother that he will save us. It is his dream, his conviction that he must do something noble in his lifetime. He is young and idealistic. He takes us to his home in Krakow and tells his wife that we are his distant cousins from Gdynia, Helena, Tomek and Maria Kowalczik, and that we will be staying with them for a little while. My mother, "Helena," has fake Polish identification papers made with our new surname, Kowalczik. *Pani* Ewa, his wife is very welcoming and pleasant to us. She has a warm, sincere smile, a dimple on her cheek, dark brown eyes. She feels familiar to me, like one of my aunts. Ewa takes us to a small room where, she tells us we can stay for as long as we like. She is kind, and she hugs my mother and gives Bubbi and me sweets.

In spite of the beautiful sights and excitement, our lives seem empty in Krakow. We have no friends, no relatives, and no cousins to play with. Sometimes we go down to the Vistula River and walk along its banks, and at other times we go to the *Sukiennice,* the marketplace and look at all things there that we cannot own: soft, warm slippers, bright peasant shawls, dolls with real hair, and funny wind-up monkeys. We stop at a bakery and buy some bread which we eat on the way back to the little apartment. Once there, we know we must be on our best behavior. Even though, *Pani* Ewa is very kind, smiles a lot and tries to engage my mother in conversation, my mother is sad and does not tell us stories or play games with us as she used to. Instinctively I know to keep quiet, behave, and not to pester anyone with my questions. Bubbi takes his cue from me. He practically becomes mute.

We stay with the Janowski family in Krakow for about two months. We go to church with them every Sunday and behave "Catholic," genuflecting at the proper times and crossing ourselves. We eat non-kosher food and say grace before and after meals. Bubbi and I have become obedient little Catholics. One day, *Pani* Ewa beckons my mother into the parlor. I watch them from a small hallway in front of the apartment. I make myself as invisible as possible and listen. They sit on the couch, close to each other. *Pani* Ewa takes my mother's hands into her own, kisses them and starts to cry. "Please, please, dear Jesus, forgive me, and you, Helena, you please, also forgive me. I am so frightened." She rubs her eyes, pulls her hair away from her face, and crushes her left hand in her right. "The neighbors are asking me questions about you, and they do not believe me when I tell them you are a relative of my husband. They nod their heads, but I know they are talking about me. They are saying that I am hiding a Jewess and her children and that I am collecting a fortune to keep you here. I would be so happy to have you stay here for free. It would buy us a place in heaven for my whole family, but I am so scared. You have no idea what my neighbors are like. For two *zlotys* they would sell your family and mine down the river of hell." She gets on her knees in front of my mother. She crosses herself and says, "I know that my Lord Jesus would never act this way, He would hide you even if it would cost Him His life," Sobbing, she adds, "It's not me I'm so worried about. I just want to protect my son. He is so little and so innocent. Please, sweet Jesus, try to understand me."

She covers her face with her hands and buries her head in my mother's lap. My mother tries to comfort her, as she herself weeps uncontrollably. "I understand the danger you are in. You were good to us and I will never forget you," she tells her. "Give me an hour or so to collect our things and we will go." I watch the interaction, terrified. I don't want to stay in Krakow, but I don't want to leave either.

"No, no," *Pani* Ewa insists. "You cannot leave now. You must spend the night here and then tomorrow you will have a whole day to prepare yourself." She cries again, but it is clear, even to me that she is relieved. My mother confides in her, "It's either the Ghetto for us or life as Catholics."

Pani Ewa nods her head, wiping her eyes with a handkerchief she pulls out from the cuff of her sleeve. "I know how hard this is, but I would suggest that you try to live on the outside. I hear that the conditions in the Ghetto are very bad. There are many people crowded into one room and there is a lot of sickness there." She continues, "Wait, and let me think" She rubs her forehead, closes her eyes, and takes a deep breath. "I have an acquaintance who owns a furniture warehouse." She walks over to a brown chest and looks through one of the drawers. She retrieves a small notebook, moistens her index finger and quickly flips the pages "Ah, here it is. Let me give you the address of a man we know. Perhaps he can help you. I know he has done it before, hidden people," she adds. She writes his name and address on a small piece of paper and gives it to my mother. "Tell him you are my relative," she adds. She hugs my mother and holds us close to her. "I will always love you," she whispers into my ear. "I will pray for you forever."

We leave the next morning. My mother has all our things in a brown, leather, bag, the last piece of the family's tannery that we will ever own.

We spend a few nights in a small hotel near the river, but our days are without purpose. In order to avoid the suspicion of the Germans milling around the hotel, we have to pretend to have somewhere to go. We leave every morning, with a seeming destination. It is early autumn, the leaves are collecting on the ground and there is a crisp feel in the air. We go to church because it is an indoor shelter and no one bothers us there. I know I am supposed to pray, but I know only one prayer, and that one is in Hebrew, I kneel in the pew and silently recite the *"Shma"* over and over again. "Listen Oh Israel. The Lord our God, the Lord is One." But really I am asking God to help us get to America and make my Mutti happy again. Although no one tells me, I can sense danger and sadness all around me.

Throughout the city I see open trucks filled with people. I can tell they're Jewish because some of the men have ear locks and beards, and the women wear *sheytls*. We stop and look. "What are they?" I ask my mother. "Where are all those people going?"

"It's a transport," she tells me without elaborating.

I spy my old nanny, from Wieliczka, on one of the trucks, with her red cheeks and thick, long black braids. She was only fifteen years old when she took care of us, but to me she was a grown up. I break away from my mother and run into the street after the truck.

"Bella, Bella, where are you going?" I shout, following the transport of unhappy people. She sees me and reaches out her arms to me, "Maidi, Maidi, I thought I'd never see you again." My mother grabs me and pulls me away.

"Don't ever do that again," yells my mother who is so angry that she shakes me, "If they catch you, you'll be shipped to a bad, bad place."

"But that was Bella, our Bella. We love her," I whine, being too young to understand

My mother ignores my protests and cautions us again "We are not Jewish, and we don't know anyone who is. Do you understand how important it is for you to remember that?" Bubbi and I nod our heads. We have never seen my mother so agitated.

We continue wandering the streets for a few more days and by that time my mother realizes that we need to make other plans. We can try to live on the outside as Catholics, find Ewa's acquaintance who owns a furniture company, or enter the Ghetto.

"We can't really stay here at the hotel any longer," she tells us. "There are too many German soldiers and I don't want them to notice me. We will go to see the man *Pani* Ewa told us about."

The owner of the furniture factory turns out to be a Turkish man who wears a red fez and speaks with an accent. A small crescent moon is pinned in his lapel. His skin is swarthy. He is so fat that his eyes look like they are folded inside his cheeks. He and my mother talk. He seems to be agreeing and nodding his head to whatever my mother tells him. He is friendly, and puts his arm on my mother's elbow, guiding the three of us into a large furniture storage area. Bubbi who has no recollection of my father lights up, "Is this our Papa?" he asks my mother tugging at her sleeve urgently. My mother smiles sadly, "no *schatzie,*" she tells him. "This nice man is going to let us live in this big room." My mother gestures towards the warehouse filled with furniture. She must have taken some money with her from Wieliczka because she is able to pay him for the rent and buy the little that we eat. She thanks the kind man and promises not to be any trouble.

"You are welcome to stay here," he assures her taking the money and smoothly sliding it into his breast pocket.

"Well," my mother sighs, "At least we have a roof over our heads. And look at all this beautiful furniture." Despite her enthusiasm about our new arrangements, she looks tired and her shoulders sag.

The factory is filled with new furniture but every chair, every table is protected, wrapped in bundles of shiny straw. Even the mattresses are covered with straw. There is a small bathroom in the factory. It contains one disgusting brown toilet bowl and a small sink that drips cold, rusty water into a dirty bowl. My mother quiets my protests at using the toilet. "Now stop it," she admonishes me. "We are lucky to have a toilet and a sink to wash up in."

At first, we each choose a different mattress to sleep on every night, making sure that we are not too far apart from one another. The factory is easy to get lost in, especially since much of the furniture is taller than we are. When we go to sleep, we brush the straw off the surface and use it to cover ourselves instead. We cannot stay in the factory during the day when customers begin to arrive so we leave promptly at nine every morning.

In truth we have nowhere to go. It is October. On cool days we spend most of our time in a church, and on warm, sunny days we hide out at the cemetery. Bubbi and I play around the headstones. Sometimes we play hide and seek; other times we play tag. My mother sits nearby on a stone bench, watching us. When we become too noisy, she warns us to keep quiet. I notice a difference in her. She is impatient with us for the first time in our lives.

When someone comes to the cemetery, she says, "Pray, pray for your grandmother." And quickly we sink to our knees in front of the nearest gravesite, cross ourselves and fold our hands in front of our chests, mumbling to the headstone.

One day, a small family comes quietly into the cemetery. The parents silently carry a small white coffin with angels carved on its side. A young man with swollen eyes and nose is followed by his wife and two young daughters. He is in a dark suit and his wife is dressed in black with a heavy veil covering her face. She holds the casket with one hand and a handkerchief to her mouth with the other. The two girls are staring straight ahead, stone faced, their lips moving in silent prayer. I stand close by, watching sadly. They carry the little casket to a grave site, and the man takes a shovel that is leaning against a nearby a tree, and starts digging vigorously. The girls and their mother sink to their knees, fold their hands in front of their chests, bow their heads and start to pray. I drop to my knees next to them, and weep and pray with them. "Please God, please let the world be happy," I pray. "Please let all this sadness stop."

Chapter Fourteen

Freezing

The weather is turning cold and the warehouse is unheated. We shiver constantly, because we fled Wieliczka wearing light summer dresses, shorts and sandals and nothing more than the clothes on our backs, we have no winter clothes, not even socks. As cold as the factory it is even colder outside, and we have no place to go. The churches are unheated and I wonder where the "coats" that my father promised are. Not only do they not arrive, but when my mother goes to the tailor shop to get the coats she had made for us in the spring time, on our way to the photographer, his shop is boarded up and there is no sign of him. A huge Swastika is painted on the door.

At night we now sleep on one mattress, huddling close to each other. My mother lies in the middle, with a protective arm around each of us. We shiver nonetheless. At one point my mother begins to pray. She thinks I am sleeping and can't hear her. But by this time I am well trained in the art of eavesdropping. I listen carefully to her quiet whispers to God. "Please God. Let me bring my children to safety. I don't care what happens to me. My children are cold and I can't go on like this much longer. Let me bring my children to their father and then You can take me," she sobs, tears sliding off her face into her ears. I don't want God to take her. What is she talking about? I resolve that I won't ever tell her how cold I am.

My mother touches my forehead. She can tell by feeling it that I am running a high fever. My throat hurts, I can't swallow, and I can hardly speak. The roof of my mouth feels as though it is caving onto my tongue, closing off my breathing. I sweat and shiver at the same time. Before long, I begin to hallucinate. "Look Mutti," I shout, "We are in a castle, in a palace. The furniture is gold. We are finally safe." The fever makes me shake. My mother holds me all night long. She knows that we have to move. We cannot stay in the freezing factory any longer. The danger of the cold is only overshadowed by the danger from the Poles and Germans. When my temperature subsides, we leave the factory.

We again walk around Krakow, looking for lodgings. The cold eats its way into my insides. It is worse than the hunger and more real than the fear. My toes, finger tips and nose hurt the most, then my ankles, wrists and knees. It is relentless. When the frost stops, the wind picks up. It slaps my face with the back of a bony hand, it burns my skin and makes my eyes water. It is worse than every pain I've ever felt and it never, ever stops.

We trudge along the streets, going nowhere, with not even a sweater to protect our shoulders and arms. Suddenly, my mother stops in the middle of the street. She gasps with a sharp intake of air and does not exhale for a long time. When she does I hear her moan quietly. There, on the opposite side of the street is a woman, walking with her two daughters, wearing identical coats. They are made of the blankets that my mother had bought so long ago and brought to the tailor to have coats made for us. Right there, on the streets of Krakow, someone is wearing our stolen coats. "Mutti," I shout, tugging at her sleeve, "they stole our coats. Run after them. Let's get our coats back." My mother sinks to her knees on the sidewalk. She buries her head in her lap, and I hear her crying softly, "What are we going to do? O God, in Heaven, what am I going to do?" Her sobs tear through her body. I am frightened. Is my mother sick? She can't be dead because she's still moving. What has happened to her? She stands up, holding her hands to her eyes and shaking her head from side to side. "Hurry Mutti, the lady with our coats is disappearing," I urge her to move.

"No schatzie," she says sadly. "If I run after the coats, the police will run after us. Those coats no longer belong to us." She looks to the sky and addresses God, "How could You God? How could You let them have our coats while my children are freezing to death?"

We walk from house to house, looking for lodgings. Is there no place in this big city for us? Is there no place in the world for us? I ask myself these questions as we are turned away from one house after another. One house has a sign in the window offering a room for rent. We knock and it is opened before we finish knocking. An elderly woman comes to the door, "are you interested in renting the room?" She looks us up and down, then she smiles revealing two eyeteeth in an otherwise toothless mouth gleaming with red gums. Before my mother can answer her she goes on, "This house belongs to my daughter, but times are so bad now, we have to take in boarders. Have you seen that flour, and eggs are not available at any price?" She beckons us into a hallway and without stopping to take a breath, continues, "I'll only rent to nice, decent people like you. I can tell a person's character just by looking into their eyes. Here," she opens a door onto a small room. "This is the room my daughter is renting." The room is bright, there are two cots on opposite sides of a wall, a small night table is between them and a crucifix is above each cot. The room is warm and inviting. The woman still has not stopped talking, "We are charging ten *zlotys* a week. A low price for you, because I can tell that you'll keep the room nice and clean and that you won't be inviting any riffraff."

She turns to us and asks, "What brings you to Krakow?" My mother is well prepared

"We're from Gdynia, in the north, but you know that the Germans invaded and we wanted to get out of there before they found out that my husband was in our Polish army at the front."

The woman utters sympathetic noises, "Such bad times," she says shaking her head from side to side. "So, tell me," she adds, "do you want to take the room? My daughter insists for me to tell you that you can have no visitors, and that you have to pay one week in advance."

My mother assures her, "there'll be no visitors here. It is all I can do to keep my children safe and warm."

She waits until my mother hands her the money. She counts it carefully and tucks it into a green cardigan with ripped elbows. "Welcome to our home. Oh," she adds, "my name is *Pani* Siepka."

The room is more than we bargained for. It is clean, it is warm and there is a nice bathroom at the end of the hallway. A burlap sack containing flour is propped up against a wall in the corner of the room under the window. Because of the cold, we remain indoors almost all the time playing and looking out of the window. When Bubbi and I are very hungry, we go to the sack of flour and scoop out handfuls. When mixed with our saliva it actually begins to taste good. Occasionally, when it isn't too cold we go out to get some food: rolls, an apple or a jar of yogurt, which we sneak back into the room. We are not allowed to use the kitchen. By the time we return, we are so happy to have a cozy, warm room that we don't want to go anywhere.

My mother spots a familiar silhouette one afternoon when we are outside on one of our food runs. She moves toward her, "Matilda!" she exclaims joyfully. It is my aunt Matilda. They hug each other, in tears and exchange whatever news they have. "How did you get to Krakow?" my mother asks. My aunt pauses, takes a breath and between sobbing and gasping, she tells us the story. "The army came to the farm," she starts out, "everyone was hiding in the bunker. We had no food, and we couldn't even whisper." She pauses, looks around as if to check that no one is listening and continues, haltingly. "I heard their boots above my head. I was so frightened. We had already lost so much, and *mamuncha,* our beloved mother was taken a few days before, when she stepped out to get some air. She was sent on a transport to Siberia."

She stops for air and goes on, "My little Miriam, my only child left before we started hiding. I only hope she is safe. She went on a children's transport to Hungary, to a cloister and is living there with the nuns. The last I heard she was christened and is living as a Catholic child among the nuns. What else could I do?" she asks no one in particular. "The police were everywhere. I knew it would only be a matter of time before they discovered us. So early in the morning, before the sun came up, I snuck upstairs, into the factory and jumped out the window. Of course one of them spotted me and started chasing me. But he was fat, and out of breath, and I was running for my life. I ran into the village." She pauses and tries to catch her breath, blow her nose and wipe the tears away, as she continues. "I ran into Shumsky's barn. You remember Shumsky?" she asks my mother. My mother nods. "Well I ran into his barn, there was nothing alive in it any more. I covered myself up with straw and waited until it was dark, then I jumped on a train, and here I am." Aunt Matilda goes on, "The Nazis and the Polish police flooded the area. I know that they got to our bunker because I met Rysek, our nephew at the train station in Wieliczka. He got away and so did a few others. Shalom (my uncle, her husband) was caught and sent to a labor camp. I don't know if he's dead or alive," she bursts out crying.

My mother too is crying at this point. "Matilda, Matilda," she says, embracing her, "We must have hope. That's the only thing they can't take from us. I never thought that I would see my sister again, and on the street in Krakow. It is such a comfort to know that at least you and Miriam are safe." Then my mother laughs cynically at her words, "Safe indeed. As if anyone of us can be safe"

My mother tells Matilda to follow us home. Once we arrive, she begs our landlady to let her sister stay in our room. "I'll have to ask my daughter. It's her house, you know. If it were up to me, I wouldn't care." She shuffles out of the room in her felt house slippers. Her daughter appears, scowling, "I said no guests, and I certainly didn't even think of people staying overnight."

My mother takes another tactic. "My sister has money. If you don't want her to stay with us, she will surely find someone else who will be happy to take her *zlotys.*"

At the mention of money, the landlady's small, yellowish eyes light up. "I'm not putting in any more beds, if all of you can manage to sleep on the two beds in the room, she can stay. But I'll have to charge you more than you are paying now. After all," she goes on, "there'll be four of you and you'll be using more water and the wear and tear on my furniture. . ."

We all pack into the tiny room. It is wonderful having Aunt Matilda with us, someone who knows us and loves us, someone we love. For the first time, since coming to Krakow, my mother's shoulders don't sag. But her revived spirit does not last long. The old landlady starts behaving strangely. She avoids us and her daughter comes to collect the rent, a cigarette dangling loosely from her mouth. She counts the money, puts it in her pocket and saying nothing walks away.

A few days later, two tall men, in civilian clothes barge into the little room.

"Here, here they are," the daughter points to our little group. "I'm not going to take any chances harboring Jews." She talks to the officers as she stands at the door watching us as if we were cats ready for mischief. "This is a respectable house and I'm not going to tarnish its image by harboring Jews." She wears a satisfied look on her face catching the ashes from her cigarette in her palm. She shrugs her skinny shoulders. "I'm only doing my duty," she tells everyone in hearing distance. "Mind if I stick around?" she asks the police. She is curious, wanting to witness our departure, hoping to have something to gossip about with her neighbors.

The men are big and noisy. One of them has a huge black mole next to his upper lip. It quivers when he shouts at my mother and my aunt. "Show me your identity papers," he yells. He rocks back and forth on his heels as my mother rushes to get them. She gives him the Polish identity papers, but withholds the ones my father had sent her about our American connection. The man with the mole scrutinizes them and hands them over to his companion who is wearing glasses, which he removes from his pale, colorless eyes, in order to read. They converse in conspiratorial whispers. "Madam, there's something wrong here. These papers state that you are from Krakow and you clearly told *Pani* Sciepka that you are from Gdynia. And if your husband is at the front, why are you staying here and paying for lodging? Don't you have any relatives anywhere that you can stay with? Something doesn't ring true. Why are you here?"

My mother trembles and Bubbi walks up to the men, "Leave my mommy alone," he starts punching their legs and kicking along their shins. "Get away from my mommy, you bad, bad men." The men have no patience for the little boy. The one with the mole shoves him away, while the other one knocks him to the floor. Two grown men overpower the three-year-old Bubbi. He never cries. He stands up and makes for their legs again. This time my mother picks him up and holds him tightly. She doesn't know what kind of anger Bubbi might provoke in them if he attacks them again. My mother pales; her lips are trembling. My aunt sits on the edge of the cot, gripping her thighs. She gets up quickly, goes to the closet and from a pocket extracts a gold bracelet and a ring. She gives one to each of the men who make them disappear like a magic trick. *Pani* Sciepka looks stunned. She has no idea that my mother and aunt had valuable jewelry. If she had known, instead of reporting us she probably would have held out for money.

"There's something wrong with these papers," the man with the mole re-peats, in a less threatening tone, "I'm not taking you in to the police station, but I am taking the documents. The captain will look them over and then we will return them to you. Stay where you are so that we can bring your papers back to you," he advises my mother and aunt before he leaves. Pani Siepka's daughter looks happy. She will probably get a reward for turning in two Jew-ish women and children. My mother is desperate because the document they took not only is counterfeit, but it also has her picture.

She keeps crying, "My picture, now they have my picture." I do not under-stand her dilemma, because in my mind nothing worse than losing her picture has happened. I think we are legitimate Catholics. I try to reassure her by tell-ing her that we can get more pictures of her when we are in America.

"Do you think he'll leave us alone?" my aunt asks my mother, "after all, he did take the jewelry."

"We can't take a chance. For the bracelet and the ring, they gave us the gift of not taking us with them. Let's not take any chances about his state of mind towards us."

Pani Sciepka asks my mother if she has any other jewelry. "Maybe we could arrange for you to go to the farm where my sister lives. She would be glad to hide you there and you wouldn't be in danger so far away from the city." She stands in front of the door, guarding it with her body.

My mother and aunt push her away and leave her house immediately. We are all running down the street while she is screaming for us to stop. We run for about ten minutes until we can no longer hear her voice and only stop several blocks further down the street where we sit down in a café and try to catch our breaths. Aunt Matilda and my mother speak in whispers. Later, my aunt tells us that she is going to try to get to Hungary to be with Miriam. We have nowhere to go. It is too dangerous for us to live as Catholics, my mother tells us. "We are going to go to a place called the Ghetto, where we will be with many other Jews. The life here on the outside is too dangerous for us."

"Can we still be Catholics?" I ask, pleading in a timid voice. By now I don't want to be Jewish.

Chapter Fifteen

The Ghetto

"*Yisgadal ve-yiskadish sh'mei raba,*" An old man is running back and forth on the streets wailing the mourner's prayer, the *Kaddish*. His palms are open toward the heavens, his eyes are closed even though he's running. He is wearing a torn black coat and his dirty ritual fringes are slapping the backs of his legs. We have passed the Ghetto many times while we walked the streets of Krakow. And now that we are inside my mother shields our eyes when we walk by. "Shhh, don't look," she says to us, afraid that we may retain some of the ghastly images. She makes us keep our eyes on the ground. No wonder. It is a glimpse into a nightmare.

The ghetto is located in Podgorze, an industrial part of Krakow Before it was turned into the ghetto 3,000 people lived there. But, by 1941, when we arrive, 21,000 Jews are crammed into its miserable quarters. A tall wall, topped with barbed wire separates the Ghetto from the rest of the city, but passer-bys hear gunshots daily as new groups of Jews are rounded up and killed on its street.

The Ghetto is filled with noise and the smell of garbage and decay. We see another old man in rags as we walk along the sidewalk. He looks dazed and approaches us, grabbing my mother by her lapels, and pulling her close to him. "Have you seen my sister Chanya?" he asks in a raspy voice. "No, I haven't," she answers him patiently. He takes hold of her hands, pulls them towards his mouth and starts to kiss them. "You look just like Chanya. Didn't you see her?" My mother is gentle with him. "I'm so sorry," she tells him, pulling her hands slowly away from his grasp. "When did you last see her?" she asks. He shrugs his shoulders. He doesn't remember. He starts to cry, "Everybody is gone. Everyone in my family is gone. Only Chanya is still alive. Have you seen her?" he asks for a second time. He sinks to the sidewalk, buries his head in his knees, and weeps.

We continue walking. A young woman, dressed in rags, holding a baby close to herself stops everyone she meets. "My milk dried up and my baby is hungry," she pleads. " Can you help me with a small amount of milk, or maybe tea?" No one pays attention to her. All around me people are weeping, begging for food, scratching their bodies and the red sores that infest them. So much pain and suffering around me. I too am grief stricken. I don't want to know why these people are being tortured; I just want it to stop. "Please Mutti," I say, "why can't we do anything for these poor people?" I look into her face and see that she too is crying.

She stops a young man in a black jacket that appears to be some kind of uniform, but his trousers are ripped and his shoes are scuffed, he wears no socks. He bears no resemblance to the well dressed officers I am used to seeing. "*Prosze bartzo,* (Please, excuse me)," she says to the young man. "Can you tell me where I can find a room?" He looks at her and laughs sarcastically. His pale face is thin, and has the unhealthy pallor of someone who hardly ever goes outdoors.

"*Pani zartuye* ,(The lady must be joking)," he answers. "This place is so full you can't get an empty paper bag into this space. Anyway, it isn't up to me. Go knock on doors. Maybe someone died and there is room in one of the flats." My mother nods, "*rozumye,* (I understand)."

Later on my mother tells me that he was a safe person to talk to as he was part of the *Judenrat,* the Jewish police. The Gestapo has rounded up the few able bodied Jewish young men and assigned them the job of policing their fellow inmates. It is their duty to enforce the rules imposed on their fellow Jews, to report any infractions, and to act as agents for the Gestapo against their fellow Jews. For this service, they are rewarded with a black uniform jacket and the illusion of power and control. While many of them are protective of the Ghetto dwellers, others become zealous enforcers of the rules, eager to catch their fellow Jews transgressing: hoping to score points with the Gestapo. Life in the Ghetto is filled with suspicions and humiliation.

A cocky teen-ager, swaggering in his new uniform stops an old man and makes him empty his pockets. He squares his shoulders insolently, hikes up his pants, and speaks in Yiddish, "Just because you are old, doesn't mean you can't smuggle." The old man shakes his head in disbelief, "Such behavior from a *Yiddishe bocher,* (a Jewish boy). That I had to live to experience such rudeness, such *chutzpah!*" This breakdown in the order of authority and respect makes everyone suspicious of everyone else.

We continue walking and looking around before approaching one of the buildings. My mother knocks on the door and a woman peers out cautiously. Her head tightly swathed in a kerchief, she is gaunt, like a pencil and her threadbare housedress hangs on her like a shroud but her eyes are on fire, and she recognizes my mother. "Freda," she exclaims, "why are you here?" She embraces my mother. It turns out that she is from Wieliczka, the rabbi's wife. "We thought you were on your way to America by now."

My mother, although frightened, seems relieved to see a familiar face. She sighs, "It feels so good to be among my own people, to know that there are still some who are alive, if you can call this being alive." She remembers the purpose of her visit and looks around the dark corridor. "Is there any room for us in your flat?"

"What do you mean 'is there any room for us?' You are us. Do you think we can't make room for one of ours? It will be an honor and a privilege to have you in our little room, although, I must warn you, it isn't what you're used to."

"What I'm used to?" my mother asks no one in particular, following her up the fetid stairs, through a narrow hallway littered with garbage and smelling of sewage. "What I'm used to is an unheated furniture warehouse and a room in the home of an anti-Semite, who couldn't wait to turn us over to the Polish Gestapo."

"This is it," she exclaims, flinging one of the doors open. "It isn't much, but you are so very welcome." It is a tiny dark room, the little bit of light that comes in is filtered through one grimy window. The room is filled with people of all ages; so close together that it is impossible to get from one end to the other without stepping over a sleeping body, or bumping into someone standing and praying. Two men, wearing black hats and *tzitzis*, (fringed garments) as commanded by Orthodox law, are standing, facing the wall, swaying vigorously to and fro and from side to side, their eyes tightly shut, praying to their unresponsive God. A red-headed, young woman sits on a red velvet chair, rocking her baby. A woman lies on a cot next to the wall, coughing uncontrollably into a blood soaked handkerchief. A teenaged boy leans against a window, his hands covering his eyes, not moving. Everyone is in his own little world.

The rabbi's wife seems to be in charge. "Move over, please, we have new guests," she tells a woman who is lying on the floor, staring at the ceiling. "We have to make room." Everyone stops what they are doing to look at us.

"God, I don't belong here," I say to myself. "I am a Catholic girl, Maria Kowalsczik. I belong in church kneeling in front of the Virgin Mary. Why am I here?" I hate this room with its awful sounds and putrid smells. I hate the dying people, the coughers, the weepers, the oozing sores, and the hopeless visions. I would rather be back in the furniture warehouse, burning up with fever and hallucinating. *I want to be anywhere but here.* All of us in this room are together because we are Jews. Aside from the rabbi's wife, we don't know anyone. We have nothing in common yet we are all staying here in one room, together. Some have given up hope; they sit and stare into vacant space. Others are waiting to be rescued. They are making plans, trading gloves for socks, belts for purses. The very religious pray for *Moshiach*, the Messiah, to come. The so -called enlightened ones are waiting for the world to come to its senses and stop these heedless killings. No one's prayers are answered.

The room has two cots and several chairs. The adults sign a list and are given a specific time to use the cots. Each person sleeps for about an hour and then the next one in turn wakes the sleeping one up by gentle nudging or assertive pushing, demanding the space. No one cares that the bedding is never changed, that lice are crawling over the blankets, that the smell of the person who just got up is rank and clinging. All they want is an hour of uninterrupted sleep; an hour to escape. Two chairs are placed facing each other, and it is on these chairs that the children take turns sleeping. Often the chairs slide apart, and then we find ourselves on the floor. After this happens to me twice, I decide that it is easier to sleep on the floor. The children almost never leave the room .We play indoors, under the table, constructing a make-believe world.

Once again, my mother, because of her Aryan looks, is pressed into service by the rabbi's wife. She hands her a black wool coat, "don't ask where it comes from," she says, "just take it and wear it. The owner will never use it again." She is sent out to forage for food for the rest of the inhabitants in our little room, a trip she will make many times in the coming weeks. She removes her Star of David armband and is escorted by one of the Jewish guards to the gate. A Jewish uniformed young man stands guard in a booth outside the ghetto walls. It is his job to check all the passes. He is an old friend of our family. He went to *cheder* (Hebrew school) with my cousin Isiek and often spent Shabbat at the farm. He is only seventeen, but already has the bearing of a man. He stands tall, refusing to be humiliated, is confident, respectful and gentle. The Gestapo trusts him, but he is ours. He protects the Jews and does not report them, even at risk to his own life. He often turns away when something suspicious is going on, such as someone coming into the Ghetto or leaving without authorization.

A Polish guard is at the sentry booth. "*Sone przepustki*? (Do you have passes)?" The officer on duty asks my mother and the Jewish escort with her, "*sone przepustki* (we have passes)! The Jewish escort guard assures him and he opens the gate for my mother. She trudges alone through the snow covered Krakow streets, bargaining with the shop keepers, for potatoes, half rotten carrots and anything else she can get for the few *zlotys* she has acquired from her roommates. She wants to pay for the food herself, but the rest won't hear of it. "We still have our dignity," a woman says, pressing two *zlotys* into her hand. My mother agrees. She may need her money for the future. She tries gathering as much food as she can. She is not particular about quality. We are many, and we are hungry but we share everything equally. The rabbi's wife tries to press some of her rations onto a nursing mother. "Come on," she urges, "You have to eat to nourish two lives."

While my mother is away, Bubbi and I stay in the room, playing under the table with the other children. In that small space we feel safe and protected until darkness comes and then panic assaults my heart. It is dark and she isn't back. I take up my vigil at the dirty window, waiting with her picture tucked up in a corner of the pane. I experience unimaginable terror; she has been caught, she is being tortured, mutilated. In my mind, I see her beaten and bloodied. I am preparing for the worst. Even though I am not yet six, I have been listening to many adult conversations for a long time and know all about the things that happen to Jews who are found outside the ghetto. I have already had first hand experience with people I love never being seen again.

It doesn't take much for my active imagination to take root and transport me to the forest of "Hansel and Gretel." My mother is gone. We are alone, lost in the woods surrounded by all kinds of danger. The horror of this reality is much more frightening than any fairy tale I have heard. "What if she never returns?" I will not be able to survive that. Bubbi and I are alone with no close relatives to turn to. Dangerous forms lurk in every shadow, just as they do in the illustrations of the frightening story my mother read to us before the horror of our reality set in. Now she is gone and it is difficult for me to separate my harsh world from the fairy tale. No one has the patience to comfort us. Everyone in the Ghetto is hungry and preoccupied. No one thinks about reassuring two small frightened children. I am dreadfully alone, afraid that we will never see her again. What will happen to us? So many people disappear. It doesn't take much imagination to see us as orphans, alone in the world with no one to take us in, a fate that so many children I know are facing.

Suddenly, she's here. She's safe and beautiful and smelling of snow. She has had an exceptional day outside the Ghetto. She comes in with a loaf of bread, three tiny potatoes, a jar of yogurt and a maggot- infested slab of meat. The kosher people won't eat the meat, but we do. "This is war," my mother tells us, "you eat whatever you can."

As long as my mother is nearby, I feel safe and protected. My mother tries hard to shelter us from devastating realities that are occurring all around us. She keeps us full of hope and promises that things will get much better when we get to America. "You'll see," she tells us, "we will have so much food that you are going to beg me to stop feeding you. You'll each have a beautiful room to sleep in, many toys, and a closet full of warm clothing."

"Will Papa play ball with me?" Bubbi asks hopefully.

"Everyday," she answers emphatically.

"And will we each have our own beds?"

"Of course you'll have your own beds; you'll even have your own rooms."

"And will papa take us to the circus?" I ask hopefully.

"Not only will he take you to the circus, he will take you to shake hands with the dancing tigers." She assures us.

"Will we be able to go to school?"

"Able?" she asks incredulously. "You *have* to go to school. In America everyone goes to school."

"Can I be Jewish in America?" Bubbi asks anxiously.

"Yes, of course you'll be Jewish. You will always be Jewish. In America, there is no anti-Semitism."

"What if I don't want to live Jewish? Will I still be able to go to church?" I want to be like everyone else. I've been Jewish longer than I want to be. "I want to be a Catholic," I protest. "I don't want to live in a Ghetto with all these Jews, with all these sad people, taking turns sleeping on a bed for one hour each night, listening to that sick woman coughing, seeing dead people taken out onto the streets, slumping against a wall, their heads rolling onto their chests. I hate the Jews. I don't want to be Jewish, not now, not ever." I am in tears. I quickly forget the promises my mother has just made to us about the wonderful life in America. In no time, I am back to reality and the sordid life we are living only because we are Jews.

"Maidi, Maidi," my mother rocks me gently. "When we get to America none of that will be happening. You can be Jewish and live in a beautiful house, with a nice big garden. You papa will buy you anything you want, and you will never have to see people suffering because they are Jewish."

I don't believe her. I resolve that when I am free, I will become a Catholic again. I promise myself that I will never be Jewish and suffer like this. But Bubbi buys into her promises. Her stories about my father are so real for Bubbi that he thinks my father is just around the corner. Every time my mother meets a male acquaintance Bubbi tugs at her sleeve, impatiently, "Ask him," he lisps, "ask him. Maybe this is our father."

My mother begins to realize that I am becoming aware of what is going on around me. She knows I no longer believe the stories she tells me to assuage my longings and fears. The conditions in the Ghetto are deteriorating and no amount of magic and make believe can make me deny what I am seeing around me. There is no longer enough food left to share and people are sick, starving and dying all around us. The illness, starvation and hopelessness of the Ghetto are taking a toll on the living.

The Ghetto is a dangerous place. Those who don't starve or succumb to illness vanish. People are disappearing daily; dragged away from the few loved ones left alive and taken to God knows where. Children and older people are dying in the streets and no one is strong enough to pick them up and bury them. All this I see with my own eyes open wide. My mother, who likes to attribute all the unpleasant things I hear and see to my imagination has stopped trying to cheer me up. She knows that she cannot erase the present with fairy tales of the future. She has had enough. One night, she collapses on the cot. She covers her face with her hands and sobs quietly.

The coughing woman has not awakened. She hasn't coughed or moved since early morning, and even I can tell that something is terribly wrong. The rabbi's wife, though weak and starving herself, takes over. "Her body can't stay in the room with us. We have to have it removed. Let me see what we can do." Three of the Jewish guards come into our room. They are going to fetch the committee in the Ghetto that prepares bodies for burial. I am not going to watch. I hide under the table and wait for them to take the coughing woman away. I don't ask where they are taking her. I'm afraid I might find out the truth and that it may be more frightening than not knowing.

Later on that very night, my mother quietly packs our few possessions, takes us with her and leaves the Ghetto with the men who are taking away the body of the coughing woman; we never find out what her name was. The guard on duty asks if we have passes to leave. My mother replies that we do, and thankfully, he does not ask her to produce them.

Chapter Sixteen

Into the Dark Woods

Outside the ghetto walls, my mother tells us that we are once again Catholic, Maria and Tomek Kowalczik. We are standing in front of a delicatessen when two German officers come out with steaming, fragrant sandwiches, smoked meat on fresh white rolls. They are laughing and conversing loudly. We follow them watching them eat. As we had hoped, they do not finish and carelessly toss the uneaten remains into waste bins. Bubbi scrambles up the bin and joyfully retrieves a meal for us, big red sausages on fresh white rolls: still warm. Nothing has ever tasted better.

In an endless search for lodging and food, we walk around for what seems like hours. All around high spirited officers speaking German push each other around good naturedly, laughing at each other's antics. I remember the uniforms from Vienna and miss my home and the handsome Nazis marching in unison. I make no connection between them and the horrors of the ghetto or the frightening punishments of the Jews. I am glad to see them again and salute them by raising my arm. "Heil Hitler," I say. They smile warmly at me, probably thinking that my blond mother is the wife of some high ranking officer.

We board a tram. When we are ready to get off, my mother takes us by the hand and prepares to disembark. A courteous German soldier pops out of his seat and offers his arm to her, helps her get off the trolley. He lifts Bubbi and me off as if weighed nothing and bows his head courteously to my mother. This, I think, is how a German gentleman behaves.

"*Grüss Gott, und danke schön.*" I thank him and curtsy as all well- bred girls are taught.

He turns to my mother, "*Wie schön, sie spricht Deutch* (how beautifully she speaks German) he tells her, smiling happily at us.

54

I quickly add in German, "Yes, right now I can speak German, but soon we are going to America, where I'll see my papa and speak English."

The soldier laughs heartily.

"The fantasy of a child," he exclaims to my mother. She smiles and thanks him in German.

My mother knocks on strangers' doors and finally finds a Polish woman willing to take in borders in exchange for a gold necklace my mother has taken from Wieliczka. We spend a few nights with her. She is kind and even brings us hot soup. But my mother is afraid. She doesn't trust any Pole, even the ones who might be kind. She won't spend more than a week with her. If the woman is sincere, then we will be putting her into jeopardy. If not, then she will betray us. We leave and this time my mother has another idea. She takes us to a jewelry store. She digs into her pocket and produces a gold bracelet with some colorful stones in it. "I know how much this bracelet is worth," she tells the jeweler. "I paid two hundred *zlotys* for it only one year ago."

He examines it through a funny little glass placed close up to his eye. "It is beautiful, the stones are real, and I can tell you that if you paid only two hundred *zlotys* you got a bargain. But these are hard times," he tells her; "I don't have many customers. Hungry people don't have money for jewelry. I'll be lucky if I can sell this bracelet to some Nazi who wants to buy his sweetheart a present. I won't get more than a hundred *zlotys* for it, if I'm lucky." He buys it for sixty *zlotys*. My mother agrees to the price. She knows she can't hold out for what the bracelet is worth. She confides in me, as though I am a grown up: "This bracelet is only good for getting us what we need to stay alive for one day at a time. It doesn't protect us from the cold and it doesn't put food in our stomachs." I listen carefully. Her tone toward me has changed from playful mother, to one adult confiding to another. I nod my head. I understand even though I am only six years old.

We approach another house and this time my mother offers the woman three *zlotys* for a room for one night. At first the woman argues with her. She wants more. But my mother has some money now and she feels a bit more secure. She refuses to pay more than three and the woman grudgingly agrees.

The next morning, there is a loud banging on the door and two uniformed officers fling it open. "Your papers; show them to us now!" The menacing Polish officers take turns yelling at us. Unlike the courteous, well-bred Nazi on the tram, these men are loud and coarse. Once again, my mother realizes we are being betrayed by our landlady who is getting even with her for not giving her more money. She looks them squarely in the eye, assuming her full stature and acting confident, aware of her blond hair, blue-eyes and aristocratic beauty. She feels she has nothing left to lose.

"I have no papers now," she spits out arrogantly. There is no point in acting scared, "all my identity papers were taken away from me by your Polish officers and they were never returned to me, as promised. Your police have them in one of their offices and now I am stuck here with no identity," she adds feigning anger in hope of diverting them.

"All they left me with is my father's birth certificate, and I doubt that it will be of any use to you, since it is written in English." She thrusts the birth certificate at them and the Polish officers scrutinize it. They speak to each other in hurried whispers. Their tone softens a bit.

"Come with us," they beckon to her, looking at Bubbi and me, suddenly taking note of our Aryan looks. "We're going to take you to the German authorities. They'll know what to do with you. Let the German devils deal with this." They treat us as equals. They look at my mother, smile and shrug their shoulders.

We follow them outside waiting for something to happen. I am trembling with fear and cold. Soon, a large, open- air truck arrives and we are quickly loaded into the back of it. There are several other people on the truck, and stops are made along the way, each time picking up additional passengers. I wonder if this is what happens to people who are being taken away every day. While the truck roars noisily through the streets of Krakow, my brother and I huddle under the black coat my mother acquired in the Ghetto, protected by her warmth. We have no idea of where we are going even though my mother automatically reassures us by telling us that we are on our way to America. She knows we no longer believe her but she can't stop herself.

"Just one of the stops on the road to see your Papa," she says optimistically.

Years later after we have gotten to America, she will answer when I ask her why she never told us the truth; "Why frighten little children with the truth? You had enough to cope with. If a little lie was going to make you less fearful, why should I deny it? Deprive you a bit of hope?" She wisely asked adding, "Besides, it certainly wasn't going to harm you if you felt there would be a happy ending to this ordeal. Whatever was going to happen would happen, whether you were frightened for a long time or just for a moment."

Chapter Seventeen

Prison

The truck finally stops in front of a huge gate surrounded by a wall topped with barbed wire. I look up to see a bird fly over the horizon. A piercingly blue sky, gazes indifferently on our little family. We have arrived at what I later learn is a huge prison, Montelupi, taken over by the Germans and now administered by the Gestapo. They patrol the corridors, wearing helmets and carrying rifles, ready for battle. The atmosphere is tense even though the waiting area is bright. There are few walls; most of the rooms are separated by stainless steel bars and tall gates that are locked with jangling keys at all times. The overhead lights reflect these separations and keep the area open and bright. We are lined up, just like schoolchildren and walk through many barred doors. At last, separated from our fellow transport passengers, we are ushered into a small room at the end of one of the hallways.

This room has real walls. We are seated in front of a big, bald German officer. His green cap sits on his desk, the eagle and swastika mounted above the visor gleam at us. He hunches over a paper, holding it close to his face and squinting at it. His glasses are resting close to the end of his pinched nostrils but he peers above them. He pays no attention to us. He studies the paper, deep in concentration. He looks at the front, turns it over and then holds it up to the light. I notice that his fingernails are neatly trimmed and polished, just like a lady's. Finally he puts the paper down on the green blotter in front of him.

"And, ...um, how did you, ahhh... come into possession, um... acquire this uh, birth certificate?" he asks my mother in halting English, pausing between words and trying to retrieve enough English to make himself understood.

She answers him in perfect German as she squares her shoulders and looks him in the eye. She has become another person, no longer frightened of the

57

stern authority figures. Instinctively she knows that it will go better for her if she commands respect rather than scorn. The Nazis have little compassion for fear. She tells me much later, when we are in America that she asked herself, what's the worst thing they can do to us? And she understands that it will be exactly what they are doing to all the others.

She pulls her chair closer to his desk, leans her elbow on it and cradles her chin. "It was in a family photo album. My father was born in America, but lived most of his whole life in Austria. I don't know why I took it with me, perhaps as a souvenir to remember him by."

The Nazi nods. "Hmmm," he muses in German and says almost like he's talking to himself, "Your German does sound like you are from Vienna." He licks his thick, red lips, and looks at the certificate again, "Ummm, Rubin Perlberger? Your father? He is," he hesitates before saying the loathsome word, "Jewish?"

"My father *was* Jewish. His whole family converted to Lutheran when he was seven years old, before they returned to Vienna."

I'm dying to ask what "Lutheran" is but have to control myself because my mother is holding my wrist so tightly that I feel like it's going to snap right off my arm.

"I see, I understand," he says, nodding his head, consulting his watch. "Very well," he says, handing back the certificate over to my mother. "The guard outside will take you to your quarters." We follow a guard through several corridors separated from each other by heavy, clanking doors. Finally, he unlocks one of the doors and we enter a large room, crowded with women and children. Bubbi and I stand at the entranceway, holding on tightly to my mother's hand while the lock behind us slides smoothly into its resting place. We look around trying to figure out where we are.

Some of the women are sitting at a long narrow table while others have brought chairs over to the window where they sit and talk to one another. They all know each other and appear to be long time friends. My mother takes a deep breath before approaching one of the women. She asks her why she is there and decides that Montelupi is just a stopping off place. "We won't be here long," she whispers to me. I nod my head knowingly. Again, she is talking to me like to another adult and not a child. "Apparently, no one stays here very long," she confides in me. Still, we are scared. Everyone is a stranger, and no one makes a move towards us.

We quickly learn the routine of the prison. Everyone sleeps on mats on the floor. In the morning the mats are picked up and stacked against a wall. The long table is brought in and stays in place until it is time to put the mats on the floor and go to sleep again.

At that table, we eat breakfast which consists of an enameled bowl of black coffee, and a saccharine tablet. The only other meal is served in mid afternoon when we receive the same bowl, only this time it is filled with sloppy, unrecognizable, slippery greasy pieces of discarded fat. It is called *Eintopf,* one pot. It consists of every piece of garbage that no one else will eat, heated up and served to us. Because I am so desperately hungry I put it in my mouth and try to chew. I can't swallow. I gag and choke before spitting it out.

Other amenities in Montelupi include a closet containing one sink with a slow leaking faucet, where all the women and their children wash up as best they can with the cold rusty water. Sometimes one manages to rinse out a pair of socks or underwear.

The first time I need to use the bathroom, I ask one of the women where it is. She takes me over to the closet and points to an enormous garbage can. "This is it," she tells me nonchalantly. I gasp. It is tall and reaches my waist. "How do I climb up?" I ask, seeing myself floating on top of the excrement. "Oh, you'll get used to it," she tells me. "Everyone hates it at first, but you get used to it." I peer inside the disgusting garbage can. I weigh the options. I can't bring myself to attempt to climb up the side of the can, but I am desperate. I run for my mother. She picks me up and holds me over the can. Still scared of landing inside, I grab onto her arms tightly. I am repulsed by the smell and use the can as seldom as possible. I try to stop going to the bathroom all together and become constipated for days. Several times a day, the can is emptied by the women who take turns with this unpleasant task but it does little to alleviate the stench and sight of it.

To augment our daily food rations, the Red Cross occasionally sends burlap bags of onions to be distributed to each of the inmates. We look forward to receiving them. We peel them and eat them like apples. We sprinkle left over saccharine powder on them and strangely enough, they begin to taste good. We elect officers, people from our ranks to be spokespersons, and things are run in an orderly manner. When the Gestapo inspects our quarters each morning, our captain, a German speaking prisoner with short hair and a loud voice calls out:

"*Achtung! Zimmer drei und dreisich, tzwei und twanzight Amerikaner, funfzehn Englender, neun kinder und ein samlung von andere auslander.* (Attention! Room thirty-three, twenty-two Americans, fifteen British women, nine children, and a collection of other nationalities)." We all spring to attention and stand ramrod straight in front of our mats, not daring to move. After the Germans take a head count, they click their boots and demand to see our papers. When that happens everyone is frightened, rushing to get whatever identity cards they possess. The officer in charge scrutinizes the documents and motions several women to leave. The rest breathe a sigh of relief. No one enters or leaves Montelupi prison willingly.

With my mother in the same quarters, I feel sheltered and protected. I know exactly where she is. She is not allowed out of there, so she cannot leave us alone. For the first time in a long time I do not have to wait for her return. It is a huge improvement over the long waiting periods I had to endure in Wieliczka and the Ghetto and I decide that Montelupi is a good place to be in.

Amazingly, extraordinary favors are bestowed upon some of the prisoners, in particular, a girl my age, Monica. She and her mother, receive chicken, grapes, salad, almond cookies and other delicacies from the outside. These come with china plates, linen napkins and silverware. Monica and her mother eat their meals on the window sill away from the rest of us, never sharing a morsel, while we choke on our slop at the communal table. I cast longing glances at their food.

The other kids and I stand around them watching them eat, despising Monica for her greed and bounty. Our gaze never strays from their food and we never miss an opportunity to tease her. "How were your grapes today, Monica? Were they fresh and tasty, or were they a bit on the sour side?" Monica looks away. She doesn't give us so much as a glance. I later wonder if the chicken, the linens and the silverware were worth the taunting we kids inflicted upon her over our next several years in captivity.

Chapter Eighteen

The Journey

One crisp winter morning several important looking Gestapo officers come into our room. They enter to the accompaniment of lots of noise and clatter. We spring to attention while they take a head count.

"Take out your identity papers," they bark today, "and line up against the wall." Panic ensues. No one knows what that means, who will be taken away or where they will be taken. The grown ups as well as the children are terrified. We all know of people who disappeared and were never heard from again.

Everyone has to get in line, many of the women praying and all of them crying and trembling, except my mother. She is standing calmly, examining a loose thread on her sleeve. In the coming years, she will recall how she had a dream the night before the Gestapo appeared in which my grandmother wearing her old green sweater with white angora trim around the collar had come to her and spoke.

"Stand tall," she told my mother. "Do not be afraid. Stand tall and act arrogant. Look everyone directly in the eye and use whatever charm you have."

That day, even as the Gestapo prowled the room, barking orders to the frightened women, the dream is stunningly vivid in my mother's mind, and when it's her turn to present her papers, she stands her full height and makes direct eye contact with the Gestapo officer. He holds the fake birth certificate, pretending to be studying it, but I can see he's really looking at her.

She smiles at him and raises one eyebrow flirtatiously. He returns her smile and winks at her. She is only thirty-four years old and beautiful. They smile at each other, as if sharing a secret. *"Alles ist im ordnung"* he assures her, motioning us to one of several lines.

Once again we are on an open truck with other passengers, fellow emigrants from Montelupi. Monica and her mother are with us. Two male drivers take turns at the wheel. We have been traveling for days through a deep, silent snow covered landscape "Mutti, where are we going?" I ask my mother for the tenth time, knowing well what her answer will be. "We are going to America to be with your Papa." I don't believe it, but somehow feel reassured when she repeats the same answer to the same question.

I persist. "But where are we now?"

"On our way to America, but first we have to make a few stops."

We ride for days through the soft, quiet countryside. We sleep when it gets dark, close to each other to conserve every bit of warmth we can generate. I wiggle my fingers to make sure they are still all there. It is always cold. I don't remember ever being warm. The drivers change places every time we come to a village. Our little transport attracts attention: old men, young women, children and a few dogs. They wave to us and smile. These towns have very little traffic the drivers tell us. Petrol is scarce and no one is going anywhere. Every now and then when we stop in a village one of the drivers jumps off the truck and returns with some bread, a bottle of water, turnips, potatoes and whatever else can be scrounged from the villagers. We take a bite and a swallow and pass it on to the others.

Several times a day the truck stops at a deserted area where most of us get off. We stretch our legs. We paint the fresh snow yellow with splotches of urine. Relieving ourselves in the cold, pristine snow is a welcome change from the loathsome cans of Montelupi. No one on the truck has any feeling of shame or embarrassment. We do what we have to do. The trip is monotonous. So quiet is the countryside, that at times people are reluctant to disturb the silence by talking.

It feels as though our journey will never end: the eternal voyage. In a strange way it is comforting. We are no longer running from the unknown. We are being driven through friendly villages by nice older men. These drivers tell us that they had been imprisoned by the British during the First World War and they remember how well they were treated. Although they are now working for the Gestapo, they are polite and kind to us.

Early one morning, just as the sun sends a pink gauze curtain across the sky to announce her arrival, four large buildings appear behind a gated wall. Our convoy arrives on a fairy tale set, complete with castles and towers. Somewhere in the distance we hear the chime of church bells. I count seven gongs. We get off the truck and stretch. Nothing is moving. No birds are chirping to complain of our intrusion, no icicles are melting from the branches, no leaf is moving, not even a breath of wind disturbs the arms of the huge evergreen trees, standing like snow- covered sculptures. The whole world is sleeping. It is a silent illustration in one of my fairy tale books.

We stand outside the truck, like statues hovering on the landscape. Four imposing stone buildings, one with medieval turrets, rise up behind the gated walls. Suddenly, the gates open to a flurry of activity. German officers greet the drivers. They shake hands, talk to each other, check some papers, and count us.

Several nuns come out to the gate to greet us. They tell us to follow them. Our contingent of women and children is taken to communal baths. We are told to undress and, to my delight, take long hot baths. It is part of the delousing project. The steam and hot water thaw my freezing fingers tips, and toes. I discover parts of my body I have forgotten in the cold, my shoulders, thighs and knees come alive and defrost. The seemingly endless supply of clean hot water and soap make for an unforgettable bath. It warms my very soul and makes me feel alive again. Welcome to my new home!

The convent at Liebenau is an operating mental institution, known as "the Asylum" in a German town not far from the Swiss border. It consists of four buildings known as the Clara House, Josef House, Cathedral and the *Schloss, or castle.* By 1940, several hundred "disposable," violent patients were gassed in order to make room for the British and American women and children; POW's who are supervised by the Swiss who visit periodically to make certain that all the rules of the Geneva Convention are observed. It is home to 600 prisoners of war: women and children. Boys are permitted to stay in the camp with their mothers until they reach the age of fourteen; then they are sent to a men's internment camp. By some miracle of fate we, Austrian-Polish Jews have ended up in an American and British POW camp in 1942.

As it turns out, the birth certificate of Reuven Perlberger, which my father had sent to us, saves our lives once again. It automatically, though falsely, makes my mother, (daughter of Reuven Perlberger) an American citizen, thereby entitling her to POW status. We are not persecuted for being Jewish, but we are a minority compared to the British and American POWs and the mental patients whom the sisters of the convent still care for.

Chapter Nineteen

A Normal Childhood
in a Mental Hospital

Miss Crew, a crisp British woman is in charge of all the children in the camp. She is thin, sharp-featured, with rosy pink skin and thick black eyebrows arching over piercing blue eyes. Her lips are narrow and barely move when she speaks, but her word is law and her manner is brusque. She hardly ever smiles and scolds us unmercifully for little things.

Before she was captured, Miss Crew, a British governess, worked for Polish royalty, the Potowskis and the Radziwills. Her job was to teach their children proper English and good manners. She lets us know that Liebenau is a major step down for her and tells us constantly how we are unlike those well- behaved children. All of us are scared of Miss Crew.

She holds our fate in her hands; telling us what to wear and how to speak. She can see whether or not we've brushed our teeth and washed our faces just by looking at us. But worst of all, she makes us go out in all kinds of weather. No matter how cold it is outside, Miss Crew insists that children must have fresh air in order to survive. And if that isn't enough, she won't permit us to wear warm clothes. I wear short skirts and light jackets on the coldest afternoons. I come inside, complaining. My thighs are red from the cold and my teeth are chattering but Miss Crew would prefer for me to freeze rather than permit the possibility of becoming overheated. "Becoming overheated," she says in a convincing tone of voice, "is inviting all sorts of diseases and germs to attack our bodies. We need to keep moving around outdoors to stimulate our circulation and keep ourselves healthy," she says, although she hardly ever goes out in the cold. I wonder how those royal children managed to stay warm in the freezing cold of Polish winter.

All the children sleep in the Clara House, in what is "the nursery." Miss Crew sits in a corner of the nursery, knitting in the dark, not leaving until she is sure everyone is sleeping. We hear her needles clicking rhythmically. She is knitting a blue jumper which she rips as soon as she finishes in order to start another one using the same wool.

One of us pretends to be snoring, making the rest of us laugh.

"Stop that at once," she orders, angrily.

We try to stay quiet, but we can't stop laughing. But every now and then another brave soul snores, and soon half the kids are snoring and the other half are laughing. Miss Crew is furious. No one is allowed to turn the lights on after dark, for security reasons, not even Miss Crew. She walks from bed to bed trying to catch the culprit. She stubs her toe on the edge of a chair and quietly curses, "Darn it!" She is determined to figure out who the snorers are. The minute she comes near one of us, we feign sleep. The room is dark and noisy and Miss Crew is furious. She is going to punish us all.

"Very well, then," she says, "since you are all misbehaving and not sleeping, you may as well stay up all night long." And with that she pulls off everyone's blanket and opens the tall windows to the blasting gusts of cold air. It does stop the laughter, but she can't keep us awake all night long either. Eventually we all fall asleep, even though we are freezing.

The food, prepared by the nuns, tastes good and is, for the most part nutritious. We are fed whatever the loonies and the sisters eat. The vegetables grown in the camp gardens are fresh in the summer and canned in the winter. Eggs are only served once a year, on Easter. When we get meat, it is usually inedible: tough, stringy, fatty, not anything I am able to swallow. There is plenty of bread and potatoes and we never have to go hungry. We also receive generous supplements from the American Red Cross. The packages are designed for the soldiers on the front and sent to us as American POWs. We each receive a parcel every few months containing cans of Spam, condensed milk, coffee, cigarettes, warm socks, playing cards, tiny chess sets, shaving kits, tooth brushes and tooth paste. We eat the Spam and enjoy teaspoons of the condensed milk sweetened with saccharine. We trade the coffee and cigarettes for luxuries: warm pull-overs, gloves, aero-grams and cold cream. We keep the cards and small chess sets, with tiny holes on the board, which hold the chess pieces. The shaving kits are exchanged for special favors from the guards: a newspaper, magazine and flash light batteries.

Every internee is allowed to send one letter a month to someone outside the camp. Since there are three of us, my mother gets to send out three letters. She writes to my father, sews several photos of us onto the inside of the aerogram sheet she is given and tells him that we are still alive, and doing very well in a protected internment camp. The minute he receives the news of our whereabouts my father goes on a wild shopping spree. He goes from the clothing store, to the book store, to the shoe store, to the toy store, to the drug store, to the food store. He's making good money, he writes to my mother. He works as a cutter in a factory that makes leather jackets for pilots and other officers. The pay is higher than anything he earned in Vienna and he has been able to set aside money for our arrival.

The packages he sends us are storehouses of luxury: pajamas, snowsuits, underwear, socks, colorful striped polo shirts, dresses, trousers, games, books, candy bars, sweaters, shoes, combs and brushes, paper dolls with fabulous wardrobes, coloring books, and crayons. When a package arrives for one of us, everyone in my mother's room gathers around exclaiming over our fortune. Suddenly we are rich! My mother is generous. She gives some things to her friends and roommates, but, Miss Crew promptly appropriates my brother's and my belongings and distributes them to other children. Before long, all the children in the camp are wearing the striped polo shirts and socks that my father sent to us. One of my snowsuits goes to Monica, the chicken eater from Montelupi. Monica never acknowledges my reluctant generosity. As far as she's concerned, the snowsuit is a gift from Miss Crew. Now I hate Miss Crew more than ever. Her control is restricted to the nursery. While she supervises what we wear and where we sleep, we usually don't see her until the end of the day at bedtime.

The rest of the time we go to school and when we are not in school, we run freely at Liebenau outdoors. We talk to and play with the patients, whom we call "the loonies." Many of them are friendly and childlike. They join us in games of hopscotch, jump rope, and ringalevio. Non–violent ones are allowed to roam freely around the camp when they aren't working in the kitchen or tending the gardens. I am fascinated by them and watch as they walk around the garden whispering, arguing, gesticulating, and nodding their heads to unseen companions. One old fellow roams around the camp cursing and shouting at the kids. We know he's harmless so we delight in his behavior. He can't stop yelling out bad words, and he enjoys the attentive, encouraging audience we make.

But not all the loonies are so benign. Luther is threatening to kill Luigi, one of the other inmates, because he claims he's heard Luigi talking to the devil, making plans to kill him.

"Calm down, Luther. You must stop," Sister Hortense says softly, trying to calm him. She is a tiny woman, with a ruddy complexion and light eyebrows.

"I've got to get him first," Luther retorts, "otherwise he and his devil friends are taking me to hell, to burn eternally. I heard them making plans." He is ranting and kicking the sisters away from him.

Sister Hortense tries again to soothe him. She is not afraid of him, even though he is a wild man, thrashing about, and trying to bite her. "Shhh, Luther, no one is going to hurt you while you are here."

He grabs her habit and starts shaking her, "Shut up, Sister, or I'll be coming for you at night with my knife," he shouts at her, "and I'll cut your lily white throat until the whole bed turns red with your blood."

We watch, awe-struck, mesmerized and scared, as he throws himself around uncontrollably. Several nuns run out of the Cloister with long strips of knotted sheets. They attempt to immobilize him by dancing around him and trying to wrap his body in the sheets, like a mummy. But it becomes impossible for the nuns to restrain him, so one of the sisters runs to the guardhouse at the entrance of the camp. She returns with two or three German guards who grab the loony under his shoulders and by his feet and drag him off. This is a routine occurrence and we know that the loony will end up in one of the two cells reserved for such misbehavior; an isolated, escape proof cell, with thick, painted windows.

When the loonies are confused we can hear their desperate raging. Some of us try to peek in through a hole that has been scratched in the thick painted glass. Others taunt these unfortunate souls, threatening them with new demons and increasing their fury and fear. I don't participate in either sport. I'm truly afraid of them.

"I'm going to get you. I'm going to tear your arms off your bodies. I'm going to kill you and rip your bloody hearts out," they scream and then they whimper, "Let me out, let me out. Oh please, let me out. I'll be good."

Their torment launches my own catastrophic fantasies. I become desperately frightened that they might escape their cells and punish us kids for taunting them. I picture them at night, climbing up the doorway, squeezing themselves through the transom and choking me. They won't know that I am not one of their tormentors. "You made fun of me? You made fun of me? Here. Here's what you get."

I am also fearful that if I talk to myself I am just one step away from madness myself. So I will myself to stop thinking, and never ever plan or practice anything in my head. I'm rarely successful in quieting my mind and when I catch myself thinking, I am convinced that I'm going crazy myself.

When I am not ruminating, I do what I assume all kids do when they are not in danger: make friends and plot against our enemies. We play games like hopscotch, cards and jump rope. We play house, school, prison, hospital and store. We put on many elaborate shows.

For Easter we put on a spectacular presentation. It is a musical comedy, written and produced by a professional actress who happens to be one of the internees, Miss Thompson from England. The main roles are to be played by grown ups but the children are given parts of singing chickens and roosters. I have the glorious distinction of having a solo and being the only rabbit in the play. We rehearse daily, stomping on the makeshift stage that is erected at the far end of a large hall. It is spring time and we are ready to put on our show.

The scenery, painted by a professional artist consists of a red barn, surrounded by a large barnyard. Six singing chickens and six dancing roosters enter the stage through a door that opens and closes in the painted barn. My costume, made by a real fashion designer, is constructed from old terry cloth towels and pink flannel from someone's discarded pajamas. The chickens and roosters wear bonnets made of crepe paper, with wings attached to their arms over the striped polo shirts supplied unknowingly by my father. When the chickens come out to do their bit, I stand up and do my solo, the chickens and the roosters sing while I jump up and down trying to scare them.

The farmer comes onstage and shoots me and a few of the chickens as well. We flop over while trying to stifle our giggles and he drags us off the stage to make his rabbit pie. The curtain comes down to the enthusiastic applause of everyone in the audience. I am thrilled with my performance and determined that I want to be an actress, singer and dancer. Everyone is invited to the performance: the sisters, the internees, the loonies, even the camp commandant. He comes with one of his fellow officers and they watch the entire performance and leave as soon as it is over, never smiling or saying anything.

Chapter Twenty

School

I wake up early on week day mornings. I want to be the first one ready for school. I wash up slowly and carefully. Much as I relished having a solo in the Easter play, school is "my turf." I sit up straight in our one room, multi- grade classroom. My hands are folded in front of the table, and I focus carefully on the teacher's face. I long for a notebook, a sharpened pencil and a backpack to carry them in. I want to be a real pupil, with homework. As soon as my hair is long enough, I insist on the pigtails older girls wear. Somewhere in my mind, there's a picture of school girls with braids. I want to be like them.

Our instructors are the British nuns and teachers, imported and employed by exclusive private schools and wealthy households. They were trapped in Germany and Poland when Great Britain entered the war. They are strict, but fair: rewarding the "good" and punishing the "bad." Although I am too young to understand why, I feel safe here, where I know what is expected. This is the first time since I was three years old that my life is ruled by predictable, reasonable boundaries.

School supplies are sparse, several English texts and story books, are brought to the camp; rescued by the teachers who could not bear to part with them. Paper is scarce and the only way we are going to learn anything is by repetition and memorization. There are about twenty of us, coming from Holland, Greece, Italy, Belgium, Germany and Poland, aged from six to eight. Monica is in my class, wearing my clothes and ignoring me. Although I try, there is no way I can upset her or get her attention.

Our lessons take place in the morning. After lunch, when the classroom is used by the older children, we are free to do as we please. I love going to school. The work is simple for me and I am eager to learn. It is one of the places I feel successful. I am a good student, receiving much praise from Sister Leticia who often scolds the other children. She is a tough taskmaster and her praise makes me feel smart and competent. I learn to read and am quickly captivated by the heroes and heroines I meet in books. Books lead me to places I have only dreamed of. They fill me with hope and glimpses into other worlds. Oh, to live in Sherwood Forest, among Robin Hood and his men, or to be Heidi, living in the Alps with her beloved grandfather. I rejoice with my heroes, they are so different from the witches and ogres that live in the fairy tales I'm accustomed to.

Hansel and Gretel, with its dark portrayals of evil and magic are much closer to my reality. I'm never completely sure that the ending will come out happily each time I hear the story and I fear for the children. In my young lifetime, I have learned always to be prepared for alternate endings: Cinderella might have not been rescued by the Prince Charming; the Seven Dwarfs do not have to appear in Snow White's forest. I am too skeptical to believe that evil is vanquished and happy endings are guaranteed. In my life wishes don't come true. I can not predict what our ending will be like, even though my mother keeps telling us that we will live happily ever after.

The heroes in my new books are real. They don't depend on the whims of magical beings, frightening ogres or evil witches. The things that happen to them can happen to anyone, even to me. It is in this little classroom where I learn to read, that I come as close as possible to having a wish granted. Reading lets me enjoy traveling to other, safer lives and escaping from the every day dangers of my life.

Chapter Twenty-One

Merry Christmas

Ironically, now that it is safe to be Jewish, I desperately want to go to mass with other children. I stand outside the chapel one morning, during Sunday morning mass, breathing in the warm and pleasant smell of incense. I am transported to the Cathedral in Krakow. I imagine I will always feel at home in a Catholic church. I hear beautiful singing coming out of the chapel. It sounds like angels. I close my eyes and imagine what heaven must be like. Suddenly, a door opens and the old priest comes out.

"What are you doing here, child?" he asks gently, smiling at me, his face is as broad as the shining sun, his blue eyes sparkle like ponds on a sunny morning.

"Oh, I don't know," I reply. "I wish I had a nice place to pray in."

"But you do," he encourages me, "Come right in and join us." He extends his pink, fleshy hand to me.

I recall the anti-Semitic girls in Poland who tormented us for being Jewish. I am certain that the priest wouldn't want me in his church if he knew I was Jewish.

"I can't," I protest, "I'm Jewish and your God doesn't want me in your church."

"Nonsense," he replies gently, "There is only one God. He loves all children, and He loves you too. Now come in with me."

I feel warmly welcomed, but I must think it over. I have a strong urge to enter a house of prayer, especially a church, where I am familiar with the rituals; and I miss them. I tell myself that I don't have to tell my mother, who would surely disapprove now that we are Jewish again. But do I have to tell her? And how could she disapprove? Wasn't she the one who first took us to church in Poland? Didn't she tell us to kneel at the cemetery? Still, I answer myself reasonably: she only did that because it was dangerous to be Jewish.

71

We had no choice before we went to the Ghetto. It was "Be Catholic or be taken away on one of those awful trucks." I struggle. I want so very much to do something I know is wrong. After lots of arguments with my conscience, I arrive at a compromise. I will attend, but only for the choir. The music coming from the church is overwhelmingly seductive. The voices of the children are so clear and pure, that I have to go in.

I join the choir, am assigned to the soprano section and begin rehearsing for midnight mass on Christmas Eve. Most of the carols are sung in German and English, and a few in Latin. I feel important. I know that I have a good voice, and I try to sing louder than all the other sopranos, hoping for a solo. I can't wait for Christmas when we finally will be able to perform for the entire camp.

Finally, it is midnight on Christmas. Outside the snow is deep and soft, reflecting the moonlight and the stars. Large evergreens stand, dignified like giant statues of brave heroes. The branches, like multiple arms are adorned with heavy sleeves of snow. The church is warm and smells of pine incense. Everyone in is seated in the pews. The "loonies" and the prisoners are dressed in their best attire. My mother unexpectedly does not disapprove of my participation. She can't bear to deprive herself or me of this pleasure, when so much already has been taken away from us. Everyone waits to hear the choir, signaling that mass has begun. We children wearing the white gowns we were given stand straight and proud in the loft, out of sight, but certainly not out of earshot.

Hundreds of soft candles cast long shadows on the silent walls. The conductor lifts her arms to our rendition of "Silent Night, *Stille Nacht, Heilige Nacht.*" Gentle harmonies, shimmering candlelight, and peaceful spirit send goose bumps up and down my arms and spine. Everyone in the church inhales deeply. Some even close their eyes and travel to their own corridors of tranquility enjoying this moment of respite from the war that rages outside our camp. When we get to the last carol, "Hark the Herald Angels Sing," we hear ominous buzzing overhead and the sad wail of the siren. We continue singing, trying to ignore the impending warning of an air raid. Surely nothing can happen to us here in church on Christmas Eve. But the bombers don't hear our voices.

The thunder of the first bomb shakes the church; we all stay put and continue singing, "God and sinner reconciled." It is a moment of peace and we want to prolong it. We linger over the last "amen," finish the mass, look at each other and quickly follow the route to the cellar of the Cloister, accompanied by the bombs blasting around us.

We sit on the whitewashed floor, our backs leaning against the walls for support. While we cringe at the sound of the shattering bombs, the patriotic

Brits applaud enthusiastically, hopeful that every blast will bring the allies that much closer to a complete victory over Germany.

"Hip, hip hooray! Our boys are getting further and further into Germany," Mrs. Furman exclaims happily, her white hair shimmers like an angel's halo around her radiant face. It must be after 2 A.M., when the all-clear siren wails. We kids run outside and claim pieces of shrapnel, too hot to touch. Strands of thin aluminum streamers are scattered among with the shrapnel. We are told that the streamers are used to confuse the enemy anti- air craft. At night, they can't distinguish between planes and the silvery decoys, which make the Nazis waste their ammunition while bombing their own country. We stand in awe, gazing at the red horizon, the result of the bombings of the nearby munitions factory.

We get up early on Christmas day to await the arrival of Father Christmas. I don't know what to expect, but I am excited. We are all gathered in the large reception room of the *Schloss,* drinking cider and eating ginger cookies when we hear a bell announcing his arrival .He is regal in his scarlet suit, red-cheeked, white bearded, his shoulders covered with melting snow, he is huffing and puffing.

"Merry Christmas boys and girls, merry Christmas," he calls out in a familiar high-pitched voice with a distinct British accent.

"Line up, presents for all the good little boys and girls. Something here for every good child." We are breathless with anticipation fearful that perhaps we haven't been as good as we should have and therefore will not receive the coveted present. All the packages are brightly wrapped and tagged with names.

"Were you a good little girl?" Father Christmas asks me smiling, before he hands me my package.

"I think so," I reply earnestly. He hands me a box.

No one is left out. Apparently we have all been good enough to be rewarded with a gift. Mine is a beautiful imitation leather sewing kit, complete with needles, a thimble and many colorful spools of thread. I am thrilled and plan a sewing project, perhaps a shirt for my brother. As we are admiring and comparing our gifts, the wailing sound of sirens announces another air raid near by. Once again, we all run down to the shelter in the cellar, clutching our gifts and feeling happy.

My brother is now "Michael". We are told that no one in Great Britain or the US has ever heard of a name like Moschel. Regardless of what they call him, I dearly love my brother. When we were in Wieliczka, I first practiced being boss. He was my closest friend, companion, doll and favorite "toy." When we were at home I dressed him up and gave him directions on the roles he was to play. He was very agreeable, and I loved him for it. Once we began to run for our lives, my feelings for him intensified. I felt responsible for him, always making sure that my mother or I was holding his hand. I feared that he might make a mistake and give away our religion so I tried to answer all the questions asked before he had a chance to respond.

Since coming to Liebenau, and being around other children, he attempts to pull away from me. He resists my interfering and prefers the company of boys his own age. This is hard on me. At first I am hurt and later angry with him. But I don't stop looking out for him, especially because our mother has been ill since we arrived here and is in the infirmary much of the time. She tells me to make sure he wears a jacket in cold weather, takes baths, does his schoolwork and is getting enough to eat. I feel responsible for him, but Michael doesn't listen to me and is hard to control. I am only eight years old and already feel like a mother who can't get her child to obey. Moreover, when he does something mischievous, like grabbing an extra helping of dessert, some of the foolish grown-ups actually come up to complain to me; as if I could really discipline him.

"Michael is being terribly rude," Mrs. Danfield complains to me. She is a short, fat woman with wire rimmed eyeglasses that look as though they are permanently imbedded in her fleshy nose. Her dull brown hair looks like a dead animal laid lifeless on her head. "He has terrible manners. I stopped him from running in the halls, and pointed out to him that not only was it dangerous to run indoors, but his shoe laces were untied, and he might trip," she continues with her diatribe, oblivious of the fact that she is talking to an eight year old. "Instead of thanking me, he ignored me and ran away." I don't know what I'm supposed to do. I listen carefully, not wanting to appear as rude as Michael has, and then I assure her that I will speak to him.

"Speak to him? Humph! He needs to be punished, not spoken to." She stomps off heavily. Now she is not only angry at Michael, but for some reason, she is angry at me also. I scold Michael as soon as I find him but he looks at me and laughs. "Mrs. Danfield is a busybody," he tells me, "next time she comes crying to you about me tell her to mind her own business."

He runs away laughing with his friends and I feel guilty, somehow responsible for his welfare. He and the other boys are taken to the nearby town for haircuts. They come home with their heads shaved laughing and pointing to each other is glee. My heart is broken for my little brother who now looks like the village idiot. I run to my mother crying and she reassures me that Michael's hair will grow back, and besides he likes looking like all the other boys.

Some of the grown ups tease him calling him "Charlie Chaplin" because can never get a pair of shoes that fit his wide foot so he wears some old grown up shoes that are much too big for him. He shuffles around trying to keep the shoes on his feet while he holds on to his trousers. He lost his belt and his pants are in danger of slipping off. He doesn't seem to mind but it breaks my heart. I take the teasing personally and end up with a lump in my throat, trying to suppress my tears. I love my little brother and feel hurt when he is being teased.

Sometimes, Michael and the other boys and girls sneak out of the camp. They climb over a fence to a nearby field and steal fruits and vegetables from the near-by farm. They don't ask me to come along and even though I would love to join them I know I would feel silly tagging along after my younger brother. I'm losing Michael to his friends and feel deprived and betrayed. Michael and the others return with their pockets bulging with little carrots and juicy peaches. They are excited, eager to share their bounty with the others. He reminds me of Robin Hood and I wish I could be more like him: brave and daring.

Eventually they are caught when Wanda, one of the pirates drops her peaches on her way back to the camp. The irate farmer runs into the camp through the front gate, stomps into the commandant in the office complaining about the ruffians. By now it has become a police matter. I am petrified to think that Michael will be taken to prison for his crime. All the children in the camp are rounded up and forced to turn their pockets inside out. Whoever is found with peaches must return them to the farmer and of course the orchard is carefully patrolled. I never eat another peach until we arrive in the U.S., where the peaches aren't very good anyway.

Chapter Twenty-Two

Denial

We are playing "hide and seek," and I am hiding at the bottom of a stair well. I am standing all alone behind the stairs, convinced that I'll never be found. That's when I hear the slapping of sandals approaching. Only one person in the entire camp wears sandals during the winter, and that's one of the loonies, a man we call *"Glatz Kopf"* or baldy. He is the only one of the loonies I've dared to tease—always from a safe distance. It is one of our games at Liebenau. I feel safe and protected when we tease him from afar.

"*Glatz Kopf*," we taunt him, "Do you wax your head?" Then we'd all run away laughing.

Now he is coming down the stairs towards me, and I am scared. He approaches me slowly, treading softly, looking over his shoulder as if expecting to see someone following. He is whistling tunelessly between his teeth. I look behind me and to my sides. There is nothing there, just a flat, straight wall. I am trapped. The feet and legs of *Glatz Kopf* steadfastly make their way down toward me. I see the brown sandals, black socks and gray trousers. I look around trying to flatten myself against the wall, become invisible. There is nowhere to run. I am trembling. I feel certain that he's going to hurt me. I know how these loonies get when they are angry. What do I do now? I try to distract him, be polite and friendly, so that he'll forget that I am one of the kids who tease him.

"*Grüss Gott*," I address him, curtsying.

He looks at me through lashless, unblinking eyelids, scrutinizing the wall behind me. He appears dazed.

Suddenly, he grabs me, holds me tightly and starts kissing me, first on my cheeks, then searching for my mouth. His rough, stubbled beard scratches my face. I am mortified. The only people who have ever kissed me are people who love me or at least like me. Why is *Glatz Kopf* kissing me? Why would

76

he like me after all the joking at his expense? And if he likes me, why won't he let me go when I struggle? I am desperate, and on some gut level I know that what he's doing is wrong, but I'm afraid to scream, scared that if I scream, I will only antagonize him. So I continue struggling.

I push him away as hard as I can, but he holds me in a tight grip and to my horror pries my mouth open with his tongue. I start gagging, shoving him away with all my strength. I clench my fists, hit him on his chest, and kick him on his shins. But he holds on tightly.

"*Ich liebe dich, liebchen*" he rasps into my ear. "I will never hurt you. Just let me kiss you and stop crying."

I can't get away from him. He is stronger than anyone I've ever met, and he holds me tightly against his sweating body. I squirm, wiggle, stiffen, twist, but I can't get him away from me.

"Oh please let me go," I plead. "I beg you. My mother is surely looking for me and so is everyone else. It's time for dinner. They'll punish me for being late." I start crying. "I'm sure everyone is looking for you as well," I tell him, "All the loonies eat before we do, and I know I'm late for dinner."

He ignores my pleas and I continue struggling. His smell is horrible and his beard is scraping my face raw. "Please, please, let me go- I must go to the bathroom," I try another ploy, "If you don't let me go I'm going to pee all over you."

He doesn't seem to care. "*Ya,* go ahead and pee, I will like that."

I struggle, uselessly against him. Alright I say to myself, you want me to pee on you, I will. And then I do, the warm liquid streams down my legs and onto his trousers, but that doesn't seem to deter him. He is licking my face, my neck, I am nauseous. I start gagging. "I'm going to throw up, vomit. You will get your whole shirt messed up."

"*Ya, ya liebchen*, soon I let you go, just one more kiss." he drools all over my face. "But you first must promise me you'll come back later, after dinner, and then I let you go now."

"Yes, yes," I assure him. "I'll be here again right after dinner. Only, please let me go. I told my mother I'd be in her room and now I'm already late."

Suddenly, he releases me, walks up the stairs, slowly; again he whistles, hissing through his teeth. He looks back over his shoulder. I do not move. I wait for him to disappear. I feel the prickly burn of his whickers and his smell as I spit on the floor and try to erase him off me. I am frightened and confused.

I wait a few more minutes until I can no longer hear his tread, and then I run for my life.

"*Glatz Kopf* kissed me all over my face and neck," I scream at my mother while gasping for breath." I hate myself. I'm not the same. "Please," I beg,

"Help me wash his smell off my face. I've got to get his smell off me. I'm scared he'll catch me again," I can't stop sobbing and shaking.

My mother looks at me disbelievingly. She shakes her head, "don't be silly. *Glatz Kopf* never kissed you. You're imagining things again, always making things up."

"Mutti," I shout, "look at me! *Glatz Kopf* kissed me."

But she won't believe me and goes on by saying, "you have such an active imagination. But you mustn't tell lies. You shouldn't pass your stories off as truth."

"I can show you where it happened," I plead with her. I am almost as distressed by my mother's disbelief as by *Glatz Kopf's* assault.

She persists in her denial, "I know, someday you're going to use your imagination to become a famous writer. I've heard that famous writers often make things up when they are children." Is she trying to distract me or can she really think I would make up such a fantastic tale?

"You don't believe me? I know it happened. I even wet myself." I insist tearfully. "Why would I make up such a horrible story?"

My mother hands me a piece of cotton soaked in disinfectant. She looks upset, but I feel like she is angry at me. She must think I'm lying.

"Forget about it. It never happened. Don't let your imagination control your thinking."

What does my mother think my imagination is like, that I would make up a story about *Glatz Kopf*? Doesn't she realize how awful I feel? Surely this is not a story I can make up and yet she keeps insisting that I have a lively imagination. As an adult I will speculate on her motives, even rationalize them. But her denial will cause me to always doubt myself, my observations, and most of all, my feelings.

Chapter Twenty-Three

Leaving Liebenau

The truck standing at the gate churns out blue smoke from its rear. Most of us look in awe at the three British Army nurses in their uniforms. We've all come to wave good-bye. They look happy, excited smiling, and waving. They will be leaving the camp. Among them is Miss Elliot, the most beautiful person in the entire camp, my mother's nurse when she was in the "sick room." I hate to see them leave and so does everyone else. Many are crying and not out of envy. We will miss them, especially Miss Elliot. Once, an army airplane swooped down to the ground and dropped two dozen red roses for her birthday in March. There are rumors that her secret admirer is none other than Clark Gable. She never tells anyone who sent the roses. She simply smiles when questioned, her dimpled cheek like a twinkling star.

A short time later, I walk into the grown up quarters looking for my mother. The women are all talking at once, excited and not listening to each other. Some of them are waving typewritten letters.

Hela Gehorsam, a young woman in her twenties, with a head of wild, curly, red hair and a face dotted with freckles is gesticulating, a letter in one hand and a piece of bread and butter in the other.

"I have to eat when I'm excited. I have to eat," she explains to the rest of the group. Her cheeks are flushed as she gobbles up her slice of bread and goes for another.

"What happened?"

"We're leaving. We're leaving and going to France to our husbands" she answers breathlessly.

"How come?" I ask.

"I don't ask questions, I just follow directions," she answers, giggling, "especially directions that are going to get me together with my husband."

Several others are going too. Exhilaration spreads like dandelion fluff among the lucky women. They are now part of a unique sisterhood, "the lucky." We watch them pack their belongings, and trade warm woolen sweaters for delicate, silky finery in anticipation of their happy reunions.

When I ask my mother why we aren't joining them, she explains that there is another camp, like ours, where the men are kept. The women who have husbands in that camp will be reunited at Vittel, another camp, which is in occupied France. Since our Papa is in America, we are not going to leave yet.

I am sad and envious and feel deprived. I hear all kinds of wonderful things about Vittel. "We are going to be living in a hotel in Vittel," says Celina Rosenzweig, a skinny woman with stringy brown hair and acne pocked cheeks. "It has tennis courts and a spa. You can leave any time you like as long as you're back at night. You can go to stores, theaters, even eat in a restaurant. They don't care what you do, as long as you're home by 9 o'clock."

"In Vittel, the married couples share villas. You don't have to share a room with anyone but your husband. Sounds like heaven to me." Johanna Stillman, her nostrils flaring like an excited horse adds in a hysterical high pitched voice. My mother pretends to be happy for them. She forces a smile but I can see her biting her trembling lower lip. She wipes a tear from the corner of her eye with her sleeve. I don't blame her for being upset, feeling left out. She is trying hard to make them think she is happy for them. I know how she feels even if she is only acting. I wonder why she is lying to them. "I wish you so much good luck," she gushes. I can always tell when she's not telling the truth, "You are going to see your husbands. That's the best part, I think, better than the tennis courts."

"Why not us?" I whine to myself. My mother has just shown me by example that nice people act happy when others have good luck. But I'm not happy—it isn't fair. "Why can't we be with our Papa?" I ask myself watching the excited preparations with a heavy heart.

Two days later the lucky board a truck that will take them to their husbands and away from here. I stand at the gate waving an unenthusiastic farewell. I feel like Cinderella watching her mean stepsisters go off to the ball. They wave and blow kisses to us from behind the gate, while I wonder if our turn will ever come.

Chapter Twenty-Four

News

"Look at this," Mrs. Ducket says to a group of women who are sitting in the common room. They call themselves the "News Club." She is reading from a copy of the London Times. "'Leslie Hore-Belisha, Former Secretary of State for War Marries Cynthia Sophie Elliot, decorated army nurse.' That's our Miss Elliot," she exclaims enthusiastically.

By now I have come to know most of the women who congregate in the room and listen to Mrs. Ducket, an authoritative, take charge British woman, who wears warm pullovers and tweed skirts all year round. About once a week, one of the guards trades an English newspaper for a pack of cigarettes. When that happens all the other women rush in to hear her read the latest news.

"How could she have married such an old man?" Angela Raynor, a chain smoker, with a nervous twitch that causes her to shake her head several times a minute asks. "He must be twenty years older than she is."

"Well," Mrs.Ducket says defensively, "he's not some bum off the street you know. He's been a member of Parliament, Minister of Transport to say nothing of being Secretary of State for War."

"But he's Jewish, isn't he?" says Mrs. Webster, scratching her scrawny head of hair with her bony index finger. She sniffs the air several times as if smelling some strange odor.

"What does that have to do with it?" snaps Mrs. Korn. She is irate, her tall thin body is rigid and her black eyes are on fire. I can't take my eyes off her. Her voice rises to a hysterical pitch, "He's good enough for the beautiful Cynthia Elliott, but he's not good enough for you Cora Webster? Is being Jewish a crime in England or just in continental Europe? Will Jews ever be considered part of the human race?" She stomps out of the room. I stand in awe of her outspokenness. I would never admit to being Jewish in a roomful of Gentiles.

A week or two later, I walk into the common room in time to see Mrs. Ducket throw a week old newspaper on the floor in dismay, only to quickly retrieve it.

"Listen everyone, listen to this headline," she shouts at the others in the room, 'Jewish Internees Sent to be Reunited With Their Families in Vittel Are Rounded up by the Nazis Occupying France and Sent to Auschwitz and Birkenau death camps.'" The women gasp in horror. The friends they had so envied were sent to extermination camps? It can't be true. "Things like that could never happen, not under the Geneva Convention," Isabella Swartz whispers. She is a small, frail woman who hardly ever expresses an opinion. Mrs. Ducket continues reading, looking for familiar names. She spots them, "Jacob and Hela Gehorsam, Theodore and Celina Rozenzweig, Chaim and Johanna Stillman, along with countless other prisoners, holding valid papers, are among those sent to Auschwitz." She shakes her head sadly, "I guess they weren't the lucky ones after all."

Disbelief and gloom settle over the room as Mrs. Ducket continues reading: "'The Germans only keep a limited number of prisoners in the POW internment camps, just enough to use as exchange for prisoners in America and the UK. When there is a surplus in Vittel, especially among the Jews, they are shipped to the death camps in Auschwitz and Birkenau,'" and then she adds cynically "with the cooperation of the Vichy government in France, of course."

"You can always trust the French traitors to do the wrong thing." Mrs. Manchester a children's writer says sadly. "Surplus, indeed, are as if human beings are goods or commodities, to be disposed of when over abundant." The women cry as they remember their friends.

I turn the word "surplus" around on my tongue. "Surplus, surplus?" I don't like the feel of the word, but I know that I've heard it before, I just can't remember where.

A few days later I approach Sister Emanuel. She has always been kind to me. I know she'll give me an honest definition of the word. She is an English teacher and she taught in a prestigious Catholic *Gymnasium* (Secondary school) in Berlin. "What is surplus?" I ask her.

She has no idea why I'm asking her. "Surplus, dear, is when there is too much of something, more than enough."

"What do they do with the surplus?"

"They give it away or get rid of it."

I shudder at the prospect. "Does that mean there could be a surplus of children, or mothers?"

She has heard about the news article and it doesn't take her long to understand my line of questioning. She bends over, and hugs me. "Don't worry, you're here, you're safe." She tries to reassure me, stroking my head gently. "Besides, you're too pretty to be surplus." I shudder.

"Look," she tells me. You're all right. Your father is in America, not Vittel. Nothing bad is going to happen to you." I don't believe a word she says. If Hela Gehorsam, with her lively head of hair and raisin like freckles can be sent to a death camp, so can I, and Michael and my mother and everyone else I love and care for.

In the coming weeks, there is no further news from Vittel. I have no idea of what is going on in Europe, especially what's happening to the Jews. I am trying to forget what I saw in the Ghetto and what I experienced on the outside hiding as a Catholic girl. I start to tell myself that it was all in my imagination. It is late autumn of 1944 and rumors circulate among the women. Most of them are kept from the children. But one day, I walk into the common hall when the News Club has gathered. Mrs. Ducket has again managed to obtain newspaper and she is reading out loud to the rest of the women.

"The Germans are retreating," she announces joyfully. "The Red Army liberated Kovno, Lithuania, and a train- load of Jews, freed from Nazi held Hungary are sent to Switzerland. The Nazis have been driven out of Russia." The women listen attentively as she comes to the end of the article. "Germany's allies in Italy and the Balkan nations are defeated and, ladies" she adds before going on, "the Americans captured the German city of Aachen; the first German city to be captured by the allies. Hip, hip, hooray. We're making progress. France was liberated in June, the allies brought Italy to its knees; we'll be going home soon!" The room is noisy, filled with applause.

She turns the page and goes on to another section of the Times. Suddenly, before reading one word to us, she gasps and coughs uncontrollably. She clears her throat but can't seem to find her voice. "Here Maxine, you read it," she whispers, handing the newspaper to Mrs. Manchester. The others are alarmed. What is going on? The strong and assertive, Mrs.Ducket is clearly not herself. Mrs. Roth quickly brings her a glass of water but she motions with her head to take it away. "I'm alright," she gasps, "Maxine, read."

Mrs. Manchester puts down her knitting, and cleans her glasses. She has a pleasant round face, frizzy blond hair and always attentive in spite of the fact that she never stops knitting. She glances at the paper, "Oh my God," she exclaims and then looks at the other women, not sure if she should read the article that Mrs. Ducket handed her. She is looking at a photograph of prisoners in Auschwitz and can't bring herself to read further.

Impatiently, Mrs. Webster grabs the paper from her and begins in a confident, husky voice. "Hitler's plan for the Final Solution has finally come to an end," she pauses to take a drink of water, "but the commanders in the camps are still killing the Jews. The starving and sick prisoners were forced to march from Auschwitz to camps in Germany: Dachau, Bergen-Belsen and Sachenhausen." Her voice trembles, she reaches for more water, wipes her brow and continues. "Those prisoners that did not die during this long march were gassed when they reached their destination. Meanwhile, the Germans and Poles are dismantling the crematoria and dynamiting mass graves of Auschwitz to hide the magnitude of their atrocities." Mrs.Webster sighs deeply, puts down the paper and shakes her head. She wipes her eyes with a handkerchief but before she can go on, she is interrupted.

"Can it be true?" Mrs. Roth, a woman with a splotchy red complexion and beige teeth shouts loudly. "How can men, women and children be taken to concentration camps to be burned while the rest of world stands by and does nothing?"

"Of course it's true, Rosa," exclaims Mrs. Oberstein, impatiently—she has dark skin and her shiny black hair is pulled back severely in a bun causing her eyes to appear slanted. "Didn't we see it with our own eyes? The trucks, the train stations, the cattle cars full of miserable people, stacked together like bales of straw? Where did you think they were going; to a resort?" She becomes agitated and little balls of spit gather in the corners of her mouth. "What do you think Hitler means when he says he is going to make Europe *"Juden rein"*? She takes a handkerchief and wipes her forehead.

"Shhh, quiet," Mrs. Manchester catches sight of me and interrupts the agitated women. She compresses her lips and points to me, saying kindly, "Rita, be a dear and go out to another room. You don't belong here, go play with the children."

I leave, positioning myself outside the door to eavesdrop. I know that grown-ups' conversation always becomes interesting when they ask me to leave. I don't know what concentration camps are. I've heard of them, of course, but no one ever told me why they exist and if they have anything to do with the war or being Jewish. I have a pretty good idea that they are awful places, where people are burned. I just don't understand why.

"No need to frighten the children, Rosa," through the door I hear Mrs. Manchester tell the other women. "They have enough to live with in here without having to worry about what's going on outside. I just can't understand how the Germans get away with all this when we are supposed to be protected by the Geneva Convention."

I heard of the Geneva Convention, but don't know what it means. Later on my mother will explain to me that the Geneva Convention is an agreement among all the civilized nations of the world. It clearly spelled out the rules of how prisoners of war are to be treated. They are to be fed, sheltered, clothed and not harmed. That's the reason why the Swiss inspectors come to our camp once a month to ensure that we are getting enough food, clothing and even medical care.

For weeks the camp has quieted down. The women go about their business silent with no friendly bantering or even noisy arguing. The children are affected also. We keep our games quiet and have given up teasing each other. We strain to listen to adult conversation. We go to school, do our homework and read or draw. It's as if something dark and scary, maybe a ghost or a skeleton is hovering above us. We are all in mourning, waiting for the next sadness to come our way, which it does.

I come into the room my mother shares with four other women. Everyone looks sad, my mother more so than the others. She sits like a grief stricken statue. Indeed she looks like some of the sculptures I have seen in churches of the Virgin Mary, bent over in grief as she beholds her beloved son hanging on the cross. I sense that something terrible has happened and hesitate in approaching her, knowing that I will not get the usual greeting of a smile, hug and kiss. She turns away from me, shaking her head. She can't talk.

I try to cheer her up. "Mutti," I start to say, "Peter promised to make a picture of the seven dwarfs for me." I am sure she'll be pleased with this bit of news. Peter is a wonderful artist and a picture from him is a prized possession. But my mother stares at me, shakes her head and then in a voice I've never heard before, she moans, hugging her knees to her chest and rocking back and forth.

"My sisters, my brothers, the children, all of them gone, perished, burned, shot", she sobs, her shoulders convulse. What happened? I've never seen anyone so distraught let alone my always optimistic, encouraging mother. She clutches a letter she received that morning from my older cousin Iziek, but it is written in Polish which I can't read so she hands the letter to another woman beckoning her to read it to me. The news is shattering. I listen, unable to comprehend.

Our entire family has been killed in Poland. Most of my aunts and uncles, countless cousins, and my little cousin Halinka, little Halinka, whom my mother thought she might be able to save by having her picture on our papers. Three year old Halinka was in Wieliczka where she was hiding with the rest of the family in the bunker underneath the factory. She had a painful sinus infection, and cried noisily and too much. In order to protect the other people in the bunker from being discovered by the soldiers upstairs, her mother put the child on her chest and covered her head with a pillow to muffle her cries. In the morning Halinka was dead: smothered. Some, like my Aunt Matilda, got away before the Gestapo came to live above the bunker, but most of the others were rounded up, sent to concentration camps, or shot in the forest close to Wieliczka. I start to cry. I know something awful has happened, but it is impossible for me to grasp the magnitude of our loss.

I try to conjure up my dead family whom I haven't seen in a long time: My aunt Angie, the funny one, made us laugh by speaking in silly voices whenever she talked to us; Aunt Paula, dark, serious and unsmiling; Aunt Fela, fat and generous, always handing us a sweet from her well stocked pockets; Uncle Motek, the only bachelor, who had a gorgeous voice and had wanted to become an opera singer; Uncle Hershel, a serious newspaper reader who gathered us together every evening to read the latest news; my cousin Isaac, fifteen, tall and thin with dark curly hairy, blue eyes and a rosy complexion, who played the violin like no one I have ever heard since; cousin Giselle, who to me looked like a grown up because she could read and write at seven and towered over me; my big cousin Rita (Ruthie), sixteen, with her long blond braids and dark brooding eyes. Rita played the piano and was my mother's first piano student. She was never seen without a book unless she was eating or playing the piano.

I can't believe they're dead. Gone, killed, tortured, gassed, shot; by those handsome marching boys in their smart uniforms. I am eight years old. I can't imagine what being dead really means.

I try to console my mother. I put my arms around her and hold her close to my little body.

"No, no," I say to her. "That is not true. It's only your imagination," using the words of reassurance I've heard so often from her when she wants to make me feel safe or help me forget. She is too devastated to hear me. I want to comfort her but don't know how. I am helpless, vulnerable and unprotected.

"You'll see," I reassure her. Squelching my fears and sounding, I hope, more grown up than I feel, "We'll pray and it will be alright." I try to soothe her even as a cold, invisible fear washes over me. So many things are going on that I don't understand, but I sense the danger. It is the first time in my life that I feel encumbered by a deep, abiding sadness that will rarely leave my side. When difficult times occur, as they do in everyone's lifetime, a feeling of familiar terror and helplessness will cover me like a gigantic wave of sadness. Little do I realize, I will never stop running, even when I am safe.

Chapter Twenty-Five

The Long Train Ride

Earlier in the month our names were finally posted on the exchange list. Monica and her mother have their names on the list as well. My mother, who is so good at bargaining, trades Camels, Lucky Strikes and Old Gold cigarettes for woolen coats, sweaters and brown leather suitcases. It is winter again and she knows we'll probably be cold. She lays the suitcases open on the floor, their lids up, yawning hungry giants waiting to be fed. We want to be ready when the transport truck arrives to take us to the train station.

My father has been notified by the State Department of our release and for security reasons, the exact date and place of our arrival are not disclosed. But as soon as he gets word of our imminent departure he writes to my mother telling her to destroy all the "coats and cover ups" that he had sent her when we were in Europe. "They are out of fashion in the U.S.," he explains, "and will make you look like foolish foreigners. Throw them into the ocean when you get far out to sea." My mother understands that "coats and cover ups" are code words for the counterfeit documents he has sent her and that they could get us into trouble with the American immigration people. If he were to write to her and tell her directly to throw out all of her papers, the message would fall into the hands of the Germans who censor all our mail. Who knows what might happen then.

The unheated train, our shelter sits in the station where it has been for hours. It lurches every now and then, raising my hopes, but goes nowhere. I'm almost nine years old, cold, hungry and hopeful; this time we are really on our way to America. The only time I'm allowed to leave my hard wooden seat is to go to the bathroom. "*Entschuldige, entschuldige uns bitte, (excuse us, excuse us, please),*" my mother disturbs the people who are sitting on the floor in the aisles while accompanying me to the toilet. It is filthy and reeks. My mother lifts me up so that my body does not come into contact with any part of the seat. "There are so many diseases that you can get off the toilet seat," she warns me. I shudder. I know. I do my business quickly in order to get out of there. I suddenly remember the can in Montelupi.

We sit, crammed. I feel the breath of the old man next to me, he snores quietly. His head falls on my shoulder and I try to move away without waking him. The scenery is the same every day: the station in front of us and bombed out cities beyond. Parts of buildings, shards of broken glass, toppled lampposts stand all around reminding me of huge, toothless ogres grinning hideously. The train only moves at night. My mother tells me that the reason we do not move during the day time is because a moving train is an easy target to spot from the air, and the Germans don't want their trains being bombed by the aircraft overhead. So we sit in a station all day long and travel for short periods of time when it is dark, coming to a halt before daylight.

Since yesterday we have been sitting for hours on this frigid train, not moving. German soldiers in their warm, woolen, green uniforms and knee high boots come through the cars shouting orders in menacing voices. Every few minutes different officers swagger onto the train. Their cheeks are red, their noses shining, and their cold blue eyes are like the icicles forming on the eaves of the stations. They look well fed and healthy though not jovial and happy like they did in Krakow. They sweep through each car, demanding to see identity papers. Each inspection presents another threat. Our survival, for this day, is at the whim of the inspecting officers. If the next officer does not approve of our papers we will be ejected from the train and left on a strange platform with no resources. We smile ingratiatingly: are polite and pleasant. My mother distracts one of them. She speaks in German.

"Where are we now?" she asks one of them.

"Nowhere special, dear lady," he answers her politely.

My fear intensifies as I watch people crying or begging for their lives being dragged from the train, pulled by their arms, pushed and kicked as they try to resist. I shudder. Are we next? I wonder.

"Move over," an officer orders us after one such intrusion, shoving the man at the end of my bench toward me. "You are being joined by new passengers." Obediently we huddle closer together. A woman and a child sit across from me. I am too numb with fear and cold to acknowledge their presence.

I sleep in an upright position as best I can, catching no more that an hour of sleep at a time. I wonder where I am when I waken in the middle of the night. The wind blows relentlessly through the unheated cars, and although we try to keep each other warm, the cold never abates. It accompanies us wherever we go. I wonder if there will be a time when I don't feel the cold? Somewhere a child is crying, a man coughing and someone is moaning. The train lurches to a stop, alerting us to another inspection.

I hear a man explaining to his teenage son that since we are out of the confines of the camp and traveling through German cities we are no longer protected by the Geneva Convention. There it is again, "Geneva Convention." Now that I know what it means I know it's not going to offer us any protection to us. The man whispers to his son. He tells his him to avoid the officers' eyes.

"Look down, Leo, don't attract any attention to yourself. The best thing that the soldiers can do to us is to ignore us."

Too often, I am back in the world of the fairy tales, where witches punish young girls for not inviting them to their wedding, where a princess is forced to marry a frog and a step- mother can cast her princess stepdaughter out of the palace from royalty to slavery. I relive all the dreadful things that can happen to children. I know they all have happy endings, but I am not there yet. I am stuck in the middle of a frightening ordeal and I'm not at all sure if the ending to my story will be happy. I've experienced enough to know that not everybody's life has a happy ending. My fears feed on more fears, like crows feed on carcasses. I am unable to let go of the terror; afraid to question my mother and that if I give a voice to my anxieties, they might become real. I also know that she will tell me it is all in my imagination as she has always done when things go wrong and I am no longer comforted by her lies.

I make a mental list of "what ifs:" "What if we get separated and can't find each other? What if one of us gets sick? What if one of us is pulled off the train and left on the platform alone? What if my mother dies? What if the train gets bombed?" The list is endless and frightening. I shift my mind to magical thinking, protective thinking: "If we only make three stops today, then nothing bad will happen. If five more people come on the train, then we will be safe. If one of the Nazi officers coughs before he speaks, we will speed off and make no more stops along the way." I play these mind games constantly, hoping to gain some sort of control. They serve to distract me from the present.

Chapter Twenty-Six

Refugee

Michael and I entertain each other playing a long noisy game called "refugee." The game involves lots of loud pleading and tears on the part of my brother who acts the part of Moishe Mogen Dovid, the poor Jew, and gesticulating and shouting by me, the officious secretary, determined to keep him from seeing the commandant.

"Please, oh please," begs Moishe M. Dovid, "I have to see the commandant. I've been waiting here all day."

"What is the nature of your business?" I inquire aggressively.

"I have some papers," he replies. His hand is shaking with fear as he extends them to me. "They have to be signed by the commandant."

I wave the papers away. "I'm sorry, but the commandant is very busy. He can't possibly see everyone who comes in here off the street."

"But listen," he folds his hands as if in prayer and places them under his chin. "I have an appointment to see him today."

"Hmmph," I, the secretary, sniff, "Lots of people have appointments. The commandant is very busy today. Come back tomorrow."

"Tomorrow? Oh, alright," Moishe responds meekly, "Can I have the appointment for tomorrow, in the morning, or perhaps in the afternoon?"

"What are you crazy?" Now I am shouting at the cowering figure of my brother "Do you think you can have an appointment on one day's notice?"

"But I have an appointment for today."

"Let me see your papers." I demand in a loud voice. Moishe hands me a piece of paper. I pretend to read it.

"This paper is no good," I say sternly, "This paper is of no use. You need a new paper." I tear the paper to shreds while Moishe looks on helplessly.

By now my poor brother is really sobbing, "I had a good paper. It was good, genuine, and now it's no good? What was the matter with it? What kind of people are you?"

"Sir," I say with disdain. "You'll have to leave the office. You are causing a commotion. We cannot have that in this office. This is not one of your little places where it is all right to scream. This is a dignified office. Now get out!"

"My goodness," a tall, woman, wearing a heavy, navy blue coat turns to my mother, "Aren't children wonderful? They manage to turn everything into a game."

My mother agrees with her, "I just wish they weren't so noisy. Some of the others are trying to sleep through this journey."

Chapter Twenty-Seven

First Stop

It is 1945, mid-January. After weeks of traveling, stopping for hours in bombed out stations, lurching backwards and forwards only to stop again, we arrive in Switzerland where the snow is deep, the sky is blue, and the air is as frigid as our hosts. Unfriendly, angry soldiers greet us; dressed in green just like the Nazis, barking out orders in a language that not one of our fellow travelers understands. I am starving, scared, and most of all, I am cold. The icy chill wraps itself around me. There is no wind but the frost stings my face, making my eyes tear. The Swiss are neutral, but they certainly are not lovers of Jews. They make this eminently clear assigning all the Jewish travelers to quarters in a freezing barn filled with dirty straw that smells like the excrement of animals it once housed. The others are assigned to a warm, heated building.

We sleep with our clothes on, our hands in our pockets and feet curled up under our bodies. Michael is not well. He is developing shiny red cysts on his neck and legs. He says they're painful and my mother moistens a handkerchief and applies it to his neck. This gives him little relief and the cysts are getting bigger and more painful every day. She is helpless. One morning he can't get out of the straw bunk. He can't talk because his throat hurts too much. The cysts have developed into swollen, shiny red boils. He is in excruciating pain, running a high temperature. One boil on his neck is so large and infected that he can't move his head or swallow. My mother is panic-stricken. Had we come all this way for her to lose her little boy to some sort of horrifying, monstrous infection? She approaches one of the Swiss guards and begs for help. Her blond hair and good looks do not impress him.

"We have no doctors here," he informs her indifferently in Pidgin German, his domed forehead as shiny as is his closely shaved face. "This is not a hospital for refugees. Nor is it a hotel for the needy. We are not responsible for the health of our non-paying guests." She carries Bubbi around covered in her coat. "Please," she implores anyone who will listen to her. "Help save my little boy. He is so hot and in so much pain." Finally, one of the men in our transport takes pity on her and offers to lance the angriest boil on Michael's neck with a penknife. Although he is not a doctor, and the conditions are far from sterile, my mother gratefully agrees. No one else has offered to alleviate Michael's condition. The man presses a handkerchief against Michael's neck as the thick pus oozes out slowly. My brother promptly passes out. When he regains consciousness he is dazed but a few days later the temperature abates and he regains his energy.

Chapter Twenty-Eight

Second Leg of Our Journey

We are once again sitting on a crowded train. Michael and I resume our game of refugee: noisy and disruptive as usual. We are traveling through neutral zones: Switzerland and occupied France. New people get on board every time we stop. The train moves quickly only stopping to take on more passengers. Bombed out cities are a rarity and we haven't heard the ominous wail of air raid sirens since we boarded in Basel, Switzerland.

Finally, in late January, we pull into Marseilles, the French seaport where three ships sit in the harbor. The biggest and most beautiful is the Swedish luxury liner, *The Gripsholm*. It is as tall as a five story building and just as wide. I crane my neck to see the three tall smoke stacks with yellow and blue stripes. Lively music is blaring from loud speakers. The *Gripsholm* sits in the harbor like a proud and haughty princess reigning over her territory. Two inferior sister ships hover nearby. One is large white ship with a red cross on its smoke stack; the other is the ugly stepsister with no promise of redemption. Small, dark and gray with rusting railings running around the deck, it cowers in the background.

I make a plea to God that we will be sailing on the big beautiful ships; sailing to the Promised Land. Two hours later we are standing on the deck of the Victoria, a dark, ugly ship, the smallest of the threesome. The cabin below deck consists of bunks, with straw mats. Tiny footfalls of rats the size of kittens scamper overhead and below our bunks. I shiver, waking to a brush stroke of fur along my arm. I'm certain it was a rat and I stay up most of the night, sickened at the possibility of another surprise encounter.

Chapter Twenty-Nine

Victor

Dr. Osiek, a young Jewish pediatrician is on our ship. We first met him on the train going to Marseilles. Victor, a little boy is with him. My mother tells us that Dr. Osiek told her that Victor is not his son.

"He is a boy he found wandering the streets of Vilna, alone," my mother informs us. "When he realized that Victor had no living relatives he took him along and now treats him like his own son."

I love the story. A little boy is lost and alone, not in the woods, but in an equally dangerous place. He is found by a big, strong man who becomes his father and they live happily ever after. It's like a fairy tale but it isn't happy for Victor. He is a beautiful child with blond curly hair and porcelain pink complexion. But he does not behave like any of the other children I have met. He is strange and seems to live in a faraway place, not talking to anyone, never smiling, crying or reacting. I am determined to get through to him.

"Victor," I nudge him, pulling on his blue sweater, "do you believe in Father Christmas? He came to our camp and he gave me a gift." I produce my precious sewing box, with all the colorful threads intact. Victor ignores me. He doesn't even look at the box. "Want to see some pieces of real bombs?" I take out my stash of shrapnel collected after air raids. Again, he does not react. He just sits on a rickety deck chair, chewing furiously on his tongue and staring at the horizon as if waiting for something to appear. I don't give up easily. I offer him some chocolate. He doesn't even look at it.

I am obsessed with Victor. I ignore all the other children on the boat and devote myself solely to getting a response from him. How can I make him answer my questions or acknowledge my friendly overtures? I am not one to ignore a challenge. I must get Victor to at least look at me. I resort to my last trick. My right hand creeps up slowly behind Victor's back. I tickle his neck hoping for the reaction I always get when I tickle someone. He doesn't even blink his eyes. "Victor! Are you dead or alive?" I scream into his ear. He continues chewing his tongue, more rapidly than before. What can I do to make him notice me? To bring him out of wherever he is? To rescue him? None of my ploys meets with success. I am terribly frustrated and suddenly burst out crying.

"What's wrong with him?" I ask Dr. Osiek. "He acts as if he's dead. Does he hate everyone? Does he ever talk to you? "

Dr. Osiek asks my mother if it would be all right for me to take a short walk with him. "Victor is a very, very sad boy," he explains to me. "He saw his mommy, his daddy and his two younger brothers, twin babies actually, killed by the Gestapo. He was hiding under the bed, or he would also have been killed as well. Victor saw a lot of blood and heard a lot of screaming." I listen fascinated as Dr. Osiek tries to explain Victor's silence. "It is very kind of you to try to make Victor happy, but it will take a long time," Dr. Osiek shakes his head sadly. "Victor is so sad that he is living in a strange world of his own where nothing can hurt him again."

"But we're going to America," I insist. "It's going to be a happy place for Victor."

"Rita, You are a sweet little girl, and kind in trying to help. But neither you, nor I, nor anyone else can make Victor forget what he's seen and heard. Only time will help him." I tear up with this sad news. Dr. Osiek pats me on the head, "but there's no reason for us to stop having fun." And with that he tells me a joke that I never forget, about two idiots caught in the rain. In spite of Victor, I have to laugh at the punch line where one of them goes home in the pouring rain to fetch his pajamas after having been invited to stay at the other's house in order not to get soaked on his way home.

I try coaxing a response from Victor a few more times, but it's no use. Dr, Osiek is right. He is not going to be distracted or brought out of his world by anyone right now. The ship sits in the harbor for days, going nowhere. Eventually, I join the other children running up and down the deck, making lots of noise, trading treasures and waiting for something to happen.

Someone has heard a rumor that our ship is bound for Africa. What has become of our voyage to America? For me, Africa is a place full of wild animals and naked cannibals. I have read about the Belgian Congo in Liebenau. I'm not going. When I ask my mother about it, she shrugs her shoulders and tells me to be grateful that at least we are out of Germany and out of danger.

"Why do I always have to grateful when something goes wrong?" I ask my mother.

"Look," she says, "there are no airplanes flying overhead, no sirens forecasting bombing missions. We are not in any danger of being killed," she doesn't even address my question. "There aren't even any shelters on the boat. We are safe. That's something to be grateful for."

"But we're standing still, and we might be going to Africa instead of the beautiful life I was promised with my Papa." I am bewildered and saddened. I make a compromise with God. If we could just get to America I won't complain about sharing my bunk with rats.

None of the ships have sailed. Several days later, with no explanation, we are taken off the ugly ship and moved to the hospital ship. What a relief. The wounded soldiers have not yet arrived and the hospital ship is full of beautiful young American nurses wearing pink striped uniforms and long red nails. They are kind and generous to us and they talk to Michael and me in serious tones. "So, when is your birthday?" Karla asks me. I tell her February second.

"Why that's today," she exclaims, "We'll have to celebrate."

I have no idea what *celebrate* means.

"We'll meet in the cafeteria in an hour and we'll have a birthday party for you." She adds.

What is a birthday party? I had never heard of a birthday party in my entire life. I know that there are parties for Christmas, for Easter, for Independence Day. But who ever heard of a party for my birthday?

I am about to find out. Michael, my mother and I come downstairs to the cafeteria where Karla has put together a wonderful celebration in honor of my birthday. There's a colorful paper table cloth on the table and many of the other nurses are there. She scoops out huge portions of vanilla ice cream, pours hot chocolate sauce over them and brings them to us.

"Stand up, stand up everybody," everyone starts singing "Happy Birthday to you."

"All for me?" I feel overwhelmed, and embarrassed. We sit down to eat and I can't believe what I'm eating. I have never tasted anything like this before. The unexpected surge of soothing, cold, smooth velvety texture in my mouth is unlike anything I've experienced. My ninth birthday is the most memorable one in my entire life. The nurses play with us and treat us as the families they left at home. Grown ups have never been so attentive and kind to us before.

Chapter Thirty

The Gripsholm

Again, and with no explanation, we are told that we will have to leave the hospital ship. By a strange unaccountable twist of fate we are taken to *The Gripsholm*. It is hard to say good-bye to the warm and generous friends we made on the hospital ship, but they hug us and wish us good luck.

The Gripsholm is an entire floating city. The decks are long and filled with cushioned deck chairs. Downstairs, beneath the deck many small boutiques are selling silk dresses, high heeled shoes, perfumes, scarves, purses and belts. The sitting rooms or salons, as they are called, are furnished with purple and green, velvet sofas. Huge gilt mirrors hang on the walls and soft carpeting lies on every floor. I listen to jazz music with new unfamiliar sounds and strong rhythms. A tall, smiling American soldier stops us on our way up the stairs. He hands Michael and me a Hershey bar and laughs when I curtsy and thank him.

"You can stop curtsying now," he tells me smiling. "In the United States, no one curtsies."

"Really?" I say, in my British accent, "Isn't that terribly rude?"

"No," he laughs at me, "pretty girls like you only have to say 'thank you' when they are given something." Soon after that, a huge African-American soldier, a chef actually, gives me an orange, and a smile that spreads across his face like silk fan. I remember not to curtsy, but I thank him and run to show my mother. I had seen pictures of oranges, but this is to be the first time I am to taste the sour juicy fruit.

Our stateroom is small and crammed full of essentials: a petite porcelain sink with hot and cold water, four bunk beds, clean linens, plenty of blankets and towels. Moreover, the room is warm, cozy and clean. For the first time in ages I forget to be cold.

The dining room with its crystal chandeliers, soft green carpeting, long tablecloths draped over round and oval tables, quiet music and embossed menus looks like what I imagine a palace must be like. We are seated at one of the many beautiful round tables, with velvet upholstered chairs, linen napkins, silverware, china plates and as if that isn't enough, Swedish cooking, with as much food as we want. I am in heaven.

I meet many children that I have never seen before. One in particular stands out in my memory. His name is Marek, and he is older than we are, about eleven. His long blond hair is slicked to the back of his head, with no part. He is wearing a black cowboy hat that hangs from a string behind his neck, a black cowboy shirt, and a jeweled belt circles his waist. Most impressive of all are the two shining toy pistols he is twirling on his forefingers. He acts smart, arrogant, with a sense of bravado, clearly enjoying the naïve fascination heaped upon his possession and mistaking it for admiration of him.

"You can get everything for *doolares*," he tells us in Polish, swaggering and taking aim at some distant object. "My mother's got plenty of *doolares*. We got them before we even started on our trip. We're rich," he brags. He comes from Warsaw and was never interned in a camp. His grandfather lives in Chicago and now he's going to live there with his family.

"Chicago?" I ask. "What's Chicago? The only American cities I've heard of are New York, Philadelphia and Hollywood where Shirley Temple lives."

"Well, little girl," he sneers at me in Polish, "You don't know everything. Chicago is a very big city in America, bigger than New York and Philadelphia combined." I realize that he doesn't speak any English and try to regain my cool.

"How are you going to get around Chicago if you only speak Polish?"

"Don't worry about me," he says disdainfully. "In Chicago, everybody speaks Polish. They even have Polish schools."

He swaggers away with a bunch of stupid boys, including my brother. What can they be thinking? That he's going to give them one of his precious guns? Boys are so dumb, I tell myself soothingly.

Suddenly the smokestacks emit several loud blasts and we are inching away from the pier. We are finally going to America. We stand on the deck, watching the land getting further and further away. When we wake up the next morning all we can see on every side of us is the ocean expanding to infinity. I feel a burden lifting from my heart. We are really going to America; this is definitely not my imagination. It's true; my mother was telling the truth.

The trip is long: three weeks. We have to travel slowly, I am told by one of the soldiers on the boat. We have to keep a sharp lookout for mines hidden in the ocean. "Mines can make the whole boat explode and the captain certainly doesn't want that to happen." By the second week of the journey

we are assaulted by tremendous winds and sky high waves. We've hit a
storm and in the North Atlantic, during the month of February storms become like raging, furious giants with waves that wash the decks with salt
water. The huge city sized *Gripsholm* sways from side to side like a paper
boat in a bathtub. Long ropes are suspended in the hallways like clothes-
lines above our heads for passengers to hold on to as they navigate from
one section of the ship to another. The dining room is half full. Many are
too sea sick to come out of their cabins and I can hear them moaning when
I pass their rooms. Then, one day, just as suddenly as it appeared, the storm
is gone. The sun is shining, the decks are washed and free of the glaze of
sea spray and the ship resumes its normal activities.

There is always something going on aboard the *Gripsholm.* Often in the
evening we watch movie and it is here that I am introduced to the famous
Charlie Chaplin. Indeed my brother did look like a small version of him, shuf-
fling around in shoes too big and baggy trousers. There is something pathetic
in the actor's eyes that only I seem to notice. Michael lacked that look of a
forlorn soul when he was running around in shoes and trousers that were too
big for him. All of us children enjoy unlimited freedom.

At night, after my mother has tucked us in, she goes out of our cabin to be
with the adults. She knows we are safe on the ship without her. She turns out
the lights, kisses us and tells us to be good, go to sleep and keep quiet. That's
when we pick up our game of "refugee." We start out quietly, whispering our
parts. Before long the game picks up momentum and our voices rise, we are
shouting and crying. We always come back to "refugee." It is an old friend
like a dog, waiting to be picked up and played with. We continue playing
"refugee" for many years, even after we are living in the U.S.

The ship's primary mission is to transport wounded American soldiers and
other soldiers whose tours of duty are over. They make up the majority of the
of the ship's population. The wounded soldiers make a lasting impression on
me. They are all handsome, wearing beautiful uniforms; they are kind and
friendly to everyone. They don't seem to notice the difference between the
Jewish kids and the Christian kids. These soldiers are nothing like the uniformed soldiers I had seen in Poland, Germany and Switzerland.

Many are amputees, some on crutches, others missing hands or arms: a set
of identical twin soldiers, who now can easily be identified, since one has
lost his right leg and the other his left leg, a handsome blond soldier walking
behind his buddy, holding onto his shoulder because he is blind and needs his
friend to take him everywhere. I am so sad when I see them coming. I feel like
I am going to cry, there is still so much sadness around me. "Is there ever a
place where everything is alright?" I ask myself. The most disturbing injury is
to a soldier whose face has been entirely burned and scarred. His skin is red,

and yellow, with little peaks and valleys, some of them oozing a clear liquid. A black opening remains in his face where his nose had been, he has no lips, but his teeth and smile are intact and although his eyelids are badly burned his blue eyes have survived his ordeal and he can see. He frightens and fascinates me at the same time. He has the body of a man and the face of a monster. I hide every time I see him coming, only stare at him from some invisible corner of the room, from behind closed drapes, crouching behind a sofa.

Underneath that frightening horror mask is an active, friendly human being. He jokes around with his buddies, greets everyone he meets with a loud "hello," plays ping-pong and seems to be unaware of his appearance. Slowly, I begin to lose my fear of him and stop avoiding him.

"Hey Blondie," he says to me rumpling my hair. "Want a candy bar?"

Nothing is as it appears. The beautiful Nazi soldiers are mean and ugly on the inside. This scarred, disfigured man approaches me with a candy bar and an attempt at a grin.

"I've got a little girl just like you waiting for me at home." I thank him and smile up at him. I know his little girl will not recognize her father. I shudder inside. What does my own father look like, I wonder? I haven't seen him in such a long time that I've forgotten everything about him.

Freda Perlberger, my mother, in Wieliczka, around 1932.

My father, Alexander Schmelkes, around 1931.

Myself and Michael in Vienna.

My family at the Perlberger estate in Wieliczka.

Myself, my Aunt Angie and Michael, in Wieliczka.
My Aunt Angie was executed by the Nazis.

My cousin, Rita (Ruthie) Birnbaum, in Wieliczka.
Ruthie was executed by the Nazis at the age of sixteen.

Family photo taken in Krakow, sent to the United States, for document purposes.

October 1943 letter written in Liebenau from Freda to her brother-in-law, Akiba (Kurt) Kornitzer, in London.

October 1943 letter written in Liebenau from Freda to her brother-in-law, Akiba (Kurt) Kornitzer, in London. Family photo is sewn into the letter.

DEPARTMENT OF STATE
WASHINGTON

reply refer to
P 740.00115 E.W.

My dear Mr. Schmelkes:

I am pleased to inform you that Fraida,
Schmelkes, Moschel Schmelkes and Rita Schmelkes have
been released by the German Government in the recent
exchange of nationals between the United States and
Germany. You will be informed when possible of the
place and date of arrival in the United States. For
reasons of security no vessels arriving in this country
can be met by any persons not having official duties
in connection therewith.

You will be informed at later date regarding
communications, transmission of funds, payment of
other costs and allied problems.

Sincerely yours,

For the Secretary of State:

Gilson G. Blake
Assistant Chief
Special War Problems Division

Mr.
2037 North Franklin,
Philadelphia 22, Pennsylvania.

Letter from the State Department notifying my father of our release from Liebenau.
My father cut out his typewritten name in order to slide it into our mail slot.

AFFIDAVIT IN LIEU OF PASSPORT

United States of America

State of .... New York ....

County of .... New York .... } S. S.

In the matter of application of .... Rita Bianca Schmelkes ....
or passport facilities:

I .... Rita Bianca Schmelkes .... whose occupation or profession is that of
schoolgirl
5 6 West 188th St. .... residing at .... New York City ....

(Number)   (Street)   (City or Town)   (State, District, Territory)

eing duly sworn, depose and say:

I was born at Vienna, Austria .... on the 2nd day of February 1 936

I have lost my nationality of origin owing to .... cannot obtain passport. ....

I am unable to obtain a passport or any form of travel document from the Government of the
country in which I now reside.

I attach hereto my photograph and personal description as evidence of my identity.

I am urgently desirous of traveling to .... Canada .... for the
following reasons: .... to obtain permanent residence in the United States.

I wish to leave on the .... beginning of February .... I intend to return to

.... NY .... after a stay abroad of not more than .... ten days ....
month's duration.

Franda Schmelkes

Rita Bianca Schmelkes
(Signature of Applicant)

Subscribed and sworn to before me this

14th day of January 1947

(Notary Public)

NOTARY PUBLIC
Notary Public, New York County
Certificates filed in
Co. Clks. No.26, Reg. No.2835
Commission expires Mar. 30, 1947

DESCRIPTION

Height 4 Ft. 10 in.   Color of eyes blue

*Affidavit issued by the US government permitting me to exit Canada
and return to the US in order to achieve permanent residency status.*

Family picture taken around 1947 at Mirka Fisch's home by Alec Fisch.

Montelupi Prison was used by the Gestapo and was where my family was detained.

Part II

IMMIGRANT GIRL

Chapter Thirty-One

Ellis Island

My mother pulls my blankets off. "Come on. Get up." She sounds cheerful and excited, "we'll be passing the Statue of Liberty this morning and I don't want you to miss it. It is a sight you will remember for the rest of your lives."

I shiver. "What *liverty?* What's *liverty?*" I mumble half asleep.

My mother laughs, "Liberty, not *liverty,* a Statue for freedom. You'll never forget the first time you see it and you'll tell your grandchildren how exciting that day was for you." She is excited and happy. Michael and I don't know what she's talking about, but we do as we are told and rush up to the deck, which is enveloped in a thick fog, a mist so dense that we can hardly see our own hands when we hold them away from our bodies. What are all these people doing here? I wonder. We see nothing in front of us and nothing above or below us. Yet the deck is full of people straining into the misty horizon, trying to see something that does not appear. We are entering New York harbor and the woman next to me tells me to keep my eyes open for "the green lady with the torch." I scan the horizon carefully, hoping to see this famous statue, but we miss her. Whether it's due to the fog or perhaps that the captain has taken a route that avoids her, we look in the distance and see land.

Three tall, red brick buildings loom on the horizon, Ellis Island, my mother tells us. She seems to have inside information. We disembark along with all the other refugees. We are processed quickly. My mother has no official documents having tossed the "covers and coats" as per my father's instruction into the ocean. She admonishes us to tell only the truth and only when we are questioned. Under no circumstances are we to volunteer any information.

"And if you're not sure what to answer, just say, 'I don't know.'"

We are taken into a small private room. My mother explains her plight to the officers behind the desk at the immigration bureau on Ellis Island who unlike the uniformed officers I'm used to seeing are wearing white shirts and black trousers, with only a small badge identifying their position. They are skeptical. She does not have the bearing of a poor Jewish woman who suffered in Europe. Moreover, her English has a strong German accent. The officers ask Michael and me a few questions: like how old we are and why do we want to come to the U.S. We answer truthfully in the upper crust British accents we have acquired in Liebenau that we want to be with our Papa. The American immigration officials look puzzled. They confer quietly thinking that I can't hear them. They must not be aware of my well developed art of eavesdropping. They whisper to each other.

"What do you think?" One of them asks.

"I don't know," the other answers, "she looks like a Brunhilde to me."

"The kids sound like Brits. You think they're legit?"

"She hasn't got a single piece of identification in her possession and she claims that her husband is living in the U.S.?"

"Could she be a German spy," one of them says. They confer, clear their throats and the spokesperson tells us that we will be detained on Ellis Island until a hearing can be scheduled to determine our status.

Michael and I hear everything but understand nothing. All we know is that we are in America waiting to see our father. We are ushered into a tremendous hall, with high ceilings and two balconies running above us, guarded by wrought iron railings. There are many doors upstairs, on each side of the hall, underneath the balcony benches and sofas stand against the wall. There is a tremendous clock standing at one end of the hallway which rings out the hours, reminding everyone that time is passing. We are taken up the stairs by a woman who is introduced to us as a "matron." She is assigned to make us comfortable and show us around. She opens one of the doors and leads us into a small dormitory like room, with three cots, a small sink, and a chair next to each cot.

"This," she tells us, "is where you are to sleep. Breakfast, lunch and dinner are served at eight A.M., twelve noon and six P.M. respectively. And," she adds, "there will be a food cart that comes around several times a day where you can get a snack: cake, fruit and candy. You are to remain downstairs during the day and only use this as a bedroom. Do you have any questions?" She is business like, but pleasant and smiles at us frequently. "Now, please follow me." She leads us to a large room where doctors in white coats check our throats, ears, eyes, hair, skin and nails. It is dark when we return to our little room and we are exhausted. It has been a very long day. My mother sits down on one of the cots, her elbows on her knees and her head hidden by her palms. She cries silently. When Michael sees this, he immediately bursts into tears himself. Only I am dry-eyed.

"Mutti, Mutti, why are you crying," I ask trying to soothe her. "We are in America. Papa will be here soon and he will take us home to our mansion."

"I know, I know," she says, "I am crying for joy," but I don't believe her. I know that there is no joy for her in a room with barred windows. We remain on the island for about two weeks. We attend school that is a real classroom, with desks firmly bolted to the floor and inkwells in the upper right hand corner. A blackboard with alphabet cards is displayed across the top. It is the focal point of the classroom. We each receive a generous allotment of school supplies: black and white marbled notebooks, pens, sharpened pencils erasers, crayons and small bottles of Waterman's blue-black ink. I can't believe my luck, all the school supplies that I have been dreaming of are now mine. A teacher comes in for two or three hours a day to instruct us in English. She holds up pictures of a window, chair, table, door, book, dog and many other everyday objects. She tells us to repeat the names of the pictures on the cards and then write them down in our notebooks. We already know how to speak English and blurt out all the answers before any one else has a chance to respond.

The lessons are easy and the school day is over at noon when we have our lunch. After lunch we play games and run around on the tiny piece of turf that is designated as the playground. There are four swings, and nothing more. It is a damp and chilly March and we look forward to four P.M. when the food cart arrives in the giant hall, and Michael and I who have recently been introduced to Drake's devil dogs sink our teeth into the two soft chocolate cake slices separated by a layer of luscious, sweet, white cream. It s the best food under the sun, and I will eat these whenever I can.

Several times during our stay a ferry comes to the island and people leave. "Where are they going?" I ask. No one knows, but the matron overhears my question answers me, "Some are going to be reunited with their families in America, and others are being investigated. They might be spies.

"What happens to spies?"

"Spies are sent back to Germany or where ever they come from," she answers casually.

I shudder. I remember that the immigration officials said we might be spies. I don't know what spies are; I don't think we're spies but suppose they think that we are? I heard what they said, and I understood what the matron said about spies. What's going to become of us? No wonder Mutti was crying. I re-enter my own world of worrying, waiting, and ruminating.

One afternoon we are told that on the following morning we will be taking a trip to New York City itself. Our destination is the immigration bureau on Columbus Circle and 59th Street in Manhattan. My father who has been notified of our arrival is catching the first train from Philadelphia where he lives and works to meet us in New York, to attend the scheduled hearing. My mother is overjoyed.

"Can it really be?" she asks me, once again assuming that I'm a grown up. "Will we finally be seeing your father?"

To my great surprise and horror I realize that I don't want to see my father. Coming to America and being with our father is a dream I have nurtured over most of my young life. It is embellished and invested in daily, but it only fits comfortably in the confines of my mind and not in the real world. I feel apprehensive and scared. I don't know what awaits me.

This place, Ellis Island is safe. I know what to expect and I don't want to face the prospect of yet another disappointment. Suppose my father is nothing like the father I have created? Suppose he is ugly, hairy and mean? What if I don't like him? Or worse, what if he doesn't like me? I don't want to see him. I don't know what I want, but one thing I am sure of; I want to remain on Ellis Island. I cannot admit these fears to anyone, especially not myself. So well am I entrenched in the art of denial that I thrust my fears away, attributing them to my "active imagination" and thereby laying a heavy layer of fear and apprehension that will reside in my heart for the rest of my life.

It's raining in the morning. Suddenly, I am very much concerned with our health. "How can we go on a ferry in the rain?" I ask my mother, hoping she'll tell the people in charge that there is no way we will be able to go on the ferry. "We're going in a small ship and we might all drown in this awful rain. Let's wait for a sunny day."

"Don't be ridiculous," she answers impatiently. She hasn't a clue why I'm telling her about the weather. "Weren't we in the middle of the ocean when it was storming?"

"Aren't we supposed to be going to school today?" I ask the matron, hopefully. Maybe she can squeeze one more day of safety on Ellis Island for me.

"Not today, dearie," she answers, "today, you will be seeing your father. And won't that be wonderful?" She has a strange accent. Much later on, when I hear an Irish brogue, I always associate it with her.

"I'm taking my school supplies with me," I announce to my mother before we are to board the ferry.

"No, you're not. You're being silly," my mother tells me. "Don't you think you will have everything you need? Your Papa will take care of everything." The ferry pulls away while I watch the island recede. I don't want to leave this place I've become comfortable in. Why do I have to abandon every place I've come to feel safe and protected: Vienna, Wieliczka, Montelupi, Liebenau, the Gripsholm and now Ellis Island. I remember leaving Wieliczka, the running in Krakow, the Ghetto, the horrible train rides, the unwelcoming stay in Switzerland. I know too well that not all change is for the better.

When we land in New York we take a taxi to our hearing. It is March. I am nine years and one month old and am awed by the sights of this city. It is pouring and I can't believe how many people are walking through the streets. All are rushing; some are carrying umbrellas, while others protect themselves by placing newspapers on their heads. No one seems to looking where they are going, but they all seem to know how to get there.

When we arrive in the hearing office, the matron who accompanies us explains that she has to leave and it will be a long wait before we see the judge. We are led to a row of chairs and told to sit there until the clerk calls our names. My mother warns us to behave. We sit silently for about a half an hour, and then we start on a "quiet" game of refugee.

I turn my chair around so that I can face Michael and appear like a proper secretary. He sits, hunched over in his seat, looking at his shoes.

"Yes?" I demand, sour pussed as possible. "What do you want?"

"Oh please, please, I have come to see the commandant," he implores.

"That is completely out of the question," I say crisply.

"Why not? I have an appointment and I have papers."

"What? You have papers. Let me see them!"

Before long, the game escalates into a shouting, crying match and my mother who is embarrassed has to separate us. She seats each of us on either side of her. We look at each other, suppressing giggles. Our fates are to be decided in this office, today and it is impossible for us to act dignified and serious.

Chapter Thirty-Two

Reunion

While we re sitting in the waiting room, trying to make each other laugh, a beautifully dressed, dark haired woman wearing lots of make-up and a wrap around purple scarf comes into the room. I point her out to my mother. "Look Mutti, are all Americans so beautiful?" My mother looks at her, and a shock of recognition registers on her face. It is her sister-in-law, Sari, my father's younger sister. I never knew we had an aunt in America.

My mother rushes towards Sari. The two women greet each other, hugging and bursting into tears. Sari, who lives in New York, has received a telegram from my father informing her of our imminent arrival. She rushes over to Columbus Circle as soon as the telegram arrives. Telegrams are the only means of rapid communication. It is 1945, and telephones are a luxury neither could consider, let alone acquire.

Some time later, a dark, unshaven man comes rushing in. He is wearing a brown hat and a black coat and he looks around, somewhat dazed, as if not sure of where he is. I make a silent wish, "please, God, let that not be my father." The wish is not granted. He recognizes my mother and runs up to us. He hugs us and I feel the sharp scrape of his whiskers on my cheek. Oh no! I am back in the empty stairwell embraced by *Glatz Kopf.*

"I left the factory in such a hurry that I didn't have a chance to wash up and shave," he apologizes for his appearance. I stare at my feet as though afraid they might take off on their own. He looks nothing like the image I had created in my fantasy. I retreat behind a wall of shyness and fear, mute, while Michael, eager to have a father, any father opens up like a gushing fountain.

"Mutti, Mutti, is this Papa?" he looks up at her, imploring her to say yes it is. We are all ushered into a room where an American judge hears our case. He is a friendly, pleasant man who wears a US army uniform. He smiles at all of us. "Believe it or not," he tells us, "I am the father of two children who

110

are the exact age of," he glances at the paper on his desk, "Rita and Michael."
He is nothing like the surly, barking officials in Poland and Switzerland. He
goes on, "I can only imagine how difficult life must have been for the four of
you to be separated for so many years. I am going to make this as easy for all
of us as I can, while staying on the right side of the law."

He asks Michael and me why we want to come to America.

"To be with our father, of course!" Michael replies in a loud voice, while
I nod in mute assent.

The judge asks my parents some other questions and I notice tears in my
father's eyes. It is the second and last time I will ever see my father cry. The
judge talks to my parents. I am not listening and if I were, I probably wouldn't
understand anything. I hear strange words like "citizenship" and "natural-
ization." What they mean when they are finally translated to me is that the
judge rules in our favor. We are permitted to leave with my father and live in
America, provided that we go to Canada for several days and enter the US as
Canadians. We don't have to return to Ellis Island where I want to go in order
to collect my precious school supplies and meager possessions.

"Today is Purim," my father tells us. I have a vague recollection of Purim
in Wieliczka when young men came to our house dressed in funny costumes,
hoping to collect a few *groschen,* pennies.

"Purim," my father reminds us is a Jewish holiday celebrating the miracu-
lous redemption of the Jews who were supposed to be hung in Persia by the
tyrant Haman.

My mother thinks he's joking, that he's making up the fact that today is
Purim. She thinks he does that for personal reasons, that it is Purim for us be-
cause we are free. She tells him so. "No, no," he assures her. Today is really
Purim, March 14, 1945. Our redemption takes place on Purim day in 1945.
Like the Jews of Shushan in Persia, we too are rescued.

Chapter Thirty-Three

Interlude

We are having dinner at Schreiber's Kosher Restaurant on the upper West Side, where we will eat for several evenings while my parents try to get acclimated to being together and making a new start. My favorite dish: the crispy kosher dill pickles. The restaurant is full of well-dressed, prosperous looking diners, but to my mother's amazement they are eating chicken with their fingers.

"That's how Americans eat chicken," Sari explains.

My mother is shocked. That could never happen in the cultured Europe she was raised. "Such bad mannered people would be asked to leave the restaurant."

By the time we finish dinner it is dark outside. New York City is ablaze with lights, even though America is still at war. To me, it is a fairy tale city: red and green traffic lights blinking on and off automatically, yellow street lamps, reflecting in the wet pavement, neon signs flashing in brightly lit store windows. The world we have just left was dark, illuminated only by the moon and stars.

"Won't the enemy planes be able to find us with so many lights on?" I ask Aunt Sari. "What happens when there is an air raid?"

"We've never had an air raid," she replies, not addressing my question.

"But what if *there is* an air raid?" I persist.

She tries to assuage my fears, "America is too far away for the Germans to get here," she declares. "We're safe. We don't even think about an air raid. We've never had one and we never will." I decide not to believe her. I know that Germany is just as close to America as America is to Germany and I remember the bombs, the air raid sirens, the loud uniformed soldiers and the warm shrapnel.

I love the lights of New York, indifferent to the war, like a wealthy princess flaunting her jewels in an impoverished world, but I worry. I am convinced we are in danger and the bright lights are disclosing our location to the enemy.

My father has found an apartment for us in the Washington Heights section of Manhattan. We aren't ready to move in yet. So Michael sleeps with my parents at a small hotel, The Endicott, on the West Side, and I stay with Aunt Sari in a room she shares with her good friend Thea. In the mornings, my parents bring Michael over to my aunt's apartment and we spend the day exploring the sights of New York, while they go out and get our new home ready.

My aunt is taking a week off from work so she can show Michael and me a good time. We leave her house early, well before noon. The streets of Manhattan are full of people in a hurry to get somewhere. We go underground, though a turnstile and enter a subway car that takes off with ferocious speed. The noisy train jostles from side to side heading for what seems like disaster in a black tunnel. We are thrown about and the noise is deafening, but no one seems concerned. Some passengers try to shout above the din to make themselves heard; others are engrossed in their newspapers, magazines and books. Everyone seems fine, not aware of the disaster that only I seem to be anticipating. Even Michael looks comfortable. Am I the only one who feels impending danger? When the ride is over we get out of the train into the bright sunlight. I question my aunt, "What is wrong with that train? Why is it so noisy and shaky? Are all of them like this? I feel like I'm going down into the very bottom of the earth and hearing the roaring of giants."

She laughs at my worries. "This is the New York Subway system, and yes, it is noisy and lurching, but it is safe and it gets people quickly to where they have to go. You'll get used to it." Then she adds, "and now that we are where we want to be, let's have some fun."

What excitement awaits us! I get to eat my first banana from one of the sidewalk fruit displays. I have only seen pictures of bananas, but I never tasted one. It is surprisingly smooth and bland and it certainly does not meet my expectations.

After the banana comes the best part. Aunt Sari takes us to the Paramount Theater to see a movie. We pass under a brightly lit marquee, through thickly carpeted, luxurious lobbies and past uniformed ushers wearing lots of brass and satin trim who help us find our seats. The theater is very dark, and the screen is huge. A pleasant smell that I will associate with movie theaters for the rest of my life permeates the auditorium. We sit in soft, comfortable seats and the music comes at us from every direction. The movie is "The Three Caballeros" which transports me to the enchanted land of animation, where every color is sharper, every sound is clearer and every costume is more outrageous than anything in the world outside. It is entrancing and I never want it to end.

From the movies, we head to the Automat for lunch, where another miracle takes place. We put nickels into a slot in the wall and a magic window opens and presents us with the food of our choice. I am now positive that America is a magical country.

Chapter Thirty-Four

516 West 188th Street

When the week is over, it is time to enter the real world. Aunt Sari has to return to work and we have to get on with our lives. My parents arrive to take us to the apartment in Washington Heights, which is on the upper west side of Manhattan, near the George Washington Bridge. The neighborhood is filled with German Jewish refugees. German is spoken on the streets, in the fruit stands and the bakery. I hate the language, guttural and dissonant. I want to forget it, but that won't be possible in Washington Heights.

We climb up five stories to get to our apartment. "Are we there yet?" I ask my father at every landing. "Not yet," he answers, trying to catch his breath. Finally, on the fifth floor he takes out a key and inserts it into the lock of one of the three doors opening onto the hallway. I have no idea of what to expect, but what I see is exciting and full of promise. Two doors are located on the left side of the dark corridor, one leading to a narrow bathroom and the other to the kitchen where we will spend most of our time doing homework, listening to the radio and of course eating. A big, bright room, with windows that face the alley, permitting me to look into our neighbors' apartments is to be our living room. The windows open onto what I think is a balcony.

"Mutti, look," I say excitedly, "we have a balcony!"

"No, no, no," my father runs over to explain. "That is not a balcony. That is called a fire escape. If there's a fire in our apartment, then we have to run down all these steps to get out of the house."

"But can't we use it as a balcony until we have a fire?" I ask hopefully.

"Well," he explains, "it can be a bit dangerous. But if you're careful, maybe you could pretend it's a balcony."

I open the window and climb out on the fire escape. Once I step onto it I freeze. Looking down I realize how dangerous it is, with its steep, narrow, long flights of rusty steps that go all the way down to the ground. One tiny misstep and I will plunge between the two buildings where I would shatter like a porcelain doll. I can see myself lying, broken on the ground. I grab hold of the rail and carefully back myself inside our new living room. This is not a balcony I will ever use.

The two other rooms are going to be bedrooms. The larger of the two belongs to my parents and the smaller one to Michael and me. Beds are already made up for us standing against two walls and one large dresser that we will share stands next to the closet. I like it. It's cozy, it's clean and it's ours. Michael and I try out the new beds. First we lie down on them, pretending to sleep, and then we jump up and down. We make lots of noise, laughing and screaming.

My father comes into the room. "Stop that," he tells us. It is the first time I hear him use a stern voice. "You're going to break the springs on the beds. Beds are made for sleeping on and nothing else."

"Alex, please," my mother says to him, "these children have had so few things of their own. What harm will it do for them to jump up and down on a bed?"

My father turns to her and I can see he is shocked by her response to scolding us. "Fredel," he says to her quietly, "did you forget that parents should never disagree in front of their children?"

My mother remembers what she learned in the *mutter schule* so long ago when she was pregnant in Vienna. She sighs. "It's been such a long time since we were able to be two parents to our children."

At night, when Michael falls asleep, I listen to my father talking to my mother in German. "You cannot imagine how hard it was to find this apartment," he tells her. "With the war still on, no new buildings are going up. Apartments are terribly scarce."

"How did you manage to find this one?" she asks, curious.

He explains that he had literally gone from one building to another, asking superintendents if they had a vacancy. By chance, he met an Austrian woman, Mrs. Flesch , who told him of this one.

He goes on to tell her what life had been for him in the United States. "You can't imagine how it was. I came here with nothing but the clothes on my back. The minute I left Vienna I was overcome with loneliness for you and the children, for my parents and, believe it or not, the city of Vienna itself. After all, I had lived there all my life, and love it or hate it, it was familiar. I knew where every street was located, where to shop and where to *daven* (pray). By the time I got to America I thought I would go out of my mind." I can hear my mother whispering but can't make out all of her responses. He continues, his voice taking on an urgency and intensity I was unfamiliar with.

"I stayed with Sari for a few weeks, but you know me. I have to be independent. At least I spoke English so that was a help. I went to *Shul* and someone told me about a job in Philadelphia, a cutter in a leather factory."

My mother is impressed. "It's wonderful that you were able, so willing to go from an office job in Vienna to a factory, working at anything that would bring you some money." She is filled with admiration for the man she married: who saved our lives, was willing to accept any kind of work and walked the streets of New York to find a suitable apartment for us. He tells her that he chose to move to New York because he knew it would be easier to bring up Jewish children in New York than any other place on earth.

"Here, in this neighborhood, we are not a despised minority," he assures her. She tells him what a wonderful choice he made. "I know that this is a wonderful apartment for us. It's a good place for the children to grow up in and learn about their new lives."

Now that my father has assured her of the appropriateness of the neighborhood he goes on to explain his having to accept a menial job. "Believe me, there were no jobs in the insurance business for refugees. Metropolitan Life, John Hancock; they would rather hire an ignorant American *Goy* than a well educated, smart refugee. As soon as they found out I was Jewish they forgot about me. They never even interviewed me. It wasn't easy going from a nice clean office, with my own desk to a dirty, noisy factory. But the money was good and I had no choice. Anyway, I have no cause to complain. Having you and the children with me? I never dreamed that I we would be together again." There are a few moments of silence and then I hear him go on.

"Sometimes I feel lost in this big country. All I wanted was to see you and the children. Now that they're here, there is so much to do in order to give them opportunities, help them understand that they're Jewish, and get them a proper education. How can I ever make up to them what they have lost?"

"Be patient, Alex," I hear my mother say soothingly. "It takes time to get used to a new life."

"I know, I know. But, believe me, here, in America, I am nothing. I have no position and no chance of becoming anything other than a factory worker. At least in Vienna our family was respected, we had relatives and friends. Here we have no one except for Sari: no family, no real friends." The contented tone of voice he had only moment ago is gone. He sounds sad.

"I hate the factory." He goes on. "You can't imagine what kind of people I work with, the lowest of the lowest." He continues and I try to stay awake, to listen in on their conversation, but sleep covers me like a warm blanket.

Because it is on the top floor, the apartment is bright and my mother does the best she can to make it as cheerful as possible. She goes to the Woolworth store and buys two potted plants and places them on the window sill. She buys an inexpensive mirror at the second hand furniture store and hangs it on the wall opposite the window. She is delighted with her decorating skills. "Look," she says to my father, "You see how the mirror reflects the windows? Now it's like we have four windows in the room instead of two."

We unpack the new dishes, pots and pans. My mother washes them in the kitchen sink, I dry them and my father puts them up on a shelf. It is an assembly line, and I'm thrilled to be part of it. The table, my father tells everyone, is made of a new product called "Formica." "You can put hot stuff on it and it won't burn the top. You can wash it with a damp rag and it won't warp. It is truly a miracle." He demonstrates its attributes by putting a lit cigarette on the table to show us that heat will not harm the new product. The top layer of Formica melts immediately. My father looks shocked and embarrassed. I laugh at the mishap as my mother quickly douses the flame.

My father becomes angry at me. "You're being disrespectful," he scolds me. "You never, ever should laugh at your parents." I don't know what to say. I'm frightened. He raises his voice and I see he's angry; and it's me he's angry with. I don't know what to do to make his anger disappear. I feel ashamed and look down at the floor, but he goes on, "I obeyed and honored my parents and I expect the same from my children."

I still don't understand what it was that I did to make him so angry. No one had ever told me that laughing at something I found amusing was bad. I turn red, squirm at his outburst, but he is undeterred, "I was a good son," he begins reminiscing, his demeanor turns from rage to sadness. "I did everything they asked of me. I sacrificed a secular education in order to respect my father's wishes and with it a chance to have a profession." I am still not sure what I did to provoke such anguish, yet I feel somehow that I must make things alright since I was the one who made my father angry. I use my mother's cheerful voice and admire the table.

"Look," I exclaim over the two extension pieces at either end of the table that slide out and have to be lifted in order to make them level. "It's almost like a piano." I turn on the radio and pretend to be playing along with the broadcast music.

My mother chides him later that night. I listen in on their conversation. "Alex. Why did you get so angry at Maidi when she laughed at your cigarette experiment? She didn't do anything disrespectful. She thought it was funny and so did I."

"She was belittling me and laughing at me," he tells her earnestly, "and that is not the kind of behavior I expect from my child. I want love and respect from my children, not joking at my expense. I may be nothing outside this family, but here, from my children, I expect appreciation and love, not ridicule."

"She wasn't laughing at you, Alex," she tells him, "she was laughing at the situation." I am happy that my mother is sticking up for me. I don't know what makes my father happy and what makes him upset. I decide to stay on his safe side, saying very little and trying to avoid him whenever possible.

I am wearing my mother's blue bathrobe, and a beret tilted on the side of my head, standing next to the wall, leaning against it. My left arm is bent at the elbow, resting on my hip, with my mother's purse hanging from it. I am putting on a show for Michael. In place of a cigarette a pencil is dangling from my lips, my eyes are half closed and I'm trying to keep the soprano pitch of my voice as deep down as it will go.

"*Unter der laterne,*" I croon. I am being Marlene Dietrich singing *Lili Marlene.*

The door opens and my father walks in. I'm surprised and embarrassed. He hasn't said a word and I'm ready to crawl under the bed. I feel as though I've been caught doing something I shouldn't be doing. He sees that I have stopped and he walks out without saying a word. I feel weird. I definitely don't want him to see me acting like myself but at the same time I feel guilty for thinking that I need to shrink away from him. I don't know right from wrong.

I take great pains to dress in the bathroom, where there is no chance of his walking in on me naked and I make sure not to sing or dance when he is in the house. I try to keep away from him as much as possible. I realize that this is the first time in years that we've had to share quarters with a man and I am uncomfortable near my father. Not only is he nothing like the man I envisioned, but he is moody, unpredictable, I never know what to expect from him. When he comes into a room, I become quiet and withdrawn, only speaking when I am spoken to. It takes a long time for me to act natural around him.

Chapter Thirty-Five

Tovah

My father who has had virtually nothing to do with our upbringing and hasn't seen us for six years is determined to take charge. Among his concerns is the fact that Michael and I know nothing about Judaism. I overhear him telling our neighbor Mrs. Flesch, that we don't know an *aleph* from a *bet*. "They're like *goyim,*" he tells her.

"Mr. Schmelkes," she interrupts him impatiently, "where were they supposed to learn Hebrew? At the Ghetto or the camp in Germany?" He doesn't answer.

He promptly enrolls us in the Yeshiva, Samson Raphael Hirsch, which is an ultra Orthodox day school. Girls are expected to wear long sleeves and boys, *tzi- tzis (*ritual fringes that hang outside the shirt). Nothing is explained to me and I don't know any reasons for what is expected of me. The school is housed in an old synagogue that has one large sanctuary and a warren of makeshift classrooms haphazardly separated by partitions and room dividers. A moveable blackboard is wheeled from one room to another and shared by all the classes.

My school day is noisy, chaotic and completely undisciplined, nothing like the regimented classroom in Liebenau or the public school, P.S. 189, across the street from our apartment. P.S. 189 is a huge brick building with a large school yard, and high windows that are opened with long poles. I watch with envy as children run around having fun before school starts, during lunch time, and when the whistle blows they quickly get into quiet lines and enter the building. I long for the disciplined atmosphere with rules and a sense of control. All the children that live on our street attend P.S.189 and they all seem to be having fun.

Since I am new at the Yeshiva and have recently come from Germany, everyone assumes that I don't know anything. I am placed in the first grade with six year olds. I am hurt, disappointed and outraged. I object loudly. What am I doing here with all these babies? I ask my parents. My mother understands, she too is upset by my being placed with first graders, but she is at a loss. She is unfamiliar with the way things are done in the U.S. and tells me to be patient.

Later on, I complain to my teacher who also tells me to be patient. I have been patient all my life; waiting to meet my father, waiting to come to the US, waiting to go to a real school. I am not going to wait patiently for another minute. Without asking permission to leave the room, I march right over to the principal's office, burst in, without knocking on the door. "I can read, I can write and I can do arithmetic. Why do I have to learn the sounds of the letters when I have already read many books?" Gone is my shyness. I speak pure British, which some Americans mistake for arrogance. Certainly I am demanding and not worried about being polite. I know who I am and what I am capable of. "I'm not a baby and I will not come to a school that can only teach me what I already know."

"Well," he answers me slowly, taken aback by my posture, "we just want to make sure you are comfortable and not in over your head."

"Over my head!? I'm drowning in boredom. I want to be with children my own age, in a class where I can learn something new, not c-a-t says cat." The years in Liebenau, when I was responsible for Michael, have taught me how to fend for myself.

He nods, "I see what you mean," he says, "let's see how you do in the first grade, and then if you do well, we'll move you up."

"Not good enough," I tell him, staunchly. "I'm not going to be in first grade one minute longer."

"Look," he says to me, "go back for the time being. I promise you that I will take care of things and have you placed in your correct grade."

I believe him and reluctantly go back into the classroom. I do my best, which is ridiculously easy. A week passes and I ask the teacher "when am I going to move up to be with children my own age?"

"I don't know anything about that," she tells me and I realize that the principal has not even spoken to her. I become disruptive in class, humming, tapping my knuckles on the table, calling out wrong answers to easy questions and confusing the little children. I am going to make them to move me up or throw me out of the school.

My tactics work. They give up and put me into third grade. I am still more than a year older than my classmates, but I give in. I know when I am beat, but I also learn how to get my way when I am incensed at injustice. The school justifies my temper tantrum promotion by assigning Tova, a pudgy third grader to help me "catch up." I don't realize this at first, but Tova is an unpopular little girl who has no friends. Tova, they figure, will be provided with a new friend and dose of self esteem by being my mentor.

"Dress, not frock, potsy not hopscotch, store not shop, cayn't not cahn't." Tova's nasal voice drills on and on. When I do things my way, she calls me "dumb." My way of writing is wrong; my way of doing subtraction and addition is ridiculous. Everything I do is criticized by Tova. During recess, she walks around the schoolyard with me while all the other girls are having fun jumping rope and playing hopscotch. She is forever correcting my pronunciation and language usage. She goes on and on.

It is clear that she does not like me but relishes her role as my boss. I understand that feeling. I have been in charge of my brother so I know how good it feels, but I am not about to take directions from some fat girl who is younger than I am and has no friends. I hate her and I hate the grown ups at the school who are allowing this.

"Quiet," she hisses at me when I raise my hand to answer a question. "You don't know the answer to that question, so put your hand down." I do know what the capital of Portugal is, and no one else in the class does, including Tova. I ignore her, and wait to be called on. "Lisbon," I reply, gloating at Tova.

For a nine year old, school is life and my life is letting me down. I looked forward to school since I was four years old and watched my older cousins go off to school in Wieliczka. I enjoyed the school in Liebenau, where even though we did not have enough supplies, I felt that I was learning and the atmosphere was disciplined. Even the little classroom in Ellis Island provided a room with a blackboard, lots of school supplies and a structured environment. This school, in America is nothing like what I had experienced, read about or imagined.

I complain to my mother, "we don't have enough of anything we need: textbooks, blackboards, maps, dictionaries. Everything has to be passed from one classroom to another. My helper Tova makes me re-write all my compositions. She checks my spelling and scribbles comments on my papers in red pencil making me do everything over again- omitting lots of my details."

I can't articulate how dreadful I feel. How does a nine year old explain the disappointment of being thrown into this chaotic environment? I don't know how to tell my mother, I don't have the language or the awareness to express my frustration. I hate my school, I hate my life. I feel more prejudice in this little Jewish school than I ever felt from any of my other teachers. The nuns and the British teachers all treated me fairly and only judged me by the quality of my work. Here I am forced to lower my standards because I was in a camp during the war.

One day I give the teacher an assignment I have completed. Tova has not done hers yet and when the teacher questions her, she complains she is unable to do her own schoolwork and supervise mine as well. I am ready to explode. Now she is blaming me for her uncompleted work. The teacher never looks at my completed assignment. She hands it over to Tova and tells her to check it before handing it back to her. In return Tova gets an extension on the assignment, and my homework is marked up in Tova's red handwriting.

I give up. I make up my mind that I am never going to return to school. The next morning I don't get out of bed. "This is not going to be a 'sick' sore throat day," I tell my parents. "This is going to be the day when I never go back to that school again." I am lying in bed, rigid and inflexible. "Michael will have to go to school without me because nothing is going to make me change my mind. There is a perfectly good public school across the street and if you want me to go to school, any school, it will be to that one." I fight a hard battle.

My mother sends Michael off alone. She sits down on the edge of my bed. "Tell me," my mother says gently. "You were looking forward to school all your life. What happened in school yesterday that is making you so unhappy?"

"It wasn't just yesterday. I have no friends, certainly not Tova. No adult recognizes anything that I am doing. I get no praise, I get no directions. This school simply does not feel right."

I burst into tears. "I hate that place. Everyone pokes fun of accent; they even call me a Nazi because I just came from Germany. The teachers never even look at my work. I have no one in that school; no one to talk to, no one to play with. I hate Tova and her bossiness. I'm not going to a school where a stupid kid who doesn't like me and whom I hate, is my teacher!" I cry and hold fast to the sides of the bed. No one is going to be able to force me out, I resolve.

My mother lets me stay home while she goes to the school administration to tell them about my feelings. I must have convinced her with my determination because she is gone for over an hour. When she comes home she reasons with me.

"I talked to the teachers and the principal. Tova will no longer be you helper," My mother pleads with me. "Try the school again and I promise you that if things do not get better, you will go to public school."

I agree and return to school the next day. Tova is relieved of her exalted position. She must be missing it or else she just misses the companionship of a playmate because she tries to win me over by showing me some of her jewelry, and offering to share a snack with me at lunch time.

Chapter Thirty-Six

Yetta

Without Tovah in tow I finally find a real friend, Yetta. She is my age and a grade ahead of me in school, but we enjoy being together. School gets better for me after I have Yetta. She is an only child and lives near the school. Yetta has a job walking two little girls home from kindergarten during lunch time. She offers to share her job and salary with me. It is a wonderful opportunity for me. We each get fifty cents a week, a veritable fortune for a nine year old in 1945. We love the job, pretending that we are mothers walking our children home from school. It provides us with money, companionship and a sense of responsibility.

To get the kindergartners home, we have to cross many streets, some of them quite busy. But we are careful and conscientious and with money in our pockets, we feel rich. Every day on our walk with the two children, Yetta and I engage in "grown up" conversations. We make plans for our futures. We will be beautiful and marry handsome boys. We will live next door to each other and our children will play together. We will visit every day and have lunch at each other's houses and then rush home to prepare dinner for our husbands.

"So, Yetta," I say, "what are you making for dinner tonight?"

"Oh," she answers, "I'm fixing up some leftovers from *Shabbes*. Sam loves the meat loaf I made, and I made enough for a couple of days."

"I'm just going to warm up the cholent and make meatballs with potato latkes."

We talk in grown up voices trying to sound like important, responsible housewives.

I try to tell Yetta about my life before coming to America. She knows I have an accent, but she doesn't care. Her parents also have accents. "You know, I have been in a real Ghetto, a prison and a camp," I tell her.

She has no idea what I'm talking about. No one has told her about the war and what has been happening to the Jews of Europe. The only thing she knows about is that her parents both come from Europe, Germany, as a matter of fact. She quickly changes the subject. "Let's talk about something else," she says. "Do you know that Fanny Rabinowitz is getting a bike? Imagine, a girl riding on a bicycle!" It is 1945 and orthodox girls are not encouraged to do anything that might compromise their hymen, be it a bike ride or a split in a gymnastics class.

Yetta is full of information. She gives me my first lessons about sex. She tells me how important it was never to let a boy kiss you because that could make you do other things. I don't understand what she means, but not wanting to appear ignorant I agree with everything she says. Why would I ever let a boy kiss me anyway? I ask myself. Boys are disgusting. The very thought of getting close to one is repulsive. They sweat, they smell.

I go over to Yetta's house after school. It's raining and Yetta suggests that I stay at her house until it stops. Her parents are much older than mine and seem like relatives to me. Her mother is short, stocky and kind. She hugs me when I come into the house. "Come in girls," her mother invites us into the kitchen. "Good you decided not walk home in this rain," she tells me welcomingly. She takes the milk out of refrigerator. "Drink, drink, it's good for your teeth," she tells us as she opens a box from the bakery and serves us chocolate éclairs. Her father comes home. He is gray and wears glasses. Like my parents, they speak German to each other and their home is warm and welcoming. I call them "*tante* and *oncle*," and feel like I am their niece. "You'll stay for dinner, ya?" her mother asks. I would love to but I must get home. My mother is surely worrying about me.

Their family comes from Berlin where her father was a physician. They emigrated to the U.S. before 1936 and Yetta was born in New York City two weeks after they arrived. Her father does not have a license to practice medicine in America, but nevertheless, my mother often consults him when any one of us is ill. He is a generous, kind man and gives freely of his knowledge. If the condition requires a prescription, he tells us to go to another doctor who is licensed to write prescriptions. But doctors are expensive for our struggling family and he often saves us money as well as our health.

I am treated as if I am their own child. They invite me to go places with them; museums, parks and the zoo. Yetta and I pretend we are sisters. In school, we tell everyone that we're cousins, that my mother is her father's sister. Her parents are better off financially than we are and pay for me to do things with her that I would never consider asking my parents for. I come home and tell them of our wonderful adventures and that they spend money on me.

"They brought money with them from Berlin and invested it," my father tells my mother. "They can afford things that are unthinkable for us. Remember, I had to leave under very bad conditions. I had to leave everything: my family, my job, my friends and my beloved parents. If I had the luxury of taking my time, I would have been able to bring more than simply money out of Vienna. Besides," he goes on, "Dr. Levy has a profession and could always get a job here if he weren't so rich and lazy." For some reason he appears to be angry at Dr. Levy. "If I had disobeyed my father, and gone to the *Gymnasium* and to the University, I would also be able to provide my children with luxuries." He sounds bitter.

"But Alex, they are so kind to Rita," my mother says to my father. "They worked for their money; got it out of Germany and now they can spend it as they wish. They deserve everything they have."

"There you go again," he tells her, "always arguing with me."

She tries to appease him, "No, no, I'm not disagreeing with you. Of course you would have brought money out of Austria, if you had the chance. But look, you did save us and bring us to America. How many people did that?" She tries to soothe him without damaging my image of the Levys. My mother is happy that I found a friend whose parents can offer me some advantages that she can't.

My father doesn't hear her, can't let go of his anger, "Do you think I like being poor?" he asks. "In Vienna I made a good living, dressed well and worked at a respectable job. I know what you went through during the war, but don't think, for one moment, that it was easy for me." I feel badly, that somehow I cause my father to be unhappy because of my friendship with Yetta. "In Vienna, at the Phoenix Company, everyone called me Mr. Schmelkes. Here, every *pischer* calls me 'Alex.' You think that's easy for me?"

Later on I ask my mother what I've done to make my father sad, but she assures me that I've done nothing bad.

"Don't worry, *Maidi*," she says to me, using my old diminutive nickname, "these problems are no concern of yours. You go on and have a good time with Yetta and her parents." She sends me off.

"Now," Dr. Levy says, "what do you girls want to do? Do you want a pony ride or a camel ride?" We are at the Bronx Zoo, standing in front of the ticket booth where kids are lined up to ride a domestic animal. The ponies and the camels smell awful, but I am not about to give up an opportunity of a lifetime. It is a hard choice but I opt for the pony, figuring it is shorter and if I fall I will be closer to the ground. Yetta's father takes my picture. They are enthusiastic and compliment me, "You looked like a real cowgirl," they say when the ride is over. I am thrilled.

School improves. I am ambitious, driven and determined to succeed. I study for tests, read books and write reports without Tova's messing them up with her ridiculous red pencil. I receive praise from my teachers and feel rewarded. I work hard get their approval. My test grades are high and I'm feeling successful. Just as I tried in Wieliczka to improve my Polish accent, I now practice speaking like an American. It isn't hard at all. "Cain't instead of cahn't, wadeh, instead of water, claiss instead of clahs, exaimple instead of exahmple, dayncing instead of dahncing." When the spring semester comes to an end, I organize the girls to put on a play. I have had plenty of experience with that sort of thing in Liebenau where we put on shows for all sorts of occasions.

We write the show. It has dancing and singing and all the girls participate. We rehearse during recess and by the time we put it on, we feel ready for Hollywood. The boys say we are a bunch of show offs, but we don't care. The teachers and the administration love our performance and we certainly love the attention and recognition we get.

Summer is coming and I overhear my parents talking about sending us to camp. I'm not supposed to be listening to their conversation, but I can't help pricking up my ears. I barge into their bedroom where they are quietly discussing my fate. "Camp? What camp?" I interrupt "You're not sending me back to camp again."

Chapter Thirty-Seven

Camp

I wake up sweating. My hair is damp, my pajama top is wet. I'm having a nightmare where I am alone in a train with no other people on it. Black, shiny birds are pecking at the windows, breaking the glass, flying into the train. I run from one seat to another, but the birds are attacking me from every direction and in spite of the heavy sweater I am wearing they are tearing my flesh. I wake up, panting and out of breath. Where am I? Where is my mother and where is my bed? I look around. Nothing looks familiar. I am not on a train. I am not on a ship, not on Ellis Island. I realize I am lost. Where, oh where am I? The room is full of cots, full of other girls sleeping, but I am lost. This is not the nursery in Liebenau. I shake my head to clear it and realize that though I am awake I'm still in the middle of a nightmare. I am in camp.

Why am I here? I sit up and let my eyes adjust to the darkness. I taste dust in my mouth and a cold empty cave lodges where my stomach used to be. I recognize it as the same one I had when waiting in Wieliczka and the Ghetto for my mother. I am so frightened. I can't crawl into my mother's bed. I can't wake up the counselor and I certainly can't go back to sleep. How did I get here?

I reconstruct the process that got me into this hell. My parents, my father really, wants me to become acclimated to America, and being Jewish. He is convinced that the most efficient way of doing this is to send me to a Jewish summer camp. I remember their conversation. My summer is settled without a word of input from me. My parents are talking, ignoring my presence in their room.

"I don't know if it's such a good idea to send the children away." My mother says. "We've only been together for three months. Don't you think they should become acclimated to us as a family before they are thrown into

128

a foreign environment? They can get used to being Jews and Americans next year."

He tries to convince her, "Fredel, you have no idea how hot, stuffy and humid New York is in the summer. There'll be nothing for them to do here. Let them go out of the city, where the fresh country air will do them good. The Jewish community thinks it's important enough to pay the camp tuition. They don't like to throw money out." He tries to win her over. "They have to learn how to live in a Jewish community. Think of what we've had to give up in order to being Jewish. Surely they can give up a summer of New York City heat and become better Jews." They'll enjoy being with other children and getting used to their lives in a free country. They have all their lives to get used to us."

She resists, "maybe we could all go for some fresh, country air and not have to send the children away the first summer we are together."

"Fredel," he tells her, "I don't know how to say this, but the children are too close to you. They have to get away from you for a short time. It isn't good to be so tied to your mother. Beside, I couldn't get away for more than one week, and that would still keep them in the hot humid city for most of the summer." He urges her, trying to get her to agree to the idea of camp. "Believe me, when the summer comes and they have no place to go, you'll realize that I was right. Only by then, it will be too late to do anything about it. The country air will give them what they can never get here in the city." They discuss it some more, while I stand frozen, horrified, listening to them making plans for my summer.

The "country air" sells her on the idea. The country is good for growing children, she agrees. "I just hope that they won't be unhappy away from us," she is not completely convinced or willing to give up the children, whom she has saved at such great effort.

"They'll have a good time in camp. All the other children there have parents in the city, and they won't be alone. Besides, they get to play and swim. This is important," he addresses her concerns.

"Please don't send me away," I beg my parents after listening in on their conversation. "I don't want to go to a camp. Besides, I can go to the country with Yetta. Her parents said I could come along."

"No, you can't go away with the Levys. I can't be taking so much from them without being able to give anything back." He speaks authoritatively although he's never been to any kind of camp. "You'll love camp," he tells me. "There are lots of other girls your age. You'll go swimming every day. Believe me, I wish I had had such an opportunity when I was a boy." I pray the he doesn't go into how much he gave up to please his parents and honor their desire to make sure he remains Jewish. Before he has the chance to bemoan his fate I jump in with my response.

"No, no. I'm not interested. I can have a wonderful summer right here in New York City." I don't want to leave my home. I just got here. Why do I have to keep leaving places as soon as I get to know them? I stand firm. "I'm not going, I don't want to go away from here," I am determined to stay in New York for the summer. My parents know of my ability to stand firm. They call in all the troops.

First, my Aunt Sari tells me that summer camp is nothing like Liebenau.

"You will love it there. Only lucky girls get to go. Imagine, you'll be living with friends, swimming, playing ball, and you'll be in the country." I don't know what she means by the "country." New York, USA is the country I'm in now and I don't want to leave my country. "Give it a try." She encourages me, "Camp is a wonderful experience and a great opportunity for you." Easy for her to say, she's never been to any camp. I stand firm. I am not going to camp. They'll have to tie me up and throw me on the train.

My cousin Elsie is called in next. It was her idea to send me to camp in the first place. She talks to me about the fun I will have in camp. She's a doctor, single, glamorous, and moreover, she herself has been to camp as a camp doctor. She knows all about it.

I protest. "I also know about camp I tell her. "I spent a long time in a camp."

"Camp in America is nothing like Liebenau," she assures me, even though she's never heard of Liebenau until she met us a few months ago. "You'll have fun, you'll have friends, you'll be happy."

"I don't want to go," I protest, beg and cajole. "Please, please, let me stay here with you. I'll be good," I promise. On some level, I think that if I say I'll be good, I'll get anything I want. It's no use. My mother sews name tags on all of my clothes and the trunk is packed.

Once again I am on a train, headed for an unknown destination, surrounded by strangers. Only this time, my mother is not with me to reassure me and tell me all unpleasant things are products of my imagination. It is the beginning of a nightmare but this time I am awake. At least, when we traveled to Switzerland and Marseilles, I thought that we were on our way to America to see my father. Now, all I am aware of is that what I am leaving is my mother, father and little brother.

I find myself in an ultra Orthodox girl's camp called *Beis Yaakov* Camp, while Michael who unlike me, wants to go, is at an equally Orthodox boys' camp called Camp *Mesifta.* One thing my father, aunt and cousin were completely right about is that: *Beis Yaakov* is nothing like Liebenau. It is much, much worse. At Liebenau I had my mother and brother near by. I was among other people in similar situations, refugees, going from one place to another. Here I am desperately alone, with no one to comfort me.

The sudden unbearable attack of loss and loneliness grabs me as soon as I say good-bye to my mother at the train station. It lodges deeper than any injury I've sustained, residing in my right shoulder and extending to the middle of my chest, between my two unformed breasts. My ribs crumble, collapsing against where I think my heart is. The ache attacks my throat, joining forces with the pain that originates from my shoulder. I can't get the clump in my throat to move aside and permit me to cry. I feel like I swallowed a rock. The waves of grief tower over me just as the ocean loomed above the Gripsholm in the middle of the frightening storm, washing the decks with salty spray. But this is not salty sea water. This is sorrow sweeping me away. This is far worse than the cold, worse even than the fear of *Glatz Kopf*. I look around at my fellow campers. They are oblivious to my pain, talking, laughing and making plans, while I am treading water, trying desperately to keep afloat and survive this ocean of panic.

I have not seen my mother for five long days. I have never been separated from her, not even for one night. Why did she permit me to be taken away from her when she held on so tightly to me before? The questions go around in my head all day and all night long. I am convinced that I will never see my mother, father or my brother again. For me separation equals permanent loss, abandonment and death. I've already had too much experience with it. My Uncle Herzl, my *Omma,* and *Oppa*, my cousins, aunts, uncles, our friends who were sent to Vittel; none of them ever came back. I suddenly understand why Victor can't talk.

The dining room is filled with the chattering and laughter of the girls. I have a mouthful of cheese and noodles and cannot get them past the massive lump in my throat. I don't swallow and I carry the chewed up mouthful with me hoping to find a place to spit it out. Finally when I get to the swimming pool, I go to the toilet and get rid of the mushy noodles. I don't speak. I haven't heard my own voice for days, and finally have to face what I have feared the most. My parents have disappeared and I do not know where to look for them.

I feel like Hansel and Gretel when they wake up in the woods; lost, alone with no one to turn to. Of all the fairy tales I've heard, I identify most closely with Hansel and Gretel. But my own version stops at the point where the woodchopper sends his children away and they realize they have been abandoned. But my story is worse. My brother is not nearby to take my hand the way Hansel took Gretel's. I have no one I can share my grief with.

The other girls get mail. I am the only one who hasn't received a single letter or post card. I am forgotten. This is further proof that something terrible has happened. I will later understand that my parents, who have no experience with camp, don't know enough to write to me. In the meantime, when I don't hear from them I have further proof that my mourning is justified. Days go by, and it gets worse and worse. I don't eat, I don't sleep, and I can do nothing to comfort myself, escape my despair. I am unable to tell anyone what is hurting me. "Oh God," I pray, "Please take me away from all of this. I really don't want to live any longer. I can't go on from here. If You can't bring me my mother, then let me die."

The camp staff is aware of my anguish, my inability to participate in even the simplest activities. My parents have no telephone and can only be reached by mail and the people in charge of the camp feel that they can't wait for a letter to reach my parents. They need to do something immediately to alleviate this child's suffering. They head counselor, a mother herself decides she will stop in at my parent's apartment when she goes into New York to buy kosher meat for the camp. She drives a big station wagon to the city every week to buy fresh supplies and she feels she must communicate my fears to my parents. She tells me nothing about this so I am surprised when I hear my name called over the loudspeaker while I am standing in the baseball field trying to swallow cornflakes from breakfast.

I am summoned to come to the office immediately. I hurry imagining the worst. My parents are waiting there to greet me. My mother is wearing a new pink sundress with a bolero. She looks more beautiful than ever. My father is wearing an open necked, short sleeved sport shirt. They look happy to see me. "How did you find me?" I ask them, not believing my good fortune at having them so close to me.

"We took a bus to Monticello in the Catskills, and a cab to Ferndale where the camp is." They have made the trip to reassure me that they are still alive. I am shocked to see them. It is as though they have returned from the land of the dead. All the tears that have solidified in my throat come pouring out. My mother takes out a hairbrush from her bag.

"*Maidi, Maidi,*" she croons, not addressing my tears, "your hair needs to be brushed and combed." She untangles my braids and brushes my hair lovingly. I feel as though I've just been saved from drowning. She tells me that she and my father are close by, at a hotel in the Catskills. They will come to visit me again in a few days. The very next day a post card arrives for me and after that, at least one piece of mail a day. I save all my letters under my pillow and reread them several times a day.

My fears have not been washed away by her appearance. I still feel ongoing anxiety gnawing at my insides, am unable to conquer the feelings of dread and doom; a prophecy of the depression waiting to descend upon me. Slowly, I begin to participate in the activities, many of which are centered on religious ritual. I learn the long grace after meals, pray in the morning, afternoon and evening, and learn many Hebrew songs and dances. I gain a great deal of knowledge about my Jewish roots.

I have always loved religion. I loved it when I was Catholic and went to church, and I now that I am beginning learn about and participate in Jewish ceremonies, I start to enjoy them almost as much as the Catholic rites.

Camp is a quick immersion into the religious pool. In addition to all the laws associated with the Sabbath, and keeping kosher, there are other holidays that have their own rituals. *"Tisha b'av,"* is a fast day which commemorates the destruction of the first and second temple in Jerusalem. It takes place in the middle of July. We are not supposed to buy or wear new clothing and not allowed to eat meat on the nine days preceding it. Most of the girls in my bunk, who like me are nine or ten years old observe it like the grown ups do. Even though they are not required to fast until their twelfth birthday, which marks the age of adult responsibility, these girls fast until one hour past sunset. We try to be serious, not joke around. We forego leather sandals wearing only canvas sneakers to show that we are in mourning for an event that took place thousands of years ago.

I love the spiritual aura that settles on the camp on Friday afternoons. We make preparations for the Sabbath "Queen." Everyone takes long showers, washes her hair and dons party dresses. *"Riva* (my Hebrew name), you look beautiful in that dress," my friend Malka says and then generously offers me her new white belt. "It will look so good with the pink flowers on the dress." It's as if we're all bridesmaids getting ready for a wedding.

The welcoming for Sabbath service is held outdoors in the sweet smelling fields, during sunset. We sing *L'cho dodi,* the prayer greeting the Sabbath Queen into our midst. I expect to see a beautiful princess in a long, white gown floating into our camp. Our simple, high-pitched young voices chant a haunting melody that surely drifts all the way to the heavens. The service ends as the sky darkens and we all walk holding hands, through the pitch black night into the bright dining room.

Chapter Thirty-Eight

The Sacred and the Profane

I am home from camp. We finish dinner and I burst into song. I am singing the long grace after meals that I learned in camp. I am eager to show off my newly acquired religious skills.

"What's this singing about?" my surprised mother asks. She is not familiar with any of this. In her family, grace was recited, not sung.

"She's *benching,*" my father tells her. "It's the Jewish-American way of saying grace."

"For ten minutes?" my mother asks, her blond eyebrows reaching her forehead. "It takes ten minutes of singing to thank God for one potato and one hamburger?"

Both my parents are astonished. They are not sure if they want such a complete transformation. But it is too late. I have been indoctrinated at camp and am hooked on Judaism. I pray three times a day, "*Shacharit, Mincha and Maariv,*" the traditional morning, afternoon and evening prayers, rocking back and forth like the girls at camp. When someone tries to interrupt me, I turn around angrily, "Shhh," I hiss. Can't they see I'm *davening*?

By my newly acquired religious standards, my parents are "*Goyim.*" My mother does not wear the traditional head covering and my father does not wear a *kippah*, even when he leaves the house and can be seen by all of my observant friends. In school, where I want to really belong, I lie. I behave as though my family is every bit as religious as anyone else's but when I get home I worry. What if we meet someone walking on the street from school and my father is seen with a *bloison kopf* (bare head)? My parents have the potential to betray me and I am embarrassed by their refusal to adhere to the principles I have been indoctrinated in. I want them to be observant. I'm scared of being "caught" with parents who act like *Goyim*.

My mother is an elegant woman. She usually wears a hat when she goes out. But my father is another story. "Please," I implore him, "can't you please cover your head when you leave the house? I want everyone to see that we are a religious family."

"No," my father tells me, lightly, "I gave that up a long time ago and I don't really believe that covering my head is going to make me a better Jew. I carry my Judaism in my heart, not my hat." I feel a sense of resentment. Why do I have to obey all of his religious edicts while he is not willing to do one single thing to meet my needs? How hard is it to wear a hat when he leaves the house? My parents won't give in. On Sabbath afternoons when all of us go to the public library, they have the potential of exposing me for what I am; not the religious girl everyone at school has been led to believe.

My father walks hatless, my mother carries a handbag; committing two sins at the same time. I consider not going to the library with them, staying home and asking them to bring me a book. But I love the library, the long, wide shelves full of all kinds of books beckoning to me, the wooden tables and comfortable chairs. I love the smell of books, and the huge selection available for nothing more than a library card. I can spend hours removing books from shelves, inspecting them, consider their worth and rejecting them or taking them home. It is always a hardship for me to limit myself to three books per week.

The children's librarian enjoys helping when I ask her for a good book for a girl my age. She introduces me to the "Honey Bunch" and, "Nancy Drew" series, "A Tree Grows in Brooklyn," Laura Ingall Wilder's "Little House" series and "Little Women." All are stories about girls my age who do courageous things. I especially loved Francie in "A Tree Grows in Brooklyn." Like me, she lives in New York City, in a similar neighborhood. She has high aspirations and like me, and she protects her younger brother. Her family, as ours, is poor but does not feel deprived. We are both avid readers and achievers and it is almost as though I am reading about my self. Her younger brother is like my younger brother. Her adventures are my adventures.

But the book that I loved the most was "Little Men" by Louisa May Alcott. In the story, Jo, one of the sisters, marries a professor and together they manage a home for motherless boys. I identify with Jo, and tuck her away in my memory, hoping someday to be just like her. What I admire most about her is the way she does things her own way. She is tomboy and she is brave. But she is kind, warm and nurturing. I would like to be as brave as she is. The best part about Jo is her love of unwanted boys; for boys like Victor and Michael. For all her unladylike behavior, she mothers them and gives them a home. That is what I want to do when I grow up; give motherless children a home.

I love the Saturday outings to the library, but I know we are committing a sin by carrying on the Sabbath. I am torn between Orthodoxy, my allegiance to my parents and the library. All the things I love are in conflict with each other. Carrying on the Sabbath, I am assured by my peers, is a very big sin. Being seen carrying on the Sabbath is even worse, because not only am I committing a sin, but it is being witnessed by some of my bossy friends. Sure enough, I get caught one Saturday afternoon as we are returning from the library.

I dread the thought of returning to school on Monday morning. I know that the "religious committee" set up by my friends will confront me. "We saw you on Shabbes with your father, mother and brother," Hannah, the ring-leader of a group of my friends accuses me, her arms crossed in front of her flat bosoms, "You were all carrying books, and your mother was carrying a pocketbook, which probably had money in it."

My face is getting hot and my heart is racing. It is the moment I have been dreading. Touching money on the Sabbath is a sin of even greater magnitude than carrying.

"My mother never carries money around," I lie helplessly. I've been caught. And on top of that, I feel compelled to lie and further humiliate myself. I feel a pulse throbbing in my neck and am sure that the girls can hear it too. I know what they say is true. They've caught me committing an unpardonable sin, something akin to shoplifting or writing on the bathroom walls. I try in vain to finagle my way out of it. It is no use. I have been caught committing a sin and lying about it; two big ones at the same time. I will now be taunted in a way I despise.

Hannah does not let go. "How could you lie to us like that?" She wants to know, "you probably don't keep kosher and I'll bet you ride on the Sabbath." The other girls stand around her, not saying a word, but agreeing with her silently. I feel their scorn.

This is too much for me to handle. "Of course we keep kosher and I have never ever ridden on the Sabbath." I fill up with self-righteous indignation. "You know what you are Hannah Werthheimer" I ask her, ready to cry? "You are a busybody. You've set yourself up to be the Gestapo of the Jewish neighborhood."

There is no room for negotiation, the girls are relentless. They position themselves around Hannah forming a circle and they look accusingly at me. I'm guilty, done, over, useless as a person, a liar, bragger, unworthy of their trust. Hannah has gotten to Yetta. Yetta, who has always been a bit of an outsider herself, is invited to join ranks with the popular girls. It is difficult to resist. At first she avoids looking at me and when that is not possible, she actually turns her back and walks away when I approach her. I can't believe it. I have lost something so important. We had such wonderful plans made for the rest of our lives. Now she is gone from my life. I feel bereft during recess. She's given my job to another girl and they walk past me as they leave the school with the kindergartners.

Someone else has taken my place. My God, I think, experience has taught me that the Catholics hate the Jews, the Jews hate the Catholics, but now I see that there are some Jews who hate other Jews. I am devastated by the loss of Yetta. I think that I'll never find another friend. Gone are the wonderful days we spent together, dreaming of the future. I begin to feel alone again. "I'm the only one of my kind," I tell myself, and I hate the way that feels. A nasty worm is boring its way into my heart. I can't explain it, and all I know is that it is with me when I wake up and when I go to sleep. It is an unwelcome addition to the seeds of depression sprouting within me. I can't seem to shake the feeling of doom and sadness. I stop singing and dancing, and only answer questions when I'm addressed. School is again becoming a burden for me. I stay indoors during recess, unable to face the joy and abandon of my former friends.

My mother doesn't notice this, and when I tell her that I am feeling sad because of Yetta, she doesn't understand. "What are you worried about? There are lots of other girls in your school. You can be friends with them."

"No, no," I say, "there will never be another Yetta. I hate America where Jews hate other Jews. At least in the Ghetto we were all nice to each other." My mother looks at me, angry, disbelieving. She scolds me and says that I am being ungrateful.

I can't even talk to my sweet, gentle mother. When I tell her how badly I feel about losing a friend, she answers by telling me that I am one of the lucky few who lost nothing I can't replace. She turns things around so that I'm always feeling guilty. "Look what happened to your cousins, your aunts and uncles. You should be grateful, count your blessings living here in America with your mother, father and brother alive." Once again, I am being told to be grateful when I'm feeling sad and alone.

Chapter Thirty-Nine

Unemployment

My mother is distracted, she looks upset. When I ask her what has happened, she tells me my father has lost his job. I don't understand.

"Why? What happened?" I ask.

"It's a long story. The war is over. The army does not need leather coats anymore. They are now making nylon jackets. We're going to have to be careful with money," she tells me.

My father is disgruntled. He's tired of working for others, answering to an ignorant foreman. He has decided to go into business for himself. He has many contacts and is able to purchase leather from a wholesale supplier. "You know what?" he asks my mother, "Leather is a luxury. Many people are not going to give it up for nylon. Leather lives for years. It is a living protective covering, leather breathes. How can anyone compare it to a chemical jacket? I may be the only one who sees a future in leather, but I am going to give it a try." He gets a loan from a distant cousin who is willing to invest in the leather business. They rent some space in Philadelphia, and my father contacts one other leather cutter; together they work in the little leather shop. When he comes home on Friday afternoons we walk on eggshells trying to cater to him and make him happy. My mother prepares all his favorite foods and serves them. Standing over him and urging him to eat. My father is wearing one of his leather jackets and brings another home to give to the generous cousin. He is in a good mood. The business is going well. My mother is happy. She is married to a manufacturer and she's proud.

In the coming weeks, he comes home less enthusiastic. "It's not so easy," he tells us, "I have to hire a salesman to go to the department stores to try and sell the jackets. I have to pay him a salary plus extra for every jacket he sells." It turns out that the inferior, ugly nylon jackets are doing very much better than the lustrous, breathing leather. One Friday afternoon, he comes home with a suitcase full of coats and jackets.

My mother's face turns white.

"What happened?"

He sighs and looks upset. "I can't sell a leather jacket for a dime. I can't even give one away. Everyone is wearing nylon. It's stronger, it's lighter and it's warmer. This was a bad time to get into the leather apparel industry."

My mother does not grasp the situation. "Does that mean that business is bad?" she asks naively.

"Business is not bad," he responds sarcastically. "The business is gone. There is no business."

My mother's head slumps on the kitchen chair, she covers her eyes. "What are we going to do?" she asks no one in particular.

Chapter Forty

A Battle of wills

My father comes back from *Shul* one Saturday in a black mood. "Some people are so lucky," he tells my mother at the table, speaking as if Michael and I are not there. "They have children they can be proud of, sons who go to *Shul* with their fathers and who *daven* (pray) with *kavoneh* (respect). Oh, what I would do to have such children." A stab from the long, sharp sword of guilt punctures my heart. We are not good enough. I know I can do what he wants of Michael, but I am only a girl, so I don't count.

My mother tries to soothe him without demolishing our egos. "Alex, darling," she says, "we are so lucky. We have come through the war and we are all alive. We have to be thankful."

He looks at her as if seeing her for the first time. "You just don't understand," he tells her, through clenched teeth, "Yes I managed to save your lives, and I got us through the war. But do you think that I didn't have to give anything up? By coming to America I lost everything: my country, parents, friends, job, standing in the community. I lost a way of life I loved. Nothing is here for me. I never even get an *alyah* (the honor of being called up to the Torah). In America they are sold, to the highest bidder." He laughs bitterly. "How can I ever spend $5.00 on such a luxury? In Europe they were honored to have me come up for an *alyah,* here I have to buy it like a bag of potatoes. What you can't understand is that the life I saved, my life, is worth nothing in this country. And my children? My children aren't anything like what I'd hoped for." My mother shakes her head. I see she looks hopeless, unable to penetrate his armor. She doesn't say a word, and clears the dishes from the table.

I want to be "like other people's children," but I don't really know what is expected of me to get to that exalted position. I want so much for my father to love me and for me to love him. But I am scared of him; I never know

140

how he will react to me. I wish for the days when he was gone all week in Philadelphia; when I could be myself and not have to worry about upsetting him. Immediately I feel guilty for my selfish thoughts and chastise myself. "Surely," I quote my mother, "I have reason to love him. After all, didn't he get us out of the hell that was Europe? Isn't he trying to provide for us? What kind of ungrateful, unloving daughter am I?" This kind of reasoning only helps to reinforce my feelings of unworthiness. Much later on, when I look back on this period of my life, I will realize how much these early feelings will contribute to my battles with depression and learned helplessness.

Michael and I do not plan to be disrespectful, but every time we do something my father disapproves of, we are accused of being disobedient and ungrateful. After all, my mother reasons with us, my father wants what he knows is best for us. We should honor him instead of trying to get our way. Even The Ten Commandments states "Honor Thy Father and Mother." It is almost impossible for me to meet his expectations, make his visions of a respectful, obedient, loving daughter become a reality. My dreams and expectations of a perfect family, seated happily on a sofa in front of a warm, crackling fire, while a beautiful mother plays the piano and a handsome father reads to his rapt children will never come to fruition.

I am constantly being reprimanded for breaking the rules that have never been spelled out for me. If I don't ask permission to play with the neighborhood kids, I am being thoughtless; if I want to spend my own money on a book I love, I am being wasteful; when I plead with my father to keep his head covered on the street, I am unreasonable. The mother I had known and loved all those years disappears. She changes, slowly and gradually becoming quiet and acquiescent. She rarely questions his motives or deeds. She is committed to the idea of presenting a united front, and is convinced that in order to do that she has to take sides; she either nurtures her children, or gives in to my father. She does not hear my silent pleas and yearning for acceptance and love.

"Be grateful that you have a father who cares about you," she tells me when I complain to her about not being allowed to play with Suzanne, "Not everybody is so lucky. Look at your cousin Miriam. She doesn't have a father anymore." I don't know what to think. Is my behavior causing my pain, or is my pain causing my behavior. Is my father angry at me because I come in late or am I choosing to be late because I dread going home?

Just as I have my dreams of the perfect father I invented over the years, he has dreams of perfect children. He wasn't there for our formative years and has now undertaken the task of shaping us to fit his concept of ideal children. He tries to mold us into the son and daughter he has envisioned: Michael into a little scholar, obedient and open to Jewish studies; me, into a little lady, polite, quiet and dainty. He is stubborn and unwilling to cut us any slack. He cannot accept the fact that his children have dreams, desires and wills of their own; that even he, with his strong dedication and commitment cannot take away our strive for independence.

I am ten years old and I want to get my long braids cut. I have had them all my life and I want to look like a grown up. There is a post-war fashion trend, called the "new look." Dresses, skirts and coats are long and hair is short. I can't have a new dress right now, but I can get a haircut like all the girls I know.

"No, I like the braids," he tells me, when I say I want to look like my friends. "You don't have to look like all the other girls who are trying to look older than they are. The braids are nice; they make you look different, unique." Different and unique is the last thing I want to be. I want to be exactly like every other girl in my school.

I have saved money from my job of walking the kindergarten girls home and I want to buy something for myself and by myself. I walk into a toy store in our neighborhood. "Do you have something for a ten year old girl for fifty cents?" I ask the elderly storekeeper.

"Hmm…" he muses "How about a book?"

A book is exactly the right thing. A book of my own to read, cherish and read again, a book that does not have to be returned to the library in two weeks. It is a perfect suggestion.

We go over to the book section and select "Little Women" by Louisa May Alcott. "You'll like it," the salesman tells me, "It is about a family of old-fashioned girls like you," he notices my long braids.

"I know. I've already read it, but I think I want to own it." My very own book, the first book I select and pay for by myself, with my own money. I skip home, happy as I haven't been in a long time. I tell the storekeeper not to wrap it and clutch it close to my bosom.

"What a ridiculous way to spend your money," my father tells me. "Go and return it. Get your money back. You can get any book that you want in the library and it's free. I don't want you to throw your money out on something you can get for nothing."

"But the money is mine," I protest, "I've earned it and saved it up for something I want." I am unable to explain my desire to own a book which I can read over and over again at my leisure. I feel completely justified demanding that this money is mine to spend any way I wish.

"It may be your money, but you are my responsibility," he counters," and it is my responsibility to teach you about money; not waste it or spend it on items you don't need. You can buy yourself some socks," he adds as an afterthought.

My mother pauses, trying to decide what to say, "Look, Rita," she says kindly, "what daddy says is true. You know you can take 'Little Women' out of the library. And if you want to read it again, you can always renew it. Maybe you could buy a game with the money?" She says it gently, but there is no mistaking it. She wants me to obey my father and return the book. At this point, the battle becomes larger than the book. It is the first of a long series of battles that my father and I will engage in: my desire to be allowed some leeway in my life against his strong need to control me. The purchase of the book was not an unreasonable purchase and I badly want them to see things my way; give me credit for being sensible.

I confront my mother privately, "Why can't I spend the money I earned the way I want to?"

"Listen to your father," she tells me, "he knows what's best for you. We want *shalom bait,* (a peaceful house)." I shake my head in disbelief. The autonomy and freedom I enjoyed while a prisoner of war, is being replaced with new rules and expectations imposed on me by my peers, teachers and most of all my parents. I refuse to return the book. I keep it and hide it under my pillow. I will read this book again and again, always surprised by how exciting it is each time I read it.

Now that Yetta is out of my life, I play with the neighborhood kids after school. We play outdoors, on the sidewalk on most days: jump rope, hop-scotch and bouncing ball games where we recite a singsong chant while doing tricks with the pink rubber ball we call a "spaldine." My new friend Suzanne comes to my house after school. After she leaves my father tells me that he doesn't want me playing with her. He doesn't want me to have non-Jewish friends. Jews have to stick together with other Jews. He tells me that all *goyim* hate Jews. Is he telling me that Suzanne hates me because I am Jewish? I can't accept his logic. I decide not to argue with him but sneak over to her house when my parents aren't home. Her mother is nothing like Yetta's mother, who feels like my aunt, offering me food and love, but she is very nice to me. How could she hate me when she invites me into her house and is friendly towards me? I get caught. My parents have come home and find me gone. When I return my father questions me; interrogates me. I blurt out the truth, trembling, I'm certain that I am going to receive one of the beatings usually reserved for Michael, but instead my father beckons me into their bedroom.

"Sit down," he tells me pointing to a spot on the bed. He goes to the closet, takes out a box that is on the shelf and produces two photographs of his parents, my *Omma* and *Oppa.* They look just as I remember them. I study the photos and wonder why my father has taken this moment to show them to me. He tells me that he has not been notified of their death and is still hoping that they are alive and that by some miracle they survived the Holocaust. He hopes to hear of their whereabouts any day now. They were in their fifties when Hitler came to Austria and he has been unable to acknowledge their fate. He searches for them fruitlessly consulting with various agencies and refuses to say *Yiskor*, the memorial prayer that children say for their deceased parents in the Synagogue. He does not light the memorial candle in his home on Yom Kippur eve. He feels that to do so would be tantamount to sentencing them to death. During the war, he was preoccupied with trying to save us. Now he begins to realize that he will probably never see them again. He starts to accept their fate.

He speaks gently to me. "These good people, my parents, I am becoming convinced that they were murdered by the *Goyim*. I don't want you to be friends with them. They hate us and they hate you too." He is very serious, "Suzanne is not a good friend for you. If her family was in Vienna during the war, they would have turned you over to the Nazis." I feel overcome with guilt. I almost wish I could agree with him, but I can't relate to what he is saying. Is he telling me that Suzanne is one of the people who had his parents killed? He is tries very hard to convince me to give up my neighborhood friends and I want to respect his wisdom, but what am I to do? The girls at school shun me because they say my family is not religious, and the neighborhood girls are either not Jewish or not religious enough. The only options I have are to be by myself all day long or disobey my father.

I look at the photographs and my heart fills with sadness. My grandparents look just as I remember them. My *Omma*, with her ill-fitting *sheytl*, tilted slightly on her head, smiling as if especially for me and my *Oppa*, a thin, half smile above his white beard, with eyes piercing and sad. I'm torn up. My father tells me that by playing with Suzanne I am betraying my beloved grandparents. I can't sustain the guilt. I give in to my father's orders and am friendless.

My father is working again. He leaves every morning to work in a factory that makes ladies' handbags and wallets. The relief of his getting a job is quickly extinguished by my mother's warning. She tells me that we are not financially secure, whatever that means. She says that my father's job is one where he can be fired or laid off at a moment's notice. "If leather bags go out of fashion," she warns, "so will our livelihood. We have to be careful with money." I don't know what she expects me to do. I have no money of my own and I certainly can't be careful with something I haven't got. I feel burdened, overwhelmed. Why has my mother told me all this? Again I worry about the future and even though he has a job I am afraid of the day when he will lose it. What will happen to us when he loses this job?

I begin to question the Orthodoxy of my school, parents and peers. With the abandonment by Yetta and my other friends, religion starts losing some of its allure for me. So many people hold so many views. What is sanctioned by my parents is viewed as sinful by my community. I am confused; I loved being Catholic, when we were in Poland; I loved being Orthodox in camp and school; I love my parents; I love my gentile friends; I love the Saturday trips to the library. All the things I love are in conflict with each other, and I am not sure what or whom to believe because clearly I am not ready to form my own set of standards. I try to adhere to my parents' principles, but realize that religion is not buying me peace or happiness I expect. When I question my father he tells me to stop asking so many questions. "Of course religion can't buy you happiness," he tells me cynically. "If it did, everyone would be religious. You just do it because you believe in it."

"But what is the "it" I'm supposed to believe in and why must it be done through laws that are meaningless for me; like not carrying or riding on the Sabbath? Or turning on the lights?"

Chapter Forty-One

Dancing

"One, two, three, four," Miss Ricky claps her hands, the pianist stops playing and we stop dancing. "Girls, girls, stop, please. Listen to the music, and for heaven's sake try to keep in time with the beat." The room with a mirror covered wall reflects nine girls of varying sizes in tights and pink ballet slippers. I am part of a dance class participating in the lessons that my parents encourage.

I beg for dancing lessons at the YMHA. They cost ten dollars for a semester of twelve weeks. My mother tells my father and they agree that dancing lessons would give me a graceful walk and improve my posture. I have something wonderful to look forward to every single week.

The ballet teacher, Miss Ricky, in her pink tights and black leotard, smiles encouragingly at my efforts. She is thin, has long arms and legs, and her hair is styled short, a stiff helmet on her head. I want her approval more than anything in the world. I strain to get the difficult positions and receive the nod of encouragement from Miss Ricky. "Good work, Rita," she tells me so the whole class can hear. A compliment from Miss Ricky is a sought after prize of recognition. The backs of my legs feel like poison has been injected into them but I am compelled to be the best one in the class, try everything and get it in as quickly as possible. I want to become an American girl, make my parents proud of me, maybe I can even to get my father to talk about me in the Synagogue and have others refer to me "...as other people's children"

My Aunt Sari, representing the Orthodox point of view frowns on the dancing lessons. "It isn't fitting for a Jewish girl to wear tight leotards and show her body off like that," she tells my father. He doesn't respond and I don't care what they think of me. I have already been excommunicated by the Orthodox kids anyway and I look forward to Thursday afternoons, where I become part of a group of the more serious students. It is a gratifying arena for me to compete in and be rewarded for my efforts. Miss Ricky tells my mother that I'm the best pupil she has all week. She wants me to come for lessons twice a week. "At no extra charge," she tells my mother. "This is strictly a well earned scholarship." My heart is bursting with happiness. Like the book I bought with my own money, I earned a scholarship on my own.

My father is quiet. He seems to take little pleasure from my scholarship. He nods his head and tells my mother that he will pick me up at the Y after my lessons. He does everything methodically, seriously, as though there is no room for light heartedness or humor. I try to engage him in dialogue and tell him that I saw a robbery on the street. This really is a figment of my imagination. "You're lying," he says. Of course he's right, but I hope he'll play along with me. I want to spark his interest, to question me, to ask me if I was scared, what did the robber look like, and what was he stealing. I want to make up a fantastic story for him to show him how smart I am. He is silent.

He is having another "black mood," raging and shouting at us. He tells me I am not behaving like the daughter he thinks I should be. I don't help my mother around the house, do not do things spontaneously and have to be told to do the obvious, like pick up objects that are out of place, wash dirty ash trays, put away books and fold laundry. He complains that Michael is stupid and lazy, preferring playing ball to studying and doing his homework. His outbursts are unpredictable and can be triggered by an innocent remark.

Chapter Forty-Two

Growing Pains

I'm standing behind Rena, waiting my turn at the jump rope. I'm next. Three girls are standing on the sidewalk behind me, waiting for their turns to jump in, sing our jingle and jump away without stepping on the rope. I jump in. "Rinny-tin-tin," I sing out but suddenly am feeling very self-conscious and uncomfortable. My breasts jiggle up and down with every jump I take. I feel ridiculous, and cross my arms in front of me. None of the other girls have such trouble. I step on the rope, miss on purpose. I don't want to be seen like this. I take my post turning the rope; it will be much less embarrassing than jumping. I become, what is called "a steady ender," someone who always turns the rope, a term usually reserved for clumsy girls.

I stand in front of the mirror. I am ten and a half years old. What is going on with my body? I have stabbing pains in my breasts, and now they are getting bigger. I touch them and they feel springy and soft, not like the flat, bony chest that I had a few months ago. No one has told me about changes that take place in a girl's body before she becomes a woman. I wonder if I'm getting fat and need to go on a diet and lose some weight. I am taller than all my classmates and my new body is getting in the way of all the games I play, not only jump rope, but hopscotch, tag and hide and seek. I feel clumsy and ugly.

I need new clothes, ones that will not stretch so tightly across my bosoms. I want to get my braids cut off so I don't have to look like a little girl with big breasts. I want to look like everyone else and at the same time, I want to be noticed. I do not want to be me. I am sad much of the time. These moods are unanticipated and come for no apparent reason. They start as a slow sense of foreboding and soon take over my conscious thinking. I feel guilty, frightened and helpless. I have no idea why I'm feeling the way I do.

I come home from the outdoors flushed and soaked. It is early June and I run up the five stories to our apartment to go to the bathroom and get a drink. My mother has just returned from a shopping trip to the Bronx, to a bargain store called Alexander's. I see two beautiful dresses laid out on her bed. One is a butter yellow piquet, with puffy sleeves and a sailor collar, the other is navy blue linen that buttons all the way down the front with a red and white belt. I am overjoyed.

"Oh thank you mommy, I am so happy." I never question whom the dresses are intended for being positive that they are a surprise for me. I shed my sweat soaked dress and stand in my underwear ready to try on the yellow one, when my mother stops me.

"No, don't. These are not for you." she tells me. I feel as though someone has slapped my face. "I'm sending these to Palestine, to Aunt Matilda and Miriam. They are so poor. They have nothing. We have to share what we can." This is not the first time my mother has done this. Only last summer an acquaintance of ours gave me a pink satin evening gown, splattered with sequins and rhinestone and covered with layers of tulle. She wore it to her sister's wedding and knew that she would never wear it again. She wanted me to have it for playing fairy tale games. "I've always wanted a dress like this when I was your age," she tells me. "At least I can make my dream come true for another little girl." I am overjoyed!

One day, when I am looking in the closet, I realize that the dress has disappeared. "Where's my evening gown?"

"I sent it Palestine, to Miriam and Matilde," she explains, not sounding the least bit apologetic for having sent it without even telling me. "They will have opportunity to wear it, and you would only use it to play dress-up."

"But it was my dress. It was given to me," I whine.

"And whom do you belong to? You're mine," she says affectionately, patting my head and kissing me.

I'm not buying into her whimsy. "I want that dress. I need it for a special occasion that will surely come along soon. Why would you give my things away without even telling me? Take it away from your own child?" I cry tears of outrage and hurt.

"Don't be selfish," she reprimands me for wanting what is mine. "You have much more than Miriam, and if we can make her life a bit more pleasant, we should feel privileged."

If she thinks I'm ashamed of my feelings, my greed, my unwillingness, no my unhappiness about having to share, she is mistaken "Share?" I scream at her. "What do I have that I can share? I haven't had a new dress since I started growing and bursting out of my own clothes. I'm too embarrassed to jump rope because I look so awful!"

She is stunned by my reaction. It was not her intention to hurt me. She just never gave my needs a thought. She reminds me as always that I still have my father and we are living in comparative luxury in the United States, while Aunt Matilda and Miriam have to share a bed in a small room.

I don't listen to her. I put on the damp dress and slam out of the apartment to hold the rope for my friends.

Chapter Forty-Three

Tenth Summer

I feel the stigma of being the oldest child in the class. I will be eleven in February and am only in the fourth grade. I realize that I am a year and a half a year behind my classmates, and to me that's a big deal. I am taller and more developed than any of the girls in my class. I very much want to make that year and a half up, and be placed with students who are my age and am willing to work as hard as necessary during the summer to close that gap. I broach the topic with my teacher, Mr. Serkin, who agrees to let me accelerate by taking home textbooks and doing pages of work to be sent to him during the summer months.

I live up to my part of the bargain spending long, hot mornings studying geography books, doing math problems, reading and answering questions about history. I read fiction and write book reports, and dutifully send my work to him every Friday afternoon. I am committed to achieving the goal of going into sixth grade in September.

It is not going to happen. When I return to school in the autumn, I find myself placed the fifth grade. My new teacher knows nothing about my arrangement with Mr. Serkin and moreover Mr. Serkin is not longer at our school. He has taken another job. I can't believe what she tells me. I made a bargain with Mr. Serkin, I kept up my end; how can the school let me down because he quit? I feel humiliated, betrayed and outraged. My class- mates make fun of me.

"So," the other kids taunt me, as they did when they discovered me coming back from the library with books in arms, and my mother carrying a purse, "you were bragging and lying, just as you were when you lied to us and told us you were religious. You were so sure of yourself that you were going to go into the sixth grade by September. Well September is here and you're still in fifth grade. TS, tough situation." I am infuriated by the injustice.

I approach the new teacher; she is young with very pale skin, rosy cheeks and she wears glasses. Her name is Miss Abromowitz and she looks kind and gentle. I tell her about my deal with Mr. Serkin. She tilts her head to one side, sympathetically.

"Nobody told me about that. I only know that you are on my class list and that this is the fifth grade."

I feel myself getting sick, choking with humiliating tears that are waiting in the corners of my eyes, ready to spill onto my cheeks. "But I made an agreement with Mr. Serkin last June. I've worked all summer long, and sent him all my assignments. This is just too unfair."

"Let me look into this," she tries to calm me. "In the meantime, stay put and do the work with all the other children in the class. I'll have an answer for you by Monday when we have our staff meeting."

I swallow hard, holding back the tears. Today is Wednesday; Monday is five long days away, interrupted by a week-end. The wait seems to go on for ages. It is unbearable. I endure the teasing of all the kids in the class, not only being left out of games but being called a bragging liar. I remain silent, refuse to defend myself. I am certain that when Monday comes, I will triumphantly ascend into the sixth grade.

On Monday morning I get to school before anyone else. I wait in front of the locked building for my teacher and there is only one thing on my mind.

"Well," I greet her expectantly at the door, my hands on my hips, "What was the decision?"

"Oh, we're not meeting until lunchtime, Rita, I'll let you know as soon as I know the answer."

It is an agonizing morning. I don't go to recess. Instead, I remain in our classroom waiting for Miss Abramowitz to return.

"What is going to happen?" I demand as soon as she gets into the room.

She looks sympathetic and bends down to my eye level. "Rita, I know how much this means to you, but none of the other people in the school know about your arrangement with Mr. Serkin and they don't know where Mr. Serkin is. He moved to another city. They can't just let you go on to sixth grade on your word alone. I'm afraid you're just going to have to spend the year in the fifth grade and then next summer I'll see to it that a proper agreement is reached." I am infuriated. This is too much. I've worked hard all summer long, kept up my end of the bargain, now I'm being punished for something I had no control over. I have no friends, no allies in this school, only taunting peers and unsympathetic staff.

I pack up my brand new notebooks, pencils, erasers, ruler and pencil case and stomp out of the classroom, out of the school and into the hot, sunny September sidewalk. It is mid- afternoon when I get home.

For a second time, I announced, "I am never going back to that school again. This time I mean it," I sob. "This is not a real school. You make agreements and work hard and they don't care. I told everyone in school that I would be in sixth grade and now they're all making fun of me. I hate that school! You don't learn anything there anyway. I'm going to a real school. I want to be smart."

My mother is appalled. Her eyes actually fill up with pain and sympathy for my plight. She watched me work all summer long, plod off to the post office and send my thick envelopes to Mr. Serkin. To her ever lasting credit, she becomes my "old" loving mother. She does not argue or try to talk me into going back. Without even consulting my father, she takes me across the street to P.S.189, to the principal's office, where I am warmly welcomed and enrolled in the sixth grade. This school began a week before the Yeshiva and things are already in full swing. A teacher gives me an achievement test and the next day, I am placed into the S.P., Special Progress class, what today is called an enrichment class.

Chapter Forty-Four

Miss Weinstein

"Boys and girls," Miss Weinstein tells the class, "this is Rita Schmelkes." She pronounces my last name correctly, I am grateful for that. Fifty eyes stare at me as though I am an alien, and indeed I feel like one. One glance at the other girls in the rooms assures me that I am wearing the wrong clothes. Everyone in the room is dressed casually, while I'm wearing my blue silk dress with a jeweled belt, the dress I wore to my Aunt Sari's wedding two years ago. The dress is tight in all the wrong places and I'm having difficulty breathing. I want to disappear, be sucked up into the air. Here I am the new kid over-dressed for what is an ordinary school day for the rest of the class. I just got here and already I feel all wrong for this school.

Miss Weinstein leads me to a desk in the middle of the room, between two girls. I look at them hoping they will like me. She returns to her stool and continues with the math lessons as though nothing has happened, oblivious to the fact that I'm burning up with embarrassment. I take a peek at her. She is tiny, bony like a small bird, perched on her tall stool. Her legs are crossed and I can see the tops of her garters.

It is afternoon, time for Social Studies. "Oh, oh," I think, "what is Social Studies?"

"Come up front Ellen," Miss Weinstein says, "let's hear your report. Quebec, Right?"

Ellen, a short, pudgy girl wearing a black jumper, glasses, and pig tails, stands up in front of the class and gives a report on Quebec. She points it out on a large map that hangs on the board like a blue, green and brown window shade. I try to listen carefully to see if I can figure out what social studies are without calling attention to myself, but I am totally distracted by the room. There are about thirty desks in the room, bolted to the floor, with tops that lifts up where books and school supplies are stored. A small round hole covered with a metal lid in the upper right hand corner is called the "inkwell." The windows are tall and occupy an entire wall; afternoon sun streams in, warming the left side of my desk. Ellen walks up to the map several times during her report to point out important facts. After she finishes, she asks for comments and criticism. The rest of the class sits up, and a few kids raise their hands.

Barry Berk, a skinny blond boy with a blond crew cut is next. His report is on Victoria, British Columbia. It is not nearly as detailed as Ellen's, but I am getting the idea. At the same time, I hear a lot of unfamiliar words like "bibliography, research, and population."

"John Reilly, you're next," Miss Weinstein says after Barry's report. "Um, your report is on Winnipeg, is that right?"

"I couldn't do it, Miss Weinstein," he tells her. "My mother was sick and I had to take care of the baby."

Miss Weinstein sighs, raising her shoulders. She looks up from her grading book. "Really?" she says. It's clear that she doesn't believe him. "Last week you didn't do your homework, used the same excuse, and now you are unprepared for you report. This is not fair to your classmates who are doing their share. I'm not going to give you extra time. You're going to have to take a zero. Rita," she turns to me, "why don't you do the report on Winnipeg and have it ready by Thursday. We need to finish up with our neighbors to the north and get started on our next project."

My face is aflame. I've only been in this room for half an hour and already am given an assignment that will put me in front of the whole class? I've never heard of Winnipeg, I don't even know that it's in Canada. I haven't the first clue about how to write a report, let alone get information. We never had reports in the Yeshiva. We never even had kids standing in front of the class talking to the whole class. I am so scared. The rest of the afternoon is spent ruminating. I badly want Miss Weinstein to like me, to think I'm smart, that she can count on me. How can I do that, when I have no idea how to gather the information and write and present a report? I'm scared of standing in front of the whole class and giving a talk, especially since I don't know how to find the information.

I must succeed in this school. It was my decision, my choice and I have to prove to my parents that I am worth listening to. But what if I fail? I ask myself. It doesn't take a minute for me to visit "Catastrophia" the country that exists in my head. My mind goes right from fear of doing the report to being kicked out of the school. I start obsessing immediately; if I get kicked out of this school, there will not be another chance. I'll have to stay at home with my mother and do nothing all day long. I won't be able to play outside because then everyone will know that I don't go to school. How am I going to find out how to do a report?

At the end of the day, I gather all the courage available, it isn't much, and I go up to Miss Weinstein. "Excuse me," I mumble, staring at my new brown, oxford school shoes, "but I don't know how to write a report."

She smiles at me, "it's not as hard as it seems," she says. "Go to the library and ask the librarian to help you find books about Canada. Then look in the index, and find all the pages about Winnipeg. Don't worry," she continues, "you are a smart girl, you can do it." She is not going to coddle me or give me a break. She is friendly but she means business. "Alright," I say," but what is an index?"

It is a Tuesday, not a library day, but my mother agrees to let me walk the ten blocks to the library by myself. The librarian, who is already my friend, is very helpful. She takes me over to a shelf and hands me five or six heavy volumes. "These should to the trick," she says. She walks me over to a table and shows me what and where the "index," is. "Now," she instructs me, "the thing we want, is to find out some important facts about Winnipeg, like the population, industry, climate, history and any famous people who come from Winnipeg." She shows me how to organize my report, how to keep it short and focused on just the important items. I sit at the library table until it is dark copying information about all the areas I will touch on.

I spend the next two days rehearsing the report in front of the bathroom mirror, and have all the information memorized. But when Thursday comes, all I can think of is 2 o'clock and how am I going to be able to stand in front of the whole class, with everyone looking at me.

I take a deep breath, swallow several times, and then, from somewhere inside my throat, I hear a voice that I don't recognize. "Winnipeg is the capital of Manitoba, on the Red River, in Canada. It is one of the coldest cities in the world and its main product is wheat..." I walk over to the map hanging behind me and locate Winnipeg as well as the Red River. Somehow, I get through my report. My cheeks are so hot that I touch my temples to see if my whole head is on fire. Ellen is the first to raise her hand when I am finished.

"What I learned from Rita's report is that Winnipeg is very cold in the winter, like some our own mid-western cities."

The comments from my classmates are complimentary. Miss Weinstein congratulates me, "You've done well, Rita," she says "especially since you had so little time to prepare." She gives me an "A" on the report and I traipse to my seat, relieved and elated.

We are ready to tackle our next project in Social Studies; Minority Groups and their Contributions to Our Country. Miss Weinstein is the first person to call my attention to the plight and the injustices that are heaped upon

Afro-Americans, only then we called them "Negroes." Negroes are the dark people you see on subway. There are none in the school and very few in our neighborhood. We open our social studies book and read about how the Negroes live in the South; persecuted and enslaved. I perk up, suddenly becoming aware of something I can identify with. I hear the word "prejudice" for the first time in my life. She defines it. I know all about prejudice. I've experienced prejudice in Austria, Poland and Germany. I even experienced it in my last school, where some of the kids shunned me because I was not as religious as they.

Miss Weinstein hits a familiar spark within me. "The Negroes in the United States are scapegoats, just like the Jews were in Germany, Austria and Poland. We must take their plight seriously." I wonder, does she know about my life in Europe? It feels as though she is speaking directly to me when she tells us about the prejudice towards the Negroes. She uses words I have to look up in the dictionary, "bias," "discrimination," "deprivation," "bigotry," "racism." I feel at home in this classroom, with so many Gentile children. Miss Weinstein is not embarrassed to use the word "Jewish." I have never been able to say it among Gentiles without feeling self-conscious. If the good citizens of Germany, Austria and Poland would have understood what Miss Weinstein was saying, then all the slaughter of the Jews would not have taken place. I adopt her outrage and sense of fair play. I promise myself that I will never sit by and watch an injustice committed against someone for reasons beyond their control.

"You count," she tells the class, "every one of you can make a difference in someone's life by treating them fairly, as you want to be treated."

I'm important I tell myself. Miss Weinstein says that we can all make a difference in the world. I can't wait to start. I join a group of young people who stand in front of the subway stations with tin cans, asking for contributions to help the Negroes in the South. We are collecting money to send school books to the children in the segregated schools.

"Marion Anderson, the great Negro singer is not permitted to sing in the Metropolitan Opera House in New York," she tells the class. "Paul Robeson cannot use the same bathrooms as the white citizens of Georgia, Lena Horne, can entertain high society, but she is not permitted to stay at first class hotels or join her white fans for dinner at a restaurant. What did the American soldiers fight for in Europe, when some Americans are not allowed to have the same rights of other American citizens?" She is sounding angry. "I thought we fought for freedom, yet there is no freedom for certain people, right here in our very own country. We need to share our freedom amongst each other." She encourages us to take a stand, talk to our parents, and ask them write letters to our Senators demanding that all Americans be treated justly.

I run home, brimming with the enthusiasm. "Did you know, Daddy that America is not truly a free country? There are all kinds of injustices heaped upon the Negroes."

My father does not approve my new concerns. "The Jews have enough trouble without taking on the plight of the Negroes. Besides, what Miss Weinstein is preaching sounds a bit like Communism," he warns me. "We can't afford to be different, to stand out." I do not listen to him. I don't even hear him. How can he possibly refuse to recognize injustice when it is perpetrated against innocent people like the Negroes? Did he forget what happened to the Jews? I worship Miss Weinstein. She is what I want to grow up to be; to teach children not to hate.

The following September, in 1948, Miss Weinstein disappears from our school. It is the beginning of the McCarthy era and the fear of Communism is as rampant as the fear of terrorism becomes in 2001. I hear whispering in the schoolyard. The kids are saying that their parents told them that Miss Weinstein has been "blacklisted." She may have been blacklisted, whatever that means, but her energy and ideals have been transmitted to many of her students.

Chapter Forty-Five

Michael

I am carrying my heavy load of books around the school and am feeling very important. I'm in seventh grade and we have "departmental," which means we go from one classroom to another for various subjects. We also get special privileges assigned to us. I get the one I want the most, being a crossing monitor. This very responsible position is allotted to only ten students in the seventh grade, and I am one of the lucky few. I get to wear a big blue button that says "J.C.G." which stands for junior crossing guard.

"Get back up on the sidewalk," I shout, "I didn't say you could step off yet." The little kids in the lower grades are scared of me. I might report them to their teachers. I love being bossy, telling children when to get back on the sidewalk, holding the hands of the kindergartners and walking them across the street, being kind or mean, whenever I want to.

My grades are excellent and my parents tell me to help Michael. He is in the Yeshiva and is struggling with all his subjects. My parents have been called in to the school and told that Michael is not a serious student, that he is playful and immature. I really don't want to help. I want to do my own work and go out to play. Michael does not want my help, he is uncooperative. Whenever I try to correct him, he tells me to "fix it up." I know I'm being bossy and officious. It's almost like playing refugee, but this time it's for real, not a game. I shout at him, "Why can't you do this easy arithmetic problem?" He shouts back at me. We get nothing done other than re-establishing the old pecking order. He fools around and tries to distract me from my "responsibility."

"You're so stupid," I tell him. "Why can't you follow a simple direction like watching your plus and minus signs?"

"You know, you're not my boss anymore," he answers me. "If you really want to help me, just do my homework for me. Nobody does homework at the Yeshiva and no one checks it either." I know this is true.

"That's cheating," I say self-righteously, "I'm not going to do that. And what are you going to do when you get tested?"

"Cheat," he says, matter- of -factly like a little psychopath.

I am appalled and attempt to teach him a lesson on morality and ethics .We argue some more. Our voices escalate and my mother comes into the kitchen. "Why can't you help your little brother without causing such a fight?" my mother asks me. "When I was young my sisters were kind to me. They fought over who would help me."

"He doesn't listen to me, and he won't do his work," I whine.

"Just show him what to do and be kind instead of mean and bossy."

"Now I'm mean and bossy?" I shout at my mother, "I want him to learn something, and you accuse me of being mean and bossy."

"It's no use," I say to myself. I take his homework and do it for him. This goes on for the rest of the year. Michael graciously accepts the homework I have done for him and turns it in as his own. The end of the semester comes and with it report cards arrive. I run up the five flights, out of breath and excited. "Look mommy and daddy, I got all A's." I'm thrilled with my achievements.

Michael is in the corner of the living room, slumped on the floor. He looks defeated. My father turns on me raging, "If you weren't such a selfish sister, you could have helped your brother. What kind of a girl is happy getting good grades when her brother has to come home with such bad marks?" Michael has already gotten his beating, now I have to be punished for only thinking of myself and my grades. "Go into your room," he tells me, angrily. I feel awful. All he cares about are Michael's bad grades. How about my good ones? Even though he hits Michael, he cares more about him than about me. I listen to him yelling.

"He's lazy. He's stupid. He doesn't know how lucky he is to be able to go to school. I never had those opportunities. If he puts his mind to his studies like he does to his playing, he could go to the university some day. What in heaven's name is going to become of him?" He is complaining to my mother about Michael, as if he were out of earshot. My mother listens, but says nothing. I am feeling weird, self-righteous, happy that I'm not being yelled at, and also guilty for being glad that it is Michael who is being punished and not me. Yet at the same time I'm jealous that he gets all the attention for being bad, while I'm ignored for being good.

My mother takes a deep breath. I hear her sigh, "Please, Alex," she pleads, "don't aggravate yourself so much. This is not the end of the world. He's just a little boy. He'll do better next time."

My father turns on her, pushing her away, "Are you telling me how to raise my son," he is irate. "It's your coddling and babying him that makes him such a dimwit."

"I have a selfish daughter and a stupid son," he tells my mother. "and much of it is your fault. I don't know what I did to earn such a reward. I want him to be successful, and he doesn't care. I want her to be generous and helpful and all she cares about is herself."

My heart has a hole in it and it's leaking with sadness. We are a source of shame for my father. My jealousy fades. I suddenly feel overwhelming sorrow for Michael and myself. My little brother, whom I had protected during our imprisonment, who was teased for looking like Charlie Chaplin, who was afflicted with painful red boils, who I love with all my heart, is being bullied and beat up because he is not smart enough. I am angry and in pain.

Why can't my father love us the way we are and not the way he wishes we were? Why must he be ashamed of us? Gone is the happy, self-righteous gloat I was sporting only a few moments ago. I should have tried to protect Michael. Instead I was feeling superior and happy. I think of what Miss Weinstein would have done had she seen someone helpless being bullied and beaten.

I make up my mind. I will go out and tell my father not to touch my brother. I am ready to defend Michael, stand up for him as I had done in Liebenau but when I open the door and see my father I shrink and my resolve blows away like smoke on a windy day. His fury is so great that I am afraid of further enraging him and getting beaten up myself. Fear robs me of the drive and ambition inspired by Miss Weinstein to defend those who can't defend themselves, and forces me to abandon my quest for justice.

I am always on guard lest I arouse his anger. I try to be "good" and do everything I can to please him, but it's never the right thing and it's never enough. I can no longer wear Miss Weinstein's mantle of outrage at injustice, and I lose much of my self-respect and value. I berate myself relentlessly for being an unprincipled coward. The bad feeling is back, and this time I invited it by and doing nothing as I watched my brother being humiliated. "When I grow up," I promise myself, "I will never witness an injustice without standing up for the victim."

Chapter Forty-Six

The Past Comes Calling

My mother and I are climbing up the steps to our apartment, after a dancing lesson. I see a tiny dwarf woman standing in front of our door. She is much shorter than I and has the blackest hair I have ever seen. I am about a flight of stairs ahead of my mother, when the woman runs over to me. She hugs me, and says in Polish,

"Freda, Freda, you haven't changed at all!" She looks astonished and chuckles in delight. I don't know who she is and why she is hugging me and calling me by my mother's name. I have no idea why she thinks I am my mother. My mother, stops in her tracks, reaches for the railing and gasps. It's as if she's seen a ghost. She stares at her, speechless and slack-jawed.

"Mirka, Mirka Fisch," my mother finally whispers. She is pale and quivering. "Can it really be you?" They hug and weep, while I stand by wondering what is going on. After a few minutes my mother turns to me. "Mirka is a dear, dear neighbor from Wieliczka. I was your age the last time I saw her in Wieliczka," she explains to me. Mirka, along with her parents and brother had left for America long before Hitler came to power. Mirka's father, who was a carpenter in Wieliczka had no trouble finding employment in the US. Good carpenters are sought after in America where new buildings are erected every day. He is and was a master craftsman.

There were no opportunities for a Jewish carpenter and his dwarf daughter in Wieliczka, so they came to America in 1915, long before anyone had ever heard of Hitler, when my mother was a little girl. Now when Mirka sees me, she sees the spitting image of my mother with two long blond braids and freckles across the bridge of my nose, exactly as she remembers her.

"Freda, my dear Freda," she speaks, this time to my mother, "I looked all over for survivors of our family, your family and anyone who might have made it out of Wieliczka and Krakow. As soon as the war ended, I went to the Hebrew Immigration Aid Society (HIAS) office in Manhattan. Can you imagine what it felt like for me to see your names? It was like seeing someone emerge from a grave. At first, I didn't believe my eyes, so I asked one of the clerks to read the name to me. When she confirmed what I was seeing and not just wishing, I cried so much that they had to show me to a seat and give me a glass of water." She continues after pausing to catch her breath, "You made it through a cyclone, an earthquake and a volcano eruption. I knew I had to see you immediately. I couldn't take the time it takes to mail a letter and await your response. So, here I am. I waited an hour in front of your apartment. I knew you'd have to get home sometime."

The reunion is tearful as my mother tells her of all our relatives who have not survived. Mirka sobs out loud.

"How can such splendid people disappear: such a beautiful family, so generous, so smart, and so talented?" Mirka and my mother both weep for a long time while I sit in the living room still wearing my coat. "Oy, oy, oy," both my mother and Mirka are now sobbing together, "how can such a family be killed so brutally? Wiped off the earth?" Even though Mirka is tiny, her emotions are big, her tears flow down her face and her feelings are overwhelming.

She tells us that her parents are still alive. They live on Division Avenue in Brooklyn, among other Chassidic families. Mirka married an American housepainter, Jack, and they live with her parents, whom she takes care of. Her parents are old and need help managing their lives.

My father comes into the house. He has never seen Mirka; she left Wieliczka before he met my mother. He is surprised to find us in the apartment, sitting with our coats on, laughing and crying at the same time. "Alex," my mother says, "this is my old friend Mirka Fisch from Wieliczka." My father does not understand.

"What?" he says in surprise, addressing Mirka, "You mean came to America now, after the war?" He is excited. It takes no time for his mind to race ahead hopefully. Maybe there are some survivors left in Poland, maybe some in Austria. He immediately thinks of his parents. Dare he think that they might be alive somewhere? He was never notified of their death.

"When did you arrive? Do you have a place to stay? How did you manage to survive?" he is full of questions.

"No, no," my mother explains to him trying to clear up his confusion. She tells him that the Fisches left Poland many years ago, before they met. "They have been here for over thirty years. They are citizens."

Mirka stays for dinner, until late at night, reminiscing with my mother. They stop often touching each not believing that they are awake and not dreaming. A visit is planned for the following Sunday. Alec, her brother will pick us up in his car, and take us to Williamsburg to visit Mr. and Mrs. Fisch.

Later on that evening, my mother tells me that Mirka is several years older than she is, even though she is not taller than a seven year old. Her family was very poor. They lived in a small hut, in the middle of Wieliczka. My mother and my aunts loved running down the hill to Mrs. Fisch's house where Mirka would read stories to them and play games. Her small size had nothing to do with her brains. She was smart my mother tells me.

We climb up a flight of rickety steps that lean precariously against a wall. It reminds me of the building my grandparents lived in. The hallway is dark, the banister is shaky. I cannot believe that such an old building is still standing. It doesn't resemble the tall brick buildings in the rest of New York. And there, at the top of the stairs, are two elderly people waiting for our arrival, looking just like my *Omma* and *Oppa:* old Mrs. Fisch in her ill-fitting *sheytl* and old Mr. Fisch in his velvet *kippah*. The little apartment is crammed full of furniture: wooden cabinets, shelves, china closets all hand made by Mr. Fisch in his spare time. The cabinets are filled with wooden carvings, miniature trees, cows, horses, a detailed chess set, all crafted by this artist- carpenter. Mrs. Fisch has roasted a large turkey. It is the first time I've seen anything like it.

"What a huge chicken," I shout.

"Dis is not uh cheeken, honey, dis is uh toiky." Mrs. Fisch laughs as she points out my mistake. It looks like a polished wooden bird, something Mr. Fisch carved in his spare time: brown and shiny. Alec has us all pose for pictures, while he stands, draped behind a tripod. He is an amateur photographer and he wants to preserve this moment. They talk in Polish, Yiddish and English, reminding each other of Wieliczka and the times they had spent together, pausing to cry and shake their heads in disbelief. How much has happened since they said good-bye to each other in Wieliczka so long ago! It is good to be together again. I feel happy here, wanted, welcomed and at home with people I love.

Mr. Fisch carves the turkey and after dinner, they catch up on the past, while Michael and I play cards. It is dark outside when we return to Alec's car. He still has a long trip, from Brooklyn to Washington Heights and then to Riverdale where he lives. Alec married an American woman and is very successful. Before we part, he invites us to his home for the following Sunday. He is honored by my mother's presence. He remembers her from Wieliczka, when she was the youngest daughter of the wealthiest town resident. Of course, he wouldn't dream of having such esteemed guests take the subway, and so he again picks us up the following Sunday in his new, green Packard.

He tells us that he is in the air conditioning business which is a brand new enterprise in 1947. We have never heard of air conditioners, but they must be something everyone wants judging by the private house he and his family live in. There is a large front yard that is covered with snow and the inside looks like my idea of a palace. It is carpeted everywhere, wall to wall in dark green pile so thick that my shoes sink into the pile. The furniture is upholstered in heavy brocade and ornate fabric drapes the windows. There are paintings hanging everywhere, and a carpeted indoor staircase that leads to the bedrooms. I have never seen such opulence. Maybe someday, I think, I too will be able to live in such a house. I am eleven years old and have spent too much time living in a fantasy world to give up my hopes and wishes.

A tall, massive, shiny, black piano stands against a wall in the living room. I salivate when I see it. A piano! I go over to it and gently stroke some of the keys with reverence. I hold my breath. I have not touched a piano since we had fled from Poland. It feels like it's been waiting for me all my life. I stroke it gently and quietly play the only thing I can, the first six notes of *La Donna Mobile*. While the grown ups go on talking, eating and making up for lost time, I spin on the piano stool, staring at the shiny dark giant, not daring to play anymore on it. Ida, Alec's wife comes into the living room with my mother and Mirka. The men stay in the dining room, smoking.

"I would love to get rid of this old piano," she mentions casually. "My girls don't play anymore and all it does is sit here and collect dust." Is this my overactive imagination hearing what it wants to hear?

"Yes," she goes on "what I'd really like to put in its place is a television set, a console. If I could find someone to take it, they can have it. All they have to do is get a mover to get it out of here."

I glance at my mother. The possibility of owning a piano is something I dare not dream about. I look at my parents imploringly.

"Really?" says my equally enthralled mother. "We would love to have it, that is, if you're sure you don't want it anymore." We leave late at night, and I fall asleep in the back of the car dreaming.

Chapter Forty-Seven

Music Lessons

An excited crowd of women is standing in front of our building, craning their necks upward to watch the swinging black giant. My piano is dangling from a crane like a yo-yo suspended from the roof of our building. The piano is held by two ropes, sliding precariously from one side of the hoist to the other. Onlookers are gazing up at it, pointing, excited, and shouting advice to the men on the roof who don't hear them. Suddenly the massive giant slides to one side. Every onlooker runs away screaming, scared that the black piano will slip from its restraints and crush them.

"Oh my God," I say as the shrieking crowd runs in every direction, fleeing the menacing ogre. Someone screams, "It's King Kong!" I don't move. I am mesmerized, certain that if I run away, the piano will somehow be lost to me. "Please don't let it fall and shatter into millions of splinters." I pray, gazing upward, my hands folded in silent supplication.

I look up at the dangling instrument. "Why are they hoisting it up through the roof, and through the front of the building when our windows face the back?" I ask my mother who alternates between watching from the outside to running upstairs to check on the indoor progress.

"They have no room in the alley for the truck or the piano," she explains. "They have to get it on the roof, move it across and over to our side of the building, and then through a window into the living room." I remain downstairs, my eyes fixed on the swinging piano. My mouth is open. I pray that it can be squeezed into our house like sardines into a flat can.

"Then what are they going to do? How are they going to get that big piano through our window?"

"They will ease it in through." She answers while gazing upwards.

I run upstairs to watch the progress from the living room. The window, the one with no fire escape, is removed and the piano is gently coaxed, on its

166

side, with the keyboard facing the window sill, through the empty frame, into our waiting living room.

The shiny dark ebony instrument is in place. It occupies an entire wall a regal, exotic African queen, glowing and resplendent. She dominates the room with haughty grandeur. She is majestic and she is ours! I am going to take real piano lessons at last. America is getting better! My mother is going to be my teacher and we are both excited.

She goes to a music store on Broadway and 49th Street, Tin Pan Alley, as it is called. "I'm going to start my little girl on piano lessons," she tells the clerk. "What would you recommend for a beginner?" He doesn't hesitate for a minute before handing her a copy of John Thompson's piano book, "Teaching Little Fingers to Play." The book is easy, and I learn all the pieces in it. It is almost like the "color by number" process. I become acquainted with the keyboard: the importance of middle C, the time value attributed to all the little eggs, black, white and dotted scattered on the five lines and four spaces, the relevance of the finger numbers placed under the notes. I especially love the two duets at the end of the book, "She'll be Comin' Round the Mountain" and "Home on the Range." My mother and I play these pieces for anyone who is willing to listen. The wild galloping rhythm of "She'll be Comin' Round the Mountain and the lazy, slow pace of "Home on the Range" are real music with rich harmonies.

I am ready to play for anyone who comes to visit us; neighbors, relatives and friends. After a bit of chatting, my mother tells everyone that I am learning to play the piano and would they like to hear me play? No one has the nerve to turn down such an offer when they are sitting in our living room eating her cookies and drinking her tea. They applaud and marvel at my progress, while envying us for having a piano.

My mother decides to consult an expert piano teacher who happens to be a cousin of hers: Poldi Zeitlin, who in addition to being our cousin, is also a niece and student of the world famous pianist Artur Schnabel. She invites Poldi over for a Sunday afternoon visit. Poldi and her husband Marc come puffing up the stairs.

She bursts into the apartment. "Goodness," she exclaims, "Freda, how do you manage these stairs? No wonder you are so thin." Poldi is a beautiful, tall imposing woman. She has short black hair, dark plucked eyebrows, pink cheeks, olive skin and the whitest, brightest smile I have ever seen off the movie screen. She is talkative, dramatic, using her hands to make every point. My mother invites everyone to the table for tea and Viennese pastries. Poldi talks with her mouth full, gesticulating expressively, with pastry crumbs flying all over the table cloth. She asks questions about our escape, and tells us about her career as a music teacher and editor. The powdered sugar collects on her chin; she talks quickly as if afraid of running out of time. After they have finished, my mother asks Poldi if she would mind listening to me play the piano.

"Mind? My dear, I wouldn't dream of leaving your house without hearing Rita play." By this time I have already graduated from "Comin' Round the Mountain" to a Sonatina by Clementi. I am very anxious to make a good impression. My mother has warned me that Poldi's opinion is vital. I have practiced hard for this moment and sit down at the piano stool. I am eleven, not yet aware of the paralyzing power of stage fright. I feel secure in executing all those running passages and trills that make me think of tiny brooks in a German forest. I put my soul into this performance and feel good about it.

Poldi goes into raptures. "*Sei ist fablehaft.* (She is enchanting, fantastic). She has only been playing for three months? *Unglaublich,* (unbelievable)!" She uses words I never heard before: "gifted, talented." I don't know what those words mean, but I know I like them because she is so very enthusiastic and extravagant in her praise.

"She must take lessons with me," Poldi exclaims and adds generously, "of course I would never charge relative for lessons, especially one so talented,"

It is decided that I will to go Forest Hills, for a lesson in Poldi's studio every other week. My mother will continue teaching me on the off week and supervise my practicing. I am eager and filled with hope. I practice every morning, before school starts, while my mother brushes and braids my hair. She strokes my head lovingly. One hundred brush strokes for each braid. Then she plaits each braid, tying the ends with ribbons she ironed the night before. I love this morning ritual when I have my mother's undivided attention and love. She is my old, sweet *Mutti* for a half an hour each morning.

We take the train to Forest Hills, to a "rich" neighborhood. Trees surrounded by small gardens with colorful flowers cast shade on the sidewalk. Poldi's building is two short blocks from the subway. It is impressive. A uniformed doorman opens the door for us and asks us where we are going.

"Mrs. Zeitlin," my mother responds.

"Ah, yes, the piano teacher."

We enter and Poldi asks us to sit in a small hallway, the waiting room, while she finishes her lesson with another student. I listen to him play. I am envious, he is playing difficult music. When he leaves, she ushers us into the living room, her studio, which has two baby grand pianos facing each other. I am overwhelmed. She motions me to sit down at one of the pianos and she sits down next to me on the piano bench.

"Well," she says to me, straightening her back, and looking directly into my eyes, "what would you like to play?"

"I can play the Clementi Sonatina."

"No, no. I've already heard that. What new piece would you like learn?" I don't know what to say. No one has ever asked me before what I would like.

"You mean to learn to play now?"

She demonstrates, playing a few selections for me and tells me to choose the one I like best. I opt for the Mozart Rondo in D major. It is a lovely, light piece of music, with lots of room for dynamics and complicated passages that will require a lot of practice.

She approves my choice. "Good," she agrees, "You will play it for the November recital." Oh, oh, it feels like the social studies report all over again.

"What is a recital?"

"A small concert, where all my students perform for each other and their parents. We have them twice a year. One in the winter and the other in the spring." She is casual, making it sound routine.

We start with scales, move on to exercises, and then go to the Mozart. I feel my excitement mounting. This is what I've been waiting for all my life. The Mozart is challenging, more difficult than anything I've tackled before and I concentrate, trying to sight read such a demanding piece.

"I don't know if I'll be able to play this for a recital," I tell Poldi.

"Don't worry," she says, "you'll learn it. Once you've played it through a few times, it will "fall" into your fingers." I go home and practice, a few bars at a time. By the time my next lesson with Poldi rolls around, two weeks later, I've memorized much of it.

Chapter Forty-Eight

The Gift

The gray November sky is not sure if it plans to bring a chilling rain or a fluffy snow before twilight descends on the afternoon. In Poldi's apartment chairs are lined up in neat rows where the excited audience made up of parents and grandparents of the anxious performers sit; waiting in rapt silence to hear their children perform. My father is at work, my aunt Sari is busy with her new baby, and my mother sits with Mirka who comes to the recital. She is carrying a large package, wrapped in brown wrapping paper, tied with string. I perform making two terrible mistakes which only I am aware of. After the recital, when we are ready to go home, Mirka thrusts the package at me.

"Open it when you get home," she tells me. "This is a gift from Harry and me, to celebrate your first concert."

I can't wait to get home and open my present and see what is inside. I rip the paper off as soon as we get home, impatient to see what it is. A wooden box with two brass hasps opens up to reveal a paint set. Every imaginable color of oil paint I have ever seen, four shades of each hue in pretty little tubes, nesting on three trays stacked up on one another. I step back in awe. I have never owned a paint set, let alone one so full and dazzling. My mother marvels over it too.

"I will share it with Michael," I tell her generously. I don't want to be greedy and I can't use it now because we don't have any drawing paper. I can't be wasting paints like these on plain paper. Reluctantly, I slide the beautiful box under my bed and start saving for a pad of good paper from the art supply store.

Every day, after school, I come home and take the set out, stroking the smooth exteriors of the metal tubes. Eventually, some of the novelty and excitement wear off and I don't check up on it every day. I take it out when I think about it. One day, I rush home from school clutching the pad of art paper that I had saved up for: fifty-seven cents it cost me. I slide my hand under my bed groping for the smooth polished surface of the box, but I feel nothing. I look under the bed thinking that perhaps it moved, slid to another spot. I do not see it.

"Where's my paint box?" I ask my mother who is in the kitchen chopping onions.

She stops to wipe onion tears from her cheeks. "Rita," she sighs deeply and sits down. I can sense something awful has happened to my paints. Before she goes on, I think that maybe Michael took them to school and lost them, or we had a robbery and someone came and stole them. Or maybe Mirka wanted them back for her nieces because I hadn't gotten around to using them yet. I was prepared for the worst.

"Be a big girl and try to understand," she starts by way of explanation. "I got a letter from Aunt Matilda, and Miriam got into a wonderful art school in Tel-Aviv." I don't bother listening to the rest of the story. I already know what happened to my paints. Just as my aunt and cousin got the dresses I thought belonged to me, the paints that I know are mine are now on their way to Tel-Aviv, to Miriam. I run to the bathroom. I can't let my mother see my tears, how upset I am. I know what she'll tell me: that I'm ungrateful, that I'm the lucky one to be living in America and still have my father alive, that I should be happy to be able to share, that I shouldn't be greedy. I am not in the mood to hear about my good luck. Right now, I just want to feel sorry for myself. How come I'm always made to feel as if I'm expecting too much? Why am I supposed to feel lucky when things are taken away from me? I feel awful, undeserving, unworthy and unentitled as well as greedy, ungrateful, and mean.

Chapter Forty-Nine

Breaking Point

My mother has the "worried" look. Her face looks pinched like it did in Krakow. I haven't seen her so distraught since we left the Ghetto. "We have to watch every penny we spend," she tells us, scratching her head and blinking. My father has lost his job again. The familiar feeling of terror that revisits much too often, returns. I look at her, afraid of the answer I will get if I ask her what is going to happen to us.

I am thirteen years old and this is not the first time my father has been out of work. But this time it's worse. My father leaves the house early each morning and returns depressed each night. The gloom that settled over our house is deeper, more penetrating than it has ever been before. He's been out of work for three months now and the whole family feels like we are wrapped in a dark, sad fog. I don't want to imagine what will happen to us if he doesn't get work soon, but the dread comes over me without my conscious provocation.

I find myself feeling sorry for him, he looks sad and lonely. He leaves the house, carrying the sandwich my mother made for him the night before, and returns every evening dejected, defeated and depressed.

I wait for him on the stairs, listening for his footsteps. I do "active waiting" again, a familiar activity, only this time it isn't waiting for my mother. I can tell by the sound of his footsteps that he hasn't found anything. His tread is slow and heavy. I run into the apartment, not wanting him to think that I'm waiting and worrying about him. That would be too embarrassing. Something tells me that he would not appreciate my concern. I bury my head in a book and pretend that everything is fine. I am already familiar with my well honed defense of denial; a personality trait that will follow me for the rest of my life. I hide behind the swinging door in the kitchen. I want to hear what he tells my mother. He sits down at the kitchen table, holding his head in his hands.

"I don't know what we're going to do," he whispers, "I go from shop to shop and there is nothing out there for me. No one is making leather jackets now that the war is over. There is no need for them. But I can cut anything; it doesn't have to be leather. I talk to the foremen in sweater factories, upholstery shops, and drapery stores. After all, if I can cut a leather jacket, I can cut a piece of fabric. I'm scared," he tells her, "what will we do when the unemployment insurance money runs out?"

I peek through the crack in swinging door that leads to the kitchen. My mother grips his hand as fear grips my heart. He looks so sad. My heart is breaking for him. The old familiar enemy is creeping back into our lives. Will we go hungry? Will we lose our apartment? Will we have to move to another neighborhood? I go to sleep every night praying that he gets a job tomorrow, scared that we will have to go into an orphanage for poor children.

Maybe he can ask Aunt Sari for a loan, he confides in my mother. He hates to borrow from her but he has to buy food. What else can he do? We have no other relatives close to us, and he certainly cannot ask a friend. He is too proud to do that. For a long time we eat nothing but potatoes. They cost twenty-five cents for five pounds and they keep us from being hungry. My creative mother doctors them up and serves them in many different ways, baked, boiled, fried, mashed, painted red with paprika, with a bit of dill on top. They're only potatoes, but they are delicious food for hungry people.

"I never had a chance to go to the University and have a profession," my father bemoans his state. "If I had, then we would never be in all this trouble now." He shakes his head, in disbelief. "If I even had a trade, like a plumber or a carpenter I would have been able to support my family. I didn't want to learn how to work with my hands. I used to think that having a trade was beneath me," he laughs mirthlessly. "How foolish I was! I used to think that smart people used their brains and stupid people used their hands." We all watch helplessly as he laments his fate. "Now I know better. Smart people work and make a living, the others, like me feel sorry for themselves. I was able to save your lives, in Hitler's Europe, but now I can't keep you alive in America. How ironic is that?"

It is July; he has not worked since March, before Passover. School is out for the summer and Michael and I spend entire days on the street in front of our house, escaping the sadness of our house. We fear the worst when we are at home: outdoors we are free. I play with the girls. Because of my changing body, I have retained the unwanted job of "steady ender," permanent rope turner. In return for this task, I get to pick the jingle and to arbitrate unfair moves. It's the prize I get for holding the rope all day long.

"My mother, your mother live across the way,
Nine-sixteen East Broadway.....

"Change it, change it. Let's move on," I call out,

"We're changing to 'Down the Mississippi Where the Boats Go Push." At least I can still be a boss over something.

I manage to distract myself from some of the awful realities in my home by practicing piano in the morning and spending the rest of the day playing on the streets.

Chapter Fifty

Rescue

"Let's take a walk, just around the neighborhood," my mother suggests one summer day. I would like nothing better. It's so seldom that I get her all to myself. When she is away from my father she often acts like her old uninhibited self, making mundane things exciting.

"Where are we going?" I ask.

"Oh, nothing special, it's a lovely day so let's enjoy it."

We amble along, window shopping and exclaiming over the displays: furniture shops with living rooms and bedrooms all laid out, dress shops with dummies posed as if caught in the middle of a party, toy stores with roller skates, dollhouses, chemistry sets; everything I want is in the window. We are talking and laughing, just like in the old days. On a side street, she notices a shop window, with darkened shades and a sign that reads "Help Wanted."

"Let's go in and see what kind of help they want?" she says.

The shop is dark and cool. It takes a few seconds for our eyes to adjust to the dimness indoors. Fans are spinning in the corners of the room blowing dust and particles of fabric around. The room smells like nail polish and several women are sitting at a long table, sewing pastel leather slippers. They are hand stitching Omphies house shoes. I realize that my mother planned this trip before we left our house. I don't know if she's looking for a job for herself, for my father or maybe even for me. What I do know, is that she's desperate to bring home some money.

"I see you have a 'Help Wanted' sign outside," she tells the forelady, a heavy woman in a housedress with a shower cap protecting her hair. "I can probably do this kind of work." She is uncomfortable. She has never asked anyone for a job before and she's not sure of how one does it. Yes, the forelady tells her, pleasantly they do need help on the week-ends, Saturdays and Sundays, when the big boss is there. She is told that she can start on the coming Saturday.

"Could I just work on Sundays?" she inquires hesitating, knowing that there is no way she could work on the Sabbath.

"No, I'm sorry," she tells her, "We can't train somebody for just one day a week." I notice she has a heavy accent. We leave the shop. Her cheerful mood is replaced by the now familiar sense of quiet desperation.

She confides in Poldi. She tells her of the dreadful financial plight she is in and how it is becoming impossible for my father to find any type of work. Poldi, in her kind, generous and impulsive way comes up with an immediate solution.

"I can help you," she offers quickly.

"No, no, please," my mother tells her. "I could never take money from you. That would be awful for me."

"Who's talking about taking money?" Poldi asks. "I have more students than I can handle. In fact I have to turn some of them away. You can become my assistant teacher."

My mother feels that she is not equal to the task. She demurs, saying that she has an accent and no experience.

"Nonsense," cries Poldi. "An accent is an asset to a music teacher. Everyone assumes you were trained by some famous European concert pianist. People want teachers with an accent. And as for experience, my dear, you are doing a magnificent job with Rita. I would love you to be my assistant."

Poldi has a way of turning everything around to an advantage. My mother's career as a music teacher is launched! A student in Forest Hills is referred to her and she is getting three dollars an hour for a weekly lesson. She takes the long subway ride penniless and returns with money in her pocket. This is the first time in her life that my mother is earning money on her own! What a sense of liberation it produces. She comes home from every lesson and places her earnings on the table. It is not much, but it buys us food to add to our potato diet. Having saved Michael and me, protected and fed us during the war seems insignificant when compared to the power of earning money.

My father is not thrilled. "First thing you know," he warns her, "is that you'll feel that now that you are earning your own money, you are free to do as you want."

"No, no," my mother assures him, handing him her earnings, "It will always be our money." This is three dollars a week they are talking about.

In addition to traveling to Forest Hills once a week to give a lesson to her student, with Poldi's encouragement, my mother gives weekly pre-instrumental lessons to children in our neighborhood hoping she might drum up some piano lesson business closer to home. She gets rhythm band instruments, tambourines, triangles, drums, bells and several music books with directions for giving young children a musical experience. She puts signs up in the grocery store, the library, and next to the mailboxes in all the buildings in the neighborhood.

It works! Her class is very successful and soon she has ten little girls coming up to our apartment for their lessons. While my mother teaches the songs and the rhythms, I accompany them on the piano. I am thirteen years old and helping my mother to earn a living. She charges 75 cents per hour for each student. That is $7.50 a week, $10.50, when you include the money she gets from her private lesson. This is more than she had in ages. She pours her soul into those lessons. I, in the meantime, am pounding on the piano, sorry to give my free time but proud contributing to the family's welfare. I would love to ask my mother for a cut of the $7.50, but I don't dare. I know I wouldn't get it but I would get a lecture on how I should feel privileged to ... blah, blah, blah.

Unfortunately none of the girls in the pre-instrumental class come back to take piano lessons after the course is over. Seventy-five cents a week for the parents of these kids is one thing, but buying a piano is another. Pianos are expensive, and moreover piano lessons will cost more than seventy-five cents. But my mother attracts another group of children and gives the same course again. Seven dollars and fifty cents an hour is a lot of money in 1949.

Even though, her plans for giving individual lessons in our neighborhood don't materialize, my mother does start teaching more and more in Forest Hills, where people are affluent. Word of mouth spreads. She is a good teacher, kind and encouraging and one student recommends another. Within one year she has enough students to make a significant contribution to the family's finances.

My father finally gets a job as a cutter in a ladies sweater factory, and we feel more secure. But his temper does not abate and the terrible rages go on, directed at Michael, myself, and sometimes at my mother, who takes pity on us and indulges us in small treats. She buys gifts for everyone. One day, I come home from school, and there, lying on my bed is a beautiful green woolen skirt with a matching sweater. I am careful lest I appear selfish. I don't even touch them before asking my mother whom they are for. She tells me they are mine. "Are they really for me?" I ask. "I thought they might be for someone special."

"They are," she answers, smiling at me, "they are for you!"

Chapter Fifty-One

Teenager

We call it cooking class, but the school calls it "Home Economics." The class is for girls only; the boys go to "shop," where they make a wooden stool or book-ends. Our section consists of four pleasingly furnished rooms: a kitchen, a bedroom a living room and a bathroom where we practice the art of homemaking. Mrs. Davis is our teacher and she sends three or four of us into the kitchen to make inedible foods like, milk toast, which we drop from the fifth floor window onto the sidewalk below, where it lands, a solid lump of clay. Another group is assigned to the bedroom to make beds with hospital corners, or to the living room to dust the furniture. When left alone, we gather in one corner of a room, whispering, and exchanging every bit of information and misinformation gathered about sex. We talk softly, reminding each other to keep our voices down.

"Did you hear that Elaine Bolkowski's sister is pregnant?" Anna asks.

"No!" we answer in a chorus, outraged. "You've got to be kidding. She's only fifteen."

"Yup," the knowledgeable Anna nods, her head going up and down. "She 'went all the way,' with Jerry O'Brien. She's easy. She's had lots of boyfriends." Anna shrugs her shoulders. "Well, that's what happens when you do French kissing. Now she has to drop out of high school." We have a vague idea of what 'all the way' means, we're not sure about what French kissing is.

"What's French kissing?" Joyce inquires. Anna tells us.

"Yuk, who would ever do that?" We groan with disgust. We hear the heavy footsteps of Mrs. Davis, coming down the hall.

"Oh, Oh, chickie the cops." We stop talking and pick up the dust rag as she comes into the room to inspect our progress.

I get my period before my eleventh birthday and I have been developing steadily, but no grown up has explained what puberty and adolescence is like. I am not totally ignorant about "the facts of life," as we call sex education in the 50's, but there are definite gaps in my understanding. Most of information I receive on this encroaching part of my own life, is what I am able to garner from my girlfriends during cooking class: never kiss on the first date, petting is necking below the neck and should be indulged in only when you're engaged and above all, virginity must be saved for the "wedding night."

Even though I know I am not the only girl in my class whose body is changing, my development seems to come at an earlier age, and coupled with the fact that I am older than my classmates I again feel different: an American living inside a refugee's body. I look at myself carefully. What is going on with me? I seem to have no control. I wonder if my newly formed curves and size 34 C bra are caused by becoming fat. Every time I ask my mother, she brushes me off, saying that what's happening is "natural." It's not just my breasts that stretch my blouses and sweaters, my skirts are too tight across my hips, my skin is breaking out in ugly zits, and my feelings are constantly bruised.

I cry when I see an old man in a wheelchair, a child with a limp, a blind person with a cane, a dog run over in the street, a lifeless bird. I think about them all day long feeling sad. What is happening to me, I wonder? Only a year ago I think I felt like everyone else. Now I feel like a freak, a spectator looking down at my life.

The reflection in the mirror does nothing to reassure me that I am today who I was yesterday. I look at myself. Pimples, like an invasion of bright red ants, march across my forehead, undeterred by my eyebrows and the bridge of my nose: an army, with daily recruits invade my territory. My father catches me inspecting myself in the mirror.

"Stop admiring yourself," he says caustically. "You are more interested in your face than your fat behind which is ten time bigger than your face."

This is how it's been for the past year and a half. Every step I take, my parents- usually my father- tries to make me take a step back. They say it's in the interest of turning me into a "decent" girl. They want me to be mature, but they won't let me grow up. I resist, I rebel but in the end I return, helpless and forlorn. My ego is not strong enough to support my will. I believe them when they tell me I am fat. I go on diets, but my body has a mind of its own, and it is filling out and developing in spite of the restraints I put on it.

Other girls in school envy me. They wish they had something to put into a bra. This is the era of Marilyn Monroe, when being sexy and desirable meant having big breasts. I envy their slim bodies, they envy my curves. My parents hate the way I look and I agree with them. I wish I could please them, but I can't control my body. I am clumsy, fat, ugly and undesirable.

It is after lunch but recess is not over. I am carrying a heavy cardboard panel decorated with sketches of a seed turning into a plant. "From Seed to Plant" is printed in bold letters across the top. This is my science project and I don't want to be pushed while standing in line. I carry this clumsy, heavy piece of oak tag. I have a pass to come up early bring the panel upstairs before the afternoon classes start. Two boys from my class follow me up the stairs.

"What are you doing here?" I ask them. "You're not supposed to be here."

They approach giggling. Paul, the taller of the two, sprouting a few black hairs on his upper lip looks at me uneasily. He takes a deep breath and walks over to me, holding his head to one side. He is very uncomfortable. Suddenly his hand shoots away from his side. He reaches over, touching my breast, intent on groping me. Burton, his friends comes up from behind and snaps my bra strap through my blouse. This is no *Glatz Kopf* experience and I am not in the least bit scared.

"Get away from me, you parasites," I snap. "Parasite" is a new word I just learned in science. I love the staccato way it bounces off my tongue and I try to use it as much as possible. "You're not gonna get a cheap feel off of me." I know all about getting felt up. All the girls in my class have been talking about it and I had been wondering when it was going to happen to me. I pretend to be outraged, but secretly, I am glad that someone finally tries it with me.

Chapter Fifty-Two

Hope

I come home from school with a blue application form for the High School of Music and Art. My father looks at it and asks "what's this? An application to high school? What's Music and Art?" It seems as though there are some things I know more about than my father.

"Every year the eighth grade students in the public and private schools in New York City try out for the 'special' high school in New York," I explain, playing the role of the patient teacher, "Bronx High School of Science and Stuyvesant High School for gifted math and science students, Hunter High School for smart girls, Performing Arts for dance, music and drama, Washington Irving for fashion design and Music and Art." He looks interested, so I go on, "I want to try out for Music and Art. You have to sign the application form that says I can take the test. And then, if I pass, I can go to Music and Art." He looks at the form, studies it, nods his head, and runs his tongue over his lips before taking out his fountain pen. He reads it carefully, sighs and nods.

He smiles and I look at him critically for the first time in my life. He is not a bad looking, I think. When he smiles, deep dimples on each side of his face imbed themselves into his cheeks. His thick eyebrows frame his dark eyes and when he looks happy he glows with pleasure. I'm pleased. I've done something to make my father smile and I don't get to do this often.

"This sounds almost too good to be true," he is enthusiastic, "only in America is there an opportunity for such an education." H e strokes his chin. "Just one word of warning," he cautions me. "This looks like a hard school to get into. Don't be disappointed if you don't get in."

"Don't be disappointed?" I ask incredulously, "I won't be disappointed. I'll just quietly commit suicide by jumping off the roof." He's smiling and I can afford a bit of humor.

"Why must you always be so dramatic?"

My best friend, Alice, applies to Bronx Science and Hunter High School. Before she takes the entrance exams she urges me to apply to both schools as well as to Music and Art. That way I will have more choices, and we'll have fun being in the same high school. I know I have no other talents. I love school and am a good student, but I really am not good in math or science, and have no desire to go to an all girls' high school. It is M&A or George Washington High.

Chapter Fifty-Three

A Glimpse of the Promised Land

I am wearing my new dress, with multi colored polka dots. My mother made it using a Simplicity pattern and fabric that she bought at a remnant store for twenty five cents a yard. My parents have finally given in and let me get my hair cut. It is gathered in a tight pony tail that swings between my shoulders. I clutch my music folder against my chest and walk slowly. I'm early for my test. It is a bright spring afternoon and I have just gotten off the IRT subway, at 125th Street. I walk through Harlem up to135th Street and Convent Avenue. As I get to the corner, I stop to listen to a soprano voice coming through one of the open windows. Ten steps further on, I hear string instruments. The music is coming from everywhere. I close my eyes and stand on the sidewalk, listening. There is no traffic, there are no other sounds. "God," I say quietly to myself, "please, please let me become a part of this."

The test consists of three parts, pitch discrimination, rhythm, and performance. The first two parts are easy. Pitch discrimination is taken in a large classroom by all the applicants. All we have to do is write "S" or "D" to designate whether the first and last note of a series of tones are the same or different. The rhythm part is taken individually, one examiner per applicant. We have to tap back a rhythmic sequence that has been presented. The rhythms become longer and more complicated, but I know I got them all right.

The performance portion of the exam is going to be hard. I wait outside of the room I have been assigned to. There are four of us prospective students waiting to go in. We listen to the hopeful applicants behind the closed door, trying to ascertain if they are better or worse than we are. We sit in the hallway and the rumors start flying.

"Someone told me that if you're very good, they stop you at the beginning," one of the girls says, "they don't need to listen to the whole piece if they can see right away that you're good."

"Now isn't that stupid?" I hear someone else say, "Why would they have to listen to a bad performance in its entirety? Why would they only spend time listening to bad music, and stop you if you're good?"

"Didn't you ever hear of giving someone the benefit of the doubt?" The first person answers, "how can they tell if you're really bad without listening to the whole piece?"

We distract ourselves from our anxiety by trying to understand the process of acceptance or rejection.

I don't know what to think as I hand my music over to one of the three examiners who will rate the performance. I take out a handkerchief and dry my sweating palms. Poldi has told me that this is what all professionals do and it is bound to impress the examiners. I play two preludes by Bach. I play the entire pieces without being interrupted. Is this is a good sign, or a bad sign? I try to read their expressions but they don't give me a clue. "Thank you for trying out for Music and Art," they tell me as they hand my music over to me. I've been in the United States for five years. I'm still not sure how to respond to certain statements.

What do I answer? "You're welcome?" Somehow that doesn't sound right to me. So I smile and say "Thank you!" Before I leave the room, I turn around and ask them, "how did I do?" I'm dying to find out, get a clue at least.

"You'll be notified in a few weeks," one of them answers not betraying any emotion.

On my way back to the subway, I start praying, making a deal with God. "Please God; I am willing to sacrifice ten years of my old age in order to get into M&A. I will make charitable contributions to the poor beggars that sit in front of the subway stations. I will never throw away any morsel of food while there are children starving all over the world. Anything You want. Just let me get into Music and Art. I will never ask You for any other favors as long as I live." I implore every Deity I can think of. It is going to be Music and Art or George Washington, the area high school. George Washington, I am told, is not a particularly "good" high school, but if I don't get into Music and Art I will not have any other option. I feel cautiously optimistic and very scared at the same time.

I go back to P.S. 189 and wait for the result. Time creeps by slowly. I have no idea of how I will be notified. "Catastrophia," my home town, dictates that I prepare for every eventuality. Will I have to be embarrassed in an assembly and told in front of the entire school that I have not been accepted, or will it be by mail? I have told every one that I am applying. Big mistake. What if I don't get in? Will I have to tell everyone that I failed? How embarrassing is that? Am I jinxing myself? Suddenly, I picture myself being rejected. I am so humiliated. Will I go to George Washington High School for one year and then apply again? Students are accepted up to tenth grade and after that, if they fail to get in, they are banished forever. Do I have chance to pass the test the second time around if I have failed it the first time? How am I going to make the days go by faster? My mind can't seem to slow down.

Finally, well into the month of June, Mr. Gross, the principal calls all of the applicants into his office. I stop breathing and concentrate only on praying. I have one last chance to convince God that I deserve a break. I feel that God still has time to intercede on my behalf. Until I hear it from the principal's own mouth there is the chance that prayer might be helpful. I close my eyes, cross my fingers and stop breathing. Mr. Gross, informs us that of the ten who had applied, three of us got in; "Marilyn Basmajian," big deal, I knew she'd get in, "Roy Hill," hmm, I didn't even know he plays an instrument and "Rita Schmelkes." Hey that's me!! He congratulates us and sends us back to our classroom and tells the others that they shouldn't be discouraged. They can always try again for tenth grade.

I can't believe my luck. Not long ago I was at the Yeshiva being bossed around by Tova and now I'm going to Music and Art! Oh Glory, Hallelujah, I'm going to live happily ever after! I run home with the good news. Both my parents are thrilled but they warn me not to tell anyone about it.

"We don't want you to brag, it isn't nice" they tell me, "everyone will find out on their own, and then we can act as if there was never a question of your not getting in. Think of how surprised they will be." I love the idea of surprising everyone, especially Monica, who I know has applied as well. I wonder if she got in. Monica's family and my family have been in contact with each other ever since we arrived in New York. I can tell from what I hear at home that my father does not like Monica's father at all, has little respect for him and his snobby ways. Behind his back he calls him *rzhygac,* which means "vomit" in Polish, instead of by his real name "Ziggy." Her parents have sacrificed everything for Monica's education. They live in a rooming house, sharing one room and using a bathroom at the end of the hall that they have to share with all the people on their floor. They have a tiny kitchen inside a closet, where Monica's mother cooks all their meals. But in spite of this, they did purchase a spinet piano so that Monica could practice. They enrolled her at the Julliard prep school. Our parents are very competitive with regard to their daughters and my mother is afraid that I'm losing ground.

"Why can't you write neatly, the way Monica writes?" my mother is looking at a composition I have just finished writing. She reads it. The content is good but the handwriting is atrocious.

"I was in a hurry to get my thoughts down and didn't have time to be neat," I reply.

Monica, unlike me, is careful and neat. Her piano playing is precise. She observes every rest, lifting her hands off the keyboard dramatically to make sure everyone can see how true she is to the composer; every dotted eighth note is held for accurate duration. I don't like her playing, it is dry. Mine is emotional, although not perfect. Our mothers make us play for them each other every time we get together and for days I hear about how clean and exact Monica's playing is.

I know that the main reason my mother doesn't want to brag about me is because she wants to astound, shock Monica's mother. I too, feel that it would be great if I could surpass her, if I got into Music and Art and she didn't. I haven't forgotten Montelupi and Monica's greed. My parents steer away from the topic during subsequent visits, but I can't contain myself any longer.

"I'm going to Music and Art in September," I blurt out. "How about you?"

"Well," Monica answers, "I go to such a wonderful Junior High School that my parents decided it would be better for me to stay there until the end of ninth grade."

"Yeah, right!" I say to myself, certain that she did not get in.

Graduation from P.S. 189 is a few weeks away and then I will become a student at Music and Art. In the meantime, the eighth grade girls are required to make their own graduation dresses in homemaking class. Boys are still working at the shop. They're making little boxes with tight fitting lids. Boys are required to wear dress shirts with ties. They're lucky. They don't have to wear their mistakes in public. Only the girls have to wear homemade dresses. Everyone goes shopping for white fabric and Simplicity, McCall's and Butterick's patterns. Most of us get Simplicity patterns or McCalls; they cost twenty-five cents. Some of the rich girls splurge and buy the expensive Vogue patterns. They cost as much as one dollar each. And the very rich girls have their dresses made by a dressmaker. Organdy, dotted Swiss, and starched pique are the standard fabrics.

We sit at the old fashioned Singer treadle sewing machines during sewing class. There are about fifteen machines in the room and all of us are busy basting, threading and pumping the machines. Even the girls who are having dresses made by professionals are sewing. They are required to wear the dresses they made, but who's going to kick them out of the graduation assembly if they show up in a dress made by a professional dress maker? It is a tedious task.

"Miss Dratty," I call, "my fabric is getting bunched up under the needle." Miss Dratty comes over. She resembles a salty brown pretzel, skinny, with a face that looks like it's made of crepe paper. She has a tiny white bun on top of her head resembling a sugar donut. "Let me see," she says in a shaky quivering voice. "Oh dear," you've got thread caught in the bobbin." She makes a few adjustments to the fabric and the machine. "Let's try it now and see how we make out."

I have little patience for sewing class. Graduation from elementary school is definitely not something to worry about. Everyone graduates from grade school, I know, but how many get to go to Music and Art? I am feeling superior and blasé about the idea of graduating. I sew as best I can, taking many short cuts and achieving a misshapen dress with a waistline that fluctuates from above my rib cage to below my stomach. The hemline dips to my ankles on one side and rises above my knees on the other. But what the heck? I've only got to wear this dress once, on graduation day.

I try the dress on as soon as it's finished. There is a big problem. I can see that it is never going to make it over my hips, let alone to graduation. I panic, and then quickly recover. I am going to be calm in the face of a crisis. This is a problem I am sure I can solve. I take the dress apart and attempt to try again. I leave more room at the seams and baste the top to the bottom. Basting stitches are the quick running ones that permit the seams come apart with one tiny pull of the thread. After securing the top of the dress to the bottom, I take a batch of safety pins and pin the dress to my slip to make sure it doesn't fall off my body. I work on it all Sunday, taking great pains to make sure it looks alright. I try the dress on struggling not to loosen one stitch lest the whole dress becomes undone. I stand in front of the mirror on the closet door and scrutinize the results. Well, it certainly is not perfect, and no one could possibly mistake it for having been made by a professional dress maker, but if I keep my arms crossed in front of my waist no one will notice how uneven it is. Besides, we're all going to be wearing white, standing close to each other. Until I walk up to receive my diploma I will be invisible. I plan to hold my arms crossed at my waistline, hiding the worst imperfections while ensuring that the bottom doesn't detach from the top. I have cheated fate. "If I don't cough or laugh too hard, or take a very deep breath, I'll be fine. Besides," I tell myself, I'll never have to wear this dress again, so who cares if it stands up to wear and tear?"

We are lined up: Girls on one side, boys on the other. The piano starts out with Sir Edward Elgar's Pomp and Circumstance March and we follow each other to the front of the auditorium. After the Pledge to the Flag we sing The Star Spangled Banner and sit down. The principal, assistant principal, and our eighth grade teacher make long speeches telling us that we're on our way towards our futures, that we are obligated to become responsible citizens, blah, blah, blah. . . . I'm not listening. I'm dreaming and planning. We line up alphabetically to receive our diplomas and stand up to sing our school song to the melody of "Auld Lang Syne."

We are serious and happy. We are going into a hopeful world. The Second World War is over, there is a United Nations Organization that will resolve all conflicts through debates, we are at peace and I will be going to Music and Art. My mother and Aunt Sari sit with all the parents. My father has to go to work but I am too happy to feel sorry for myself for not having him present. Everyone is proud of their child, but my mother is the proudest. Her daughter has been accepted to one of the most prestigious high schools in the city, perhaps in the United States. I graduate with a gold seal on my diploma.

Chapter Fifty-Four

Music and Art

For graduation I get exactly what I ask for: a brown leather loose-leaf book, with a zipper that goes all the way around, and my initials RBS stamped in gold on the front. It is a beautiful gift and I know that it cost a lot of money. My parents had to save up for it and I feel rich and privileged, and above all worthy. Inside there are pockets for stray papers and a zippered case for pens and pencils. I have filled it with three holed paper and have even put in subject dividers. I stroke it, smell the familiar odor of leather, and hold it against my cheek. I plan for my first day of school, what I will wear, how I will act, and how I will wear my hair.

"How does it look better?" I ask Michael holding onto my leather loose-leaf, "in front of my chest, held with both arms? That's how the girls in George Washington carry their books, or held in one hand against my body, looking more casual?"

I hope I'll be popular, have girl friends and boyfriends, be smart and fit in. I'm wondering. Should I take the beautiful leather binder to school on the first day? I really want to but something tells me not to bring it on the first day. It is a bit too much. The voice tells me not to call attention to myself; to go to school with nothing but an assignment pad to write down what sorts of school supplies I'll need. I ignore the voice. I've waited too long for this treasure to leave it at home for one day longer than necessary. Most of my classmates in P.S. 189 had such a binder when they entered a seventh grade, departmental class. Against my better judgment, I decide to take it.

Horror of horrors! Not only am I the only student in the entire school to be carrying such an obvious loose leaf, but I am also the only girl not wearing lipstick. I feel so conspicuous, like I'm wearing a black satin evening gown to a class picnic. I look around, my face is on fire. I am sure that everyone is staring at me, laughing, and saying to each other, "did you ever see such a refugee in your life? Doesn't she know better than to bring such a loose-leaf on the first day of school? She must think she's terrific to own such a beautiful loose-leaf. Doesn't she know that we've all had those since we were in seventh grade?" Once again, I am feeling like the outsider, the refugee. I am unable to take notes, pay attention to the teachers, or get my bearings. All I am able to think of is how everyone must be whispering about me behind my back. I slide the binder under my seat. I wish I could disappear with it.

After school, instead of getting off at my bus stop, I get off at 181st Street and head directly for the Woolworth, Five and Dime Store. I know exactly what I want; a Pond's lipstick, the shade called "honey." It is bright, bright red, comes in a small aqua tube, and it costs ten cents. I buy it, put it on and smile at my reflection in the small mirror provided by the cosmetic counter. I feel much better. My teeth are sparkling, my lips are red, shining, and I am glamorous. All the girls I know are wearing that shade of red. Some of them even used it while at P.S.189, wiping it off upon entering school, and putting it on as soon as school ended. I, however, obeyed my parents and resisted buying the lipstick while in elementary school. All the girls in high school are wearing bright shades of lipstick and after this humiliating first day, I am determined to look as much like everyone else as possible.

I wipe the lipstick off before my father comes home from work. I will tackle the lipstick problem on the Sabbath, when my father might be in a good mood. We sit down to Friday night dinner and that's when and I make my proclamation, "From now on," I start bravely, "I am going to be wearing lipstick and dungarees to school. Every day," I add.

My father recoils with indignation at my announcement, "No you're not," he declares, "that's not at all what we have in mind for you."

I persist. "Every other girl in school wears it. Why do I have to look so different?"

"We want you to look like a decent girl from a good family. Teachers will like you much better if they see that you don't paint your face. You need to make a good impression."

"What are you talking about?" I interrupt, hysterically. "This is America. The teachers here don't judge you by whether or not you're wearing lipstick. Besides, if they think badly of me then they'll have to think badly of all the girls in the school, because they all wear lipstick."

We go back and forth, I keep insisting that I will wear whatever I please, and they're united as always. Neither one of us is going to budge. "We know how grown ups think. Only cheap, trampy girls wear lipstick and disrespectful dungarees."

With this declaration, my father turns his back and makes for the door. He has said his piece and his word is final. I run after him, trying to get him to at least hear me out. He turns around to face me, "I know. I know, I'm only the father in this house," he looks at me pointedly, raising his hands shoulder level, palms out, in a mock pose of surrender, "I only love you more than anyone else. I saved your life, and I support you. So why should you listen to me?" he says sarcastically grabbing the doorknob in his hand. He turns away and then changes his mind facing me, "you are not going to wear lipstick to school while you're living in my house," and he closes the door.

I wish my mother would intercede on my behalf as she had done in Liebenau, but by now I know that she won't. She stays silent, perhaps because she is afraid to contradict him, and is committed to the "united front." It is not the lipstick I am fighting for. The issue for me has little to do with lipstick. If I want to, I can put it on every time I leave the house and wipe it off when I return. It's more important for me to prove a point and get them to hear me than it is to wear the lipstick. I am trying to assert my independence and still gain their approval. It is not going to happen. "Let me grow up," I scream inside my head, "and accept my ideas once in a while. Or, at least hear my argument before closing the door on further discussion."

Chapter Fifty-Five

Thanksgiving 1951

Now, that my mother is teaching piano every day, the house is empty until 5:30. Michael, who attends the Yeshiva University Prep School, starts to bring his friends over to the house. Their school is around the corner from my house and this is a very convenient place for them to congregate. His friends are good looking, funny and "regular guys," which means that they are athletic and prone to mischief. I love it when they come over. Today they are all cutting 8th period and playing cards and smoking. I run back and forth from the kitchen to the living room, providing the boys with drinks. One of them, Wally, pays a lot of attention to me. I find him staring at me and he manages to brush up against me whenever he gets the opportunity. He runs his hand down my arm and I shiver, feel myself turning red; painted with a brush dipped in blood. I run to the bathroom to catch my breath and look in the mirror. Wally follows me and closes the door.

"Hey, Rita," he says, leaning against the wall, a cigarette dangling from his mouth, "how would you like to go to Fort Tryon Park with me on Saturday?" Fort Tryon Park is an easy fifteen minute walk from my house. I don't want to appear too eager, but on the other hand I don't want to discourage him either.

"Well," I hesitate. I'm dying to go with him but I'm also scared, unsure of myself. I don't know how I'm feeling. I wonder, is he asking me out on a date, is he just being friendly, or is he setting me up, just testing me to see if I'll show up? I don't trust boys yet and I certainly don't trust myself. I have to make a quick decision. It will just be a walk in the park on a Sabbath afternoon. I don't say "yes" or "no."

"Why don't we meet at the front gate of the park on Fort Washington Avenue at three o'clock, weather permitting, of course?"

Wally is very tall, has long arms and legs, a slow sexy smile and wavy black hair. His friends call him the *shlang*, the snake. He looks so handsome,

I would love to carry his picture in my wallet and tell my friends in school that we are going steady. But I'm scared to meet him in the park. I'm not sure if he's asking me for a real date or just suggesting that we meet. If I'm there and he doesn't show up I will die of humiliation. My dilemma is solved by Mother Nature. It pours on Saturday so there is an opportunity to buy time. I wish he'd ask me out on a real date.

Whenever he comes over we escape into the bathroom where we neck and grope each other. We practice French kissing, something I had found so repulsive only a short time ago and now can't get enough of. It is Wednesday evening, the night before Thanksgiving. I am so excited. I have made wonderful plans for the week-end. Tomorrow we will be having Thanksgiving dinner with my Aunt Sari and Uncle Avrom. Friday will be spent catching up on what I normally do on Sunday, and on Sunday Michael and I will go out on a double date. I have been carrying my brother's picture around in my wallet and showing it to all my friends.

"Oh, he is gorgeous, adorable, sexy," my friends all agree. And indeed he is. He is six feet tall, has black hair, well defined eyebrows, long black lashes that brush his cheekbones, sideburns and a fuzzy black moustache. He is "tall, dark and handsome." All my girlfriends want to get fixed up with him even though he is a year younger than they are. I fix Mike up with Sandra Manly, a good friend of mine. I will be going with Wally. We will all go to the movies on Sunday afternoon and then get a soda afterwards. We are both happy. We are discussing our plans for Sunday, when my father overhears us.

"What's that you're planning?" he asks

Innocently, I tell him that Mike, Wally, Sandy and I are going to the movies. "On a double date, so Mike and I can look out for one another," I add to reassure him that I won't be alone with Wally.

"What date?" he asks. "Who said you had permission to go on a date, and make one for your brother?" I have once again, inadvertently, provoked his fury. "You know you still live here, and it would be nice if you consulted with your mother and me before you make plans not only for yourself, but for Michael." I'm still waiting to hear what I did or said to provoke such an outburst.

"What's the big deal?" I ask, my voice quaking with fear. "We're all going to the movies together, Michael and his friend, me and my friend. We're paying for ourselves."

"And who gave you permission arrange this date?"

"I don't know," I lie, "it just sort of came about."

"Well, Michael is not going to the movies with any of your girlfriends."

"Tell me, what's wrong with going to the movies?" My fear is quickly turning to anger.

"Plenty's wrong with that. You are not going to decide when, where and whom your brother is going out with. He's a poor enough student and doesn't need to be thinking about girls."

I feel a hot spark of defiance streak through my upper body. I take a deep breath, "we made plans and we are going." I don't know where I get the courage, but I am determined not to give in, not to disappoint Sandy, not to lose out on an opportunity to be a real teenager on a double date, just like Archie, Betty, Veronica and Reggie. "We're going," I shout, "and that's final."

"Watch your mouth," he warns me. "It is not your place to decide what Michael is going to do. I'm saying he is not going and that's final!"

I stamp my foot, and shout at him. "You're always keeping me from doing what I want to do. When I'm religious, you're a goy. When I want to do something like go to the library on Shabbat, you suddenly pull it away from me. You think you own me and that I have to be forever grateful to you for saving us. Well I'm not grateful." I stop just short of telling him I hate him. But he gets the message.

His hand flies away from his wrist. Suddenly, I feel a sharp blast across my cheek. It sends me sprawling onto the bed behind me. I shake my head, trying to catch my breath. He can beat me to death, but I'm determined to get my own way. Something in me refuses to budge. "You can kill me, but I'm not going to listen to you."

Michael and my mother cower behind the doorway in the hall. My father grabs me by my blouse and slaps me again and again, holding onto my upper arm so that I cannot fall back onto the soft bed. "You are not going to win a fight with me, young lady" he shouts, "I might not count for much out in the world, but in this house, I am the boss." He lets go of me, leaves me to fall back on the bed. "This is one Thanksgiving you will never forget." Time will prove him right. I have underestimated his power.

I sob. I hate my father, for what he's done to me, Michael and my mother; for what he wants me to be, for not caring about my feelings. I'm supposed to be an obedient puppet, with no rights to my opinions, not worthy of being heard. I cry on my bed until I fall asleep, exhausted. When I wake up, my father tells me that I will not be going with the rest of the family to my aunt on Thursday. I am being punished for my fresh mouth and bad behavior. I'm glad. I don't want to go anywhere with my parents. My mother only cares about my father and Michael. She never stands up for me. I look in the mirror and I see bruised cheekbones and two black eyes. My arms are black and blue from my elbows to my armpits. When everyone leaves the house, I pick up the phone and call Sandy. She's disappointed but says she understands.

On Monday I return to school, my bruises have turned green and yellow, a hideous map across my face. I tell my curious friends that I tripped over a wire in the night and fell against a table.

Chapter Fifty-Six

Odd Girl Out

"Let's go to Lord and Taylor on Saturday," my friend Sandy suggests. "They're having a sale on sweaters." I can't tell her that there is nothing in that store that I could ever afford. So I tell her the other truth about myself.

"I can't, I'm religious."

"Oh yeah, I know. Like kosher."

Music and Art opens a glimpse into a world I can't belong to, but am dying to enter. As long as I was attending P.S. 189, I was in a homogenous environment. None of the kids there had much more than the others. We never felt poor, because most of the families were just like ours, struggling immigrants, trying to make ends meet, battling unemployment and acclimating to the American dream. Only a few were comfortable enough to have dresses made by a dressmaker or shop at Lord and Taylor.

Music and Art is totally different and although I feel completely accepted and have many friends, I know that I am different. The special high school draws students from all over New York City and offers them what no public or private school can. I am the only immigrant in Music and Art that I know of. Most of the other kids come from middle class families, many of them wealthy, living on Park Avenue and Central Park West. Their fathers are doctors, engineers, business men and lawyers. A few, as I, come from less affluent families, living in working class neighborhoods, but they are tough on the outside, noisy, and wild. They run into the bathrooms between and during classes and smoke cigarettes. They play drums and saxophone, while we play piano and violin. I feel more comfortable with the rich kids, the ones that use expressions such as, "my mother will kill me for not wearing a sweater," or "I've got to be home right after school, my family rule." Those are the values that my own parents espouse. Norman, one my friends, comes over to our table. He is carrying a tray which holds a steaming red frankfurter, cuddled in a soft white roll and topped with a mountain of sauerkraut. I look at it and suddenly I am in Krakow, starving while soldiers are coming out of the delicatessen laughing and eating. I stare at Norman's lunch, salivating. I know I can't have a frankfurter, for one thing, it isn't kosher, but I want it badly. I don't ever tell anyone in school about my background. I am not willing to appear any more different than I already am. I want so badly to fit in and be like everyone else, almost as badly as I want that frankfurter. Most of us bring a lunch bag to school. Some of us buy a snack, milk, tea and ice cream for dessert. A few buy hot lunches every day, most are able to afford them and everyone can eat it. Not me. I cannot afford anything other than an ice-cream sandwich which costs a dime and I can't eat anything that is not kosher, which, the school lunches certainly aren't.

When my friends go shopping or to the movies on Saturdays, I stay home and go to synagogue. They are considerate and invite me to join all their activities. I, of course, cannot participate in anything that would violate the Sabbath. I can only attend Saturday night parties after the Sabbath is over. During daylight savings time, I can't leave the house until as late as 8:30 P.M. after dark. Music and Art students live all over the city and I often have to travel over an hour to get to a party. I have a mid-night curfew. My mother waits for me to return by 12. She is sitting in the living room holding a hot water bottle against her nightgown to ease to pain of her ulcer. The condition is aggravated by anxiety and my being out late at night certainly contributes to her worry. I know only too well what waiting for a loved one to return feels like. I don't want to make her wait and I don't want to be grounded for breaking curfew.

Sometimes I don't get to the party until 10:00 P.M., only to put in a quick appearance and leave alone at 11:00 P.M. Sometimes, a boy offers to take me home but I refuse. I don't want to appear dependent and more than that, I don't want anyone to feel sorry for me. I am determined to be independent and self-reliant.

I wait on deserted subway platforms, in the middle of the night. Then, when I get to my stop, I have to walk from the subway to my house, on empty streets, through a neighborhood that is not all that safe. My parents feel that a "nice, decent," girl has to be home by mid-night. They don't take into consideration that the distances I have to travel to get to where I am going take up most of the evening, and that by enforcing such a strict curfew, they are putting me in danger. There is no way to reason with them. The united front is solid and once my father announces his proclamation, he is finished. There is no discussion, no appeal. My father says what he has to say and leaves the room.

The reality of who I am and who I want to be widens. It is not just my parents' restrictions that set me apart from my peers. I come from another world. I was born across the ocean and though I live in New York, my home life is different from theirs. While they are enjoying freedom and independence, having choices, encouraged to shop for their own clothes, I am kept in a strict protective environment where I am not even permitted to choose my wardrobe. They joke around with their parents, are given allowances while I have to keep a careful lid on my emotions, stay respectful and "decent." At times it appears as though I am still a continent away from where I want to be. In many ways Music and Art is my salvation, but it also defines me as an outsider.

My own family, although goal oriented toward success and achievement is economically disadvantaged when compared to my friends. I often envy the girls with cashmere sweaters and matching skirts, new loafers and haircuts at Best & Co. My best friend's father is a lady's clothing manufacturer. She wears a new outfit to school every day, while I make do with hand-me-downs from Mirka's nieces.

I don't know one other Orthodox girl in the school whom I can be friends with. If there is, I have never met her. I am the only girl in my group of friends who lives by a different set of rules. I am embarrassed to talk about being Orthodox. I'm forever hiding from the real me, unable to acknowledge myself to myself. I want to fit in everywhere and sense that I fit in nowhere. I am ashamed to be the daughter of a factory worker who is often unemployed. Since my father is now working in a sweater factory, I tell everyone at school that he is a sweater designer. I try to be part of the middle class group.

Chapter Fifty-Seven

My School

Located on 135th Street and Convent Avenue in Manhattan's upper west side, Music and Art is right in the middle of Harlem, next to City College. The students call it the "Castle" and indeed it looks just like one. It is seven stories high, the top floor being a tower, with tiered seating, where the junior choir meets every morning at 7:30, before school starts. It is a beautiful room with a high ceiling, flawless acoustics, and a stage with a piano.

I join the choir even though I am not a voice major. I am assigned to the first soprano section. We are singing Haydn's "Creation." It is written in four part harmony, rousing and inspiring. I am not used to singing with baritones and basses; in the Glee Club at P.S. 189 we only had sopranos and altos. I am immersed in the harmonies when, suddenly, I hear the purest, crystal clear, soprano voice coming from the rear of the room where the basses are sitting. I turn around, as do all the others to see, Thomas Young, a big, muscular, Black he-man, singing with the voice of an angel. He has decided to join the choir. He is the last person, I think, who would be interested in doing anything he doesn't have to do, but his voice is magnificent. Usually, he sits in the back of the classroom, cracking jokes under his breath and making the rest of laugh. I try to sit close to him in our classes, and catch all his hilarious mutterings.

He explains that the only reason he has joined the choir is because he has nothing else to do early in the morning before classes start. His father, a biology professor teaches at City College, next to our school, and he drops him off early at school. I don't know if my ears or my eyes are deceiving me. How can such a high, pure voice be coming from such a big man? No one dares to tease him, he is too big and strong and we respect him for his gorgeous voice. He refuses to take solos. "That belongs to the girls," he tells our director, grinning.

Every piano student is required to take an orchestral instrument. I am assigned to the French horn, because I am one of the few ninth graders who is not wearing braces on my teeth. I don't want to play the French horn. It looks like brass intestines, rolled up and held on the lap. I have my heart set on the cello. There are four of us in the French horn room, two boys and two girls. I am lucky. Thomas Young is in all my classes including instrumental music. In addition to having the most beautiful voice in the choir, Tommy never stops making us laugh. We hold the horns to our mouths, giggling hysterically each time the teacher leaves the room. There is no way to play the horn while laughing. And since our teacher is out of the room part of the time, instructing other brass sections, Tommy has free reign. The individual rooms are soundproofed and Mr. Lawson, our teacher does not suspect that we are fooling around instead of practicing.

In spite of all this fun, some of us do manage to make progress. Instruments can be rented from the school for the week end for five dollars a month. I don't ask my parents for such a sum. I know they can not afford that, and I have learned never to ask for what I can't get. So, between all the fooling around during practice time and no opportunity to work more seriously at home, I do not become a very proficient player. Nevertheless, at the end of our freshman year, we are all assigned to an orchestra or a band. The difference between the two is that there is no string section in the band. There is no fooling around either. I am assigned to Junior Orchestra where I play with three other horns. Goose bumps crawl over my arms when the string section floats over to the back of the orchestra where the brass section sits. I am engulfed by the music and enjoy listening to it so much that at the first few rehearsals I miss every cue.

In addition to daily practice and orchestra periods, music majors are required to take theory, harmony, keyboard harmony, counterpoint, and dictation. Not all of these courses are offered in the same year, but we all have at least three periods of music per day, in addition to all the academic courses we are required to take. Our school days are longer than the average high school, and all of us have to travel to get there. But no one ever complains.

Chapter Fifty-Eight

Opening Doors

Music and Art has a profound impact on my life. It shapes me, directs my goals and opens a world that could never have been entered through any other passageway. I am changing and I will never be the same again; playing and listening to music with my friends, discussing the merits of the figured bass as compared to the *continuo,* happy to woo a common lover, the music. We share a joint "sameness" while being uniquely different from each other. This is the only time I will live in such a dream world.

During lunch, we sit at tables singing Bach's Two Part Inventions, folk songs accompanied by a guitar, and top hits, with clarinet and saxophone music in the background. I float from table to table. I love listening to the Inventions and singing the folk songs. My friends and I communicate non-verbally on spiritual levels. As we play or sing, we make eye contact and a message has been sent or received, with only a gesture, a smile or raised eyebrow, an acknowledged agreement. Making music together is making profound connections. I go to school with kids from every socio-economic and ethnic background. In this school it is only talent that counts. We feel that we are part of an elite group. We are snobs and look down on kids from the neighborhood schools.

The teachers are the best that the city has. My voice, my opinions and ideas are listened to in my classes. No one puts me down for asking a question or saying what I think. Here I win some respect which is so lacking in my "other" life." Mr. Gross, my algebra teacher is kind and patient with me, even though I am an idiot in math. Dr. Sayers, the ninth grade English teacher makes the Iliad and the Odyssey as real as today's headlines. Dr. Patterson opens my eyes to Renaissance, Roman, Romanesque, and Gothic architecture; and there are examples of it all over the city, from the Romanesque Cloisters in Fort Tryon Park to the Gothic St. Patrick's Cathedral on Fifth Avenue.

We meet and go to free radio broadcasts on Sundays and week nights at the Frick Art Gallery, the NBC Orchestra, and "The Firestone Hour," where I listen to Fritz Kriesler play the violin, Laurence Melchoir, Jan Pierce and Jussi Bjorling sing and Arturo Toscanini, Bruno Walter and Guido Cantelli conduct. Thirty-five cents buys us seats at the Lewissohn Stadium to hear young Leonard Bernstein play the piano as he conducts Mozart's 17th Piano Concerto, and in Carnegie Hall, we watch and listen to Erica Morini play Brahms violin concerto. In the middle of the performance, she pops a string, turns to the concert master, exchanges violins with him and continues without missing a beat. We see "Porgy and Bess," at the City Center, and on a Saturday night in October, I meet up with classmates to listen to Artur Schnabel play four Beethoven piano sonatas at Hunter College. While I am too young to appreciate the extent of my education and the unusual opportunities afforded me by the generosity of New York City's cultural events, I will never forget them.

We aren't serious all the time. We make lots of room for fun. Once, on April Fools' Day, the entire orchestra decides to play a trick on the teacher who the conducts the orchestra. We are rehearsing Aaron Copland's "Fanfare for the Common Man," a piece of music that starts out with an ear splitting clash of the cymbals and roll of the bass drum. The conductor raises his arms, poised to cue in the percussion section. His baton comes down swiftly, the percussionists stand mute. He shakes his head, raises his arms and gives the signal. Nothing happens, utter silence.

He raps his baton, "O.K., let's try this again." The cymbal player stands with the cymbal poised against his chest making direct eye contact with the conductor who again signals for the clash and roll of the percussion section. Stunning silence. "What the heck is going on?" he blurts out. "Am I going deaf or are you guys crazy?"

"April Fool," we scream in unison.

Another time, the senior orchestra conductor is absent and a substitute teacher comes in to take his place. He is a capable musician and looks forward to substituting at our school. It is time for another trick. All the kids exchange instruments. Violinists take the oboes, the horns take the cellos. No one is holding his own instrument when the teacher ascends the podium. I don't remember what we are playing, but it must be a classical selection. He picks up his baton and raises his arms. A cacophony of noise, in unison assaults him.

"What's going on?" he asks, stunned. "Isn't this senior orchestra? You're supposed to be the best of the best. You sound like you can't even play your own instruments." We shrug our shoulders, desperately trying to suppress the laughter that is threatening to explode.

Chapter Fifty-Nine

Chameleon

At home I behave like a "decent," religious girl who doesn't wear lipstick or slacks But as soon as I leave the house, I become someone else. I remove the skirt under which I rolled up my trousers, put on lipstick and get on the subway. I try to act like what I think regular teenagers act like. Archie, Betty, Veronica and Jughead are my models. Of course, no one I know acts like them, but I talk the way my peers do. I say "cool, dig, hip," words my parents wouldn't understand. I interject the word "like" into every sentence; "'like' I was going to 'like' the subway, when I 'like' met this weird character. 'Like' he was smoking on the train." I sneak on the forbidden lipstick every time I leave the house and even try smoking outside the building before school starts. I have memorized the words to the latest songs on the Hit Parade and sing along with my friends during lunch or on the subway. I love Tony Bennett, Dinah Shore, and Les Paul with Mary Ford and Nat King Cole. I also love Artur Rubenstein, Rudolf Serkin, Isaac Stern, and Roberta Peters.

I get a pair of white bucks; the white buckskin tie shoes that everyone, boys as well as girls are wearing, a felt skirt with a poodle painted on it. I earn the money for these luxuries by babysitting on the Saturday nights that I don't go to a party. I am working hard to fit in and on some levels I think I may be succeeding. I hear my father's voice.

"You can't wear that bathing suit," he yells at me. His voice and manner remind me that I am not like everyone else. It suggests that only he knows what is best for me. Under the guise of constructive criticism, he is insulting and humiliating me.

"Why not? I like it, I think it looks great, my friend Myra thinks it looks good on me and I paid for it with my own money."

"Don't you see how you look?" He asks me, "Do you really think your friends want you to look good? The worse you look the better it makes them look," he continues with his crazy logic. "That suit is not for you. It makes you look fat and it's indecent."

"Indecent?" I ask, "How is it indecent? It's one piece. Nothing is showing that shouldn't be."

"First of all it's strapless and cut low and second of all it makes you look fat." He walks out of the room, leaving me to contemplate my dilemma. I bought a bathing suit, with my own money. I have just spent $10.99 earned by baby sitting. Bathing suits cannot be returned and all my friends are going swimming at the St. George Hotel on Sunday. I look at myself in the mirror. I know that I'm not perfect, but I like the suit, it fits and I think it looks good on me. I want to obey but I want to go swimming with my friends even more. I rationalize: If I could return the suit, I would probably do it, but at fifty cents an hour, which is what I'm paid, eleven dollars is an awful lot of money to lose on a bathing suit that looks fine.

He returns to the room to remind me, "Your rear is huge in that suit and I'm only telling you this for your own good. If I didn't love you and have your best interest at heart, I wouldn't be telling this."

I'm supposed to feel grateful to be the recipient of so much love. I start crying.

"Stop your stupid sniveling," he shouts. "I hate to see you cry like a baby because you're hearing the truth." He is relentless and I am inconsolable. "Your girlfriends will always say you look good when you don't. They are happy when you look fat, it makes them feel beautiful. Only I will tell you the truth." I continue sobbing. Even my father thinks I'm ugly.

I wear the suit. I put it on under my dress, take a towel and go to the pool. I've made a decision to do what I want, wear what I like, not ask for permission and not worry about the approval I might or might not get.

Nevertheless, everyone in the family is enlisted to help me become a more attractive person. My cousin, Elsie, who is the doctor, puts me on a diet, and prescribes appetite curbing pills. I wonder why I can't sleep at night. I am, as it turns out, on speed, the reducing drug of choice during the early 50's. In my memory my adolescent self, is a fat, ugly, graceless girl, but later on, when I look at pictures of myself, I see an average sized, developing young woman, with bright eyes and an eager smile.

Chapter Sixty

A Cold and Empty House

I carry the heavy books up to our apartment, drop them at the door and take the key out of my pocket book. I hate coming home, leaving the "castle" for the dungeon. The apartment is always cold. Ever since we have come to live here the superintendent of the building has been skimping on the heat.

"Go down and ask the super for some heat," my father tells me. I hate these trips to the dark basement. The damp smell of the cellar brings me right back to Liebenau, the bottom of the steps and *Glatz Kopf's* slobbery kisses. I knock on the super's door. One eye peers out of the open crack.

"Yeah, whaddaya want?"

"Could we please have some more heat? We are freezing upstairs."

"Yeah, Okay." He slams the door in my face. When I get up to the fifth floor I tell my parents that he said okay. We wait for the heat to come hissing through the radiators. We are all wearing our winter coats waiting for the welcoming sound of sputtering, a sign that the heat is going to be up soon. We hear nothing. My father starts banging on the pipes, sending a message to all the tenants. Everyone below us joins in, banging, trying in vain to get a response from the super. We go to sleep wearing our coats over our pajamas. Will I always be cold, like I was in the furniture factory in Krakow, on the journey to Liebenau, on our trip to America, and as cold as we were in Switzerland? I feel like I'll never get warm in the winter.

A note in my mother's European handwriting is lying on the kitchen table; "Dear Rita, peel four or five potatoes, boil them, then you can mash them with some oleo. The meat is already sliced, so you only have to warm it up. Cut up an onion and fry it, then add the meat. Please, also, prepare the string beans that are in the fridge. I'll see all of you around 8 o'clock." The house feels so empty and lonely without her. In the past I used to come home to the sound of the radio, the smell of something cooking and the heat from the stove. Now that my mother has so many piano students and has to leave the house before 2 o'clock in order to get to Forest Hills by 3, I am in charge of getting dinner on the table. I'm feeling overburdened, overwhelmed and unappreciated. Between 4:30, when I get home from school and 10 P.M., when I go to sleep, I have to do my homework and spend at least two hours practicing. Dinner has to be ready by 5:30 when my father comes home, and I'm to clean up the kitchen. The rest of the evening is devoted to homework and practicing. I know my mother is keeping us afloat financially as she goes from one house to another giving piano lessons, but I miss her warm companionship and I resent the new tasks that are expected of me. I'm sixteen and I'm not ready to give up my mother's companionship.

During this time, my father is becoming more and more observant. New edicts are issued every week. Gone are the long Saturday afternoon trips to the library, he wears a hat every time he walks out of the door. "It is a sin to carry on Sabbath," my father tells us, as if I didn't pay dearly for that bit of knowledge. "It is a sin to turn on the lights, listen to the radio, write, answer the phone and tear on the Sabbath." We tear toilet paper squares on Friday afternoon, stash them in the bathroom and avoid a sin. We get a Sabbath clock which is plugged into a lamp. It turns the lights off on Friday night, whether I've finished what I was doing or not. When the lights go out, there is nothing to do other than to go to bed. I long to read, but it's too dark. The lights are turned on again of Saturday afternoon, at the same time, whether it is dark or not

It is Saturday afternoon; we are sitting at the Sabbath table finishing lunch. The table is made festive by a white table cloth protected by a plastic sheet, tall shining silver candle sticks that used to belong to my grandmother, a square bottle of purple Manischewitz kosher concord wine, and crumbs from the challah. My father and brother are wearing embroidered yarmulkes, long white sleeved shirts and ties. They have returned from the synagogue and we have finished eating. We are all relaxed and looking forward to the week end. We are chanting the *Birchat ha Mazon,* (grace after meals). The mood is suddenly shattered by my father's angry outburst.

"Lechem, not lehem," he spits out at me, emphasizing the guttural Hebrew ch sound. "Can't you learn to say it right?" His outburst is explosive, sudden and unprovoked. It shocks my whole body. I feel so dumb. I start to cry.

"Leave the table," he bellows, pointing his finger accusingly at me. "You're pissing through your eyeballs at my *Shabbes* table. You're disturbing my *Shabbes.*"

I run into the bathroom, hot with shame while the rest of the family returns to the *Birchat* as though nothing has happened. How clumsy and stupid I am. I hate myself. I resolve that I shall never cry again. I press my frozen tears into icicles and store them somewhere between my ribs and my stomach. I shall never cry again, I promise myself.

My father comes home between 5:30 and 6. He is unsmiling and uncommunicative at the dinner table. He berates Michael for coming home late and not getting to his homework on time. I feel desperate at these belittling sessions. I get angry at Michael myself. Why can't he do what he is supposed to do? Why does the atmosphere at the table always reek of anger? It's Michael's fault that my father is in a bad mood.

Michael appears unscathed by the verbal assaults. He is nodding his head as if in agreement with my father. It's as though he were talking about someone else; some stranger my brother would not bother defending. Michael is enjoying his dinner, which I prepared. I'm incensed. Why does he get all the attention for being bad, while I don't even get a "thank you" for preparing the dinner? I'm jealous of Michael. It's not only the attention he's getting. I envy his popularity with the opposite sex, his popularity among his own friends, his thinness, his unblemished complexion and his relaxed acceptance of my father's anger. I'm absorbing the brunt of rage over Michael's behavior, while Michael is nonchalant and seems entirely removed from it.

I'm angry at everyone in my family, especially Michael, who in spite of my father's wrath seems to be carefree, happy and popular. He's got everything I want, while I carry the guilt for his behavior strapped to my heart. One Saturday, I decide to rat on him. I tell my parents that he has gone to a friend's dormitory room at Yeshiva University Prep School, where several of his friends meet to smoke cigarettes and listen to the baseball game on the radio; all on Sabbath. My father reacts exactly as I had expected him to. He is furious. The cinders of his rage swirl about my head and shoulders.

"My son brings me nothing but shame!" he shouts at my mother and me. "He not only desecrates the Sabbath, but he does it in a religious school. Listening to the radio on *Shabbes* is not enough for him. He has to smoke as well." My father is out of control. "Whose room is he in that he feels comfortable smoking and listening to the radio?" I don't want to tell. At first I say I don't know. He persists, I must tell him or else, he threatens, he will go to the dormitory and bang on all the doors in order to find Michael and the rest of his hoodlum friends. If I didn't know him better, I might take this as an idle threat. But I'm familiar with his rage. When he's this angry nothing can restrain him. Now I have lost complete control of the situation and will have to deal with the demons that will pop out of the Pandora's Box I have brought into the house. I tell, I reveal Michael's accomplice.

"Really!" He exclaims, smiling, suddenly pleased, "Sammy Ehrnfeld? What a hypocrite his father is. He goes around the *Shul* telling everyone how *frum* (religious) his little Sammy is. My father rubs his hands in glee. His sense of vindication far outweighs his rage. "After *Shabbes* I'll give him a call and tell him what a "wonderful" son he has." My father can't wait for sundown. He derives visible satisfaction at being told about someone else's "bad" son. His anger at Michael subsides perceptibly.

Now I have not only ratted on Michael but on his friend as well. Michael comes home at sundown and is immediately dispatched to his room. "So, you were listening to the radio and smoking in Sammy's room today," my father accuses him, slapping his face. Michael doesn't wince. He's gotten big and strong, he doesn't cry anymore. "Get out of my sight. I'll deal with you later. First I'm going to make a phone call to that bragging hypocrite." My brother glares at me. There is only one person who could have betrayed him to my father and gotten his best friend into trouble at the same time.

I hear shouting from the hallway where the telephone stands on a little table.

My father comes into the living room. He is livid. "Imagine the nerve," he splutters to my mother. "Instead of being grateful that someone is looking out for his son's welfare, he tells me to mind my own business. He actually hung up on me. No wonder his son smokes on *Shabbes*. Ehrenfeld has no manners, he's not only disrespectful, he's rude. Imagine the nerve!" His angry mood is restored. Michael is forbidden to ever talk to Sammy again. "He's a bad influence on you," my father tells him. "His parents can't even take care of their own son. He lives in the dormitory because his parents are divorced and he has much too much freedom. Be happy you've got parents who care about you." Michael nods his head. He willingly agrees to sever his friendship with Sammy, as though it doesn't mean a thing to him, while I do not collect my reward for tattling. I am left with an empty feeling of betraying my friend and ally.

The only time I gain positive attention from my father is when I play the piano. He loves classical music and he enjoys listening to me. Although he never tells me directly, I believe that he thinks I am talented and I thrive in his silent praise.

"Play that passage again?" he asks me. I do as I am told.

"I would play it softly, *pianissimo,*" he advises, showing great interest and sensitivity to the music.

He sits back, reading the paper, listening carefully. He interrupts me every now and then with a comment or suggestion. I try to do as he says. I am finally being heard. He is actually listening and sharing his opinions with me without dictating or forcing his will on me. He often tells me that he would surely have played an instrument if given the opportunity. I love playing for him. I f eel as though we have a common bond; a silent language around the music that I am struggling with. It has nothing to do with Michael, this is all about me. His praise is hard to earn, and I am thrilled when he says "wonderful," after one of the pieces I play. I know that he looks forward to his evenings listening to me. I do my practicing after the dinner dishes are done so that I can bask in my father's appreciation.

Chapter Sixty-One

Forest Hills

My parents are arguing in the kitchen. "The rents in Forest Hills are very high. It is out of the question," I hear my father tell my mother when she broaches the topic of possibly moving. "Besides, I have my *shul* here, Sari lives nearby. We will not discuss it anymore." He makes his pronouncement and leaves the room.

Life continues at a predictable pace. Mike is being bad, punished and berated, while I am being "good," but not good enough to be rewarded, not even so much as an acknowledgement for the fact that I am now doing most of the household tasks in addition to my school work and practicing. My mother's schedule is becoming more and more hectic. She wants desperately to move to Forest Hills, where she could eliminate her travel time of two hours a day. My father won't hear of it. He's made his proclamation and as far as he's concerned the case is closed. Even though she contributes more money to our financial welfare than he does, he does not treat her as an equal. He is satisfied in Washington Heights, and Washington Heights is where he says he's staying.

My mother is not going to give up easily. Leaving of the house to go to work and bringing in money has given her new self-esteem and confidence. Without his knowledge, she has been investigating apartments in Forest Hills. She comes home one night and she is excited, she has found an apartment in Forest Hills that charges affordable rent. "I left a small deposit with the superintendent, and told him I'd be back to see it with my husband." She begs and cajoles my father into at least looking at it. He resists. "I told you weeks ago that the case is closed. I will not move to Forest Hills. If you love it there, then you go and move by yourself. Nobody cares about my needs," he adds.

The power of earning money has given her the gumption to stand up to him. "All right Alex, I understand how you feel, but I'll have to cut back on some of my lessons. I can't continue to teach four hours a day and spend two and a half hours on the subway. If you can't at least look at that apartment with me on Sunday, I will cut my schedule even though we've come to rely on the money. You know that I'll never move away from you, but I will take better care of myself."

I listen to her, astounded. "Atta girl!" I cheer silently, even though I don't want to move. "Show him he's not the only person in the world." This is the first time I've heard her challenge him and I realize that he's afraid she means what she says. She sounds strong, not the meek little person she's become since coming to America. Reluctantly, he agrees to look at the apartment, assuring her that it is only a look and not any kind of a commitment. On the following Sunday, they explore the neighborhood and my mother points out several synagogues, kosher butchers and bakeries. He spots two men walking on the street wearing skull caps, deeply engaged in conversation. This doesn't look as bad as he thought it would. He becomes less resistant to the idea of moving.

I am not happy. I have finally found a group of observant Jewish teenagers, girls and boys, who congregate in the neighborhood park on Saturday afternoons. I hate the idea of moving away from Washington Heights and giving up this bit of socializing, especially since my father has warned me that I could only date Orthodox boys. The Saturday meetings are informal, but they give me something to do on the long afternoons in the spring. I look forward to them eagerly. The boys are dormitory students at the Yeshiva Michael has been expelled from. He still has many good friends there and I tag along, happy to hang out with them and flirt with religiously acceptable boys. For the first time I am happy that the Saturday afternoons in the springtime are endless. A lot of good looking boys hang around in the park and I sense that they enjoy my company as much as I do theirs.

I get my first glimpse of the new apartment on moving day, a balmy day in March, when I take a day off from school to help. In no way does it compare to my expectation. I thought we'd be moving into a Forest Hills apartment building like Poldi's, with a uniformed doorman guarding an opulent lobby. Instead we move into a dark, ground floor apartment that doesn't have a lobby or carpeted hallways. The windows look out onto street, and when I peer outside, the view is one of shoes attached to legs, but no torsos or heads. The kitchen is too small to accommodate our formica table from Washington Heights and it can only fit two chairs and a small square card table.

"Gosh it's small," I tell my parents. "What are we going to do?" I ask "Take turns eating? We can't all fit inside this kitchen." My parents ignore my comment. They are busy directing the movers. There are two bedrooms; the smaller one can only accommodate a small bed and an unpainted dresser which doubles as a desk. Since Michael and I are much too old to share a room, we will take turns sleeping in this tiny space. For one week he will sleep in the living room on the sofa while I sleep in the little bedroom and then we will switch. The week ends in the living room are hard on us. The sofa has to be made up early, and we will not be able to catch up on our sleep for two weeks every month. Privacy is not even taken into consideration. The one sleeping on the sofa has to take clothing to the bathroom in order to get dressed. With one bathroom which doubles for a dressing room, and four people in the apartment, everyone is clamoring for its space every morning.

"Hurry up, you've been in there for an hour," I bang on the door to get Michael out. I have to get ready for school and there is no way I'll be on time if he hogs the bathroom all morning long. He takes his time. He is in no hurry. He's shaving and his school starts later than mine.

Getting to Music and Art, involves four train changes, and a one hour ride to and from school. In spite of the inconvenience I look forward to the travel. I get to ride with all my friends who live in Queens. We shout to each other to make ourselves heard above the roar of the train, scramble madly for empty seats, and sing the latest hits oblivious to the deafening noise and the amused or annoyed glances from our fellow passengers.

Michael and I have made several friends in the new neighborhood. They attend the same synagogue and are our age. We join a youth group that meets on Friday evenings after dinner at each house. We hang out in front of the synagogue on Saturday mornings and when the weather is good meet at the local park in the afternoon. I still miss the get-togethers with the Saturday afternoon kids, but I'm managing.

The move marks a significant change in the way my parents start to regard me. I hear talk about finding a suitable *shidduch* (marriage match). Are they serious? I ask myself. I'm only seventeen, still in high school. What sparks this sudden interest in my marriage-ability is the engagement of one of my new friends, Naomi. She has just gotten engaged and she's only seventeen.

My Forest Hills girl-friends and I are standing outside the synagogue one Saturday when Naomi comes flouncing down the street, holding her hand in front of her face, admiring it so attentively that she trips over a crack in the sidewalk.

"Hello ladies," she chirps. "Wanna see something gorgeous?" She holds her left hand up for inspection.

"Wow, what a rock!" Regina exclaims, squealing, grabbing Naomi's hand and holding it up to the sun. "Tell all!"

We crowd around her. Naomi is a pretty girl, tall thin, with long blond hair which she wears in a page boy. She goes to Forest Hills High School and I know she is a member of ARISTA, the honor society.

"It was a blind date, (which I happen to know is the Americanized term for *shidduch* in an arranged match) He is just what I've been dreaming about all my life."

"What does he look like? How old is he? What does he do?" We bombard her with questions. We need to know everything about him.

Naomi savors her celebrity status. "Well," she hesitates before going on, "he's much older than I am; well, twenty-two, but he's very smart."

"Yeah, what is he? What does he do? Is he still in school? What's he studying?" The questions come at her so quickly, she can't respond rapidly enough to satisfy our curiosity.

"He's in the diamond business. This stone is two and a half carats and perfect, blue-white." Naomi smiles, holds up her left hand, admiring her ring.

"Did he go to college? What did he study?" We're eager; we surround her, clamoring for answers.

"Um, no. Well... yes," Naomi is not sure how to answer. "He takes courses at City College," she pauses, "at night," she adds." He's studying Business."

"When do we get to meet him?" Maya asks.

"When are you getting married?"

"What does he look like?"

Our curiosity is only overshadowed by our envy. Me? I am slowly turning the color of lettuce. What I wouldn't give to be engaged!

My father comes home from Shul that afternoon. "Such a wonderful *shidduch*," he says. "She managed to get the richest boy in the diamond club." I can see that I am not the only one who is envious. Marriage is the ultimate goal for every girl in the 50's, especially within the Orthodox community. Being an old maid is a fear that is harbored in my breast as well as in all my girlfriends' breasts. I am hardly eligible for old maid status, but already minds are spinning. I love the idea of getting married young, being desirable and pursued. I haven't had a serious boyfriend yet, but that doesn't keep me from dreaming. I believe in love at first sight and hope I meet him soon.

And then I meet Richard, Naomi's fiancé. He comes to spend *Shabbes* with her family and she brings him to *Shul*. He is an ugly, little man, with a thick pot belly, receding hair line and is perspiring visibly under his gray fedora. He stares at the ground as she introduces him. I don't believe my eyes. How could she settle for someone is so dull, so homely? He is about four inches shorter than she is and looks like an old man: thirty, at least. He is wearing a navy blue suit that stretches across his middle. I look at his feet, his shiny black oxfords, tiny, like a little kid's. I can't imagine going to bed with someone who must have such white feet. How is Naomi going to spend one night with him, let alone a lifetime? I feel resentment creeping up against her, betrayal, disappointment and anger. She "copped" out, took herself off the marriage market, and for what? I am positive that she can't be in love with him. Is she so afraid of being an old maid that she needs to settle for him at this point in her life? She has violated some private ethic that I must be harboring; done what I swore I would never do: marry someone I wasn't in love with. I cross her off my list. I have lost all respect for her.

I look around at my other friends. No one seems as disapproving as I am feeling.

"Are you getting married after graduation, next year?" Randy asks her.

"I'm not going back to school in September," she tells us. "I don't need any diplomas or degrees now," she says confidently. "I'm getting my MRS. and that's good enough for me: my own apartment, my own dishes, a big bedroom with beautiful furniture, a living room set with a sectional sofa. What else do I need?"

I am annoyed with myself. Why am I taking this so personally? Am I scared that I too might feel pressured into marrying an ugly, old man? Everyone else is taking it in their stride, while I'm so upset with his appearance. I imagine giving up romance and love for the sake of safety: cooking, shopping and cleaning for this little man, for rest of my life. Is this what it's all about, I ask myself? The ring is beautiful and Naomi appears to be happy. Well, at least Naomi did not get the best man possible. There's still a chance for me.

In Music and Art being popular with the opposite sex is a valued asset. Many of the popular girls are pinned to college men. On Mondays the girls talk about their dates on the weekend. I talk also, but most of my dates are the result of imagination and wishful thinking. In my generation, having a date on Saturday night is a critical symbol of desirability and status. Rules of dating are clear. This is before a girl would dream of phoning a boy. No self respecting girl would ever admit to phoning a guy. Some of the boys in school call me and ask me out, but they are the ones who are unappealing. I couldn't think of kissing them good-night. Most Saturday nights, I choose to baby-sit or stay home and dream about my ideal boyfriend; tall, thin, curly dark haired, funny and smart and with preferably blue eyes. So far, I have never met such a man, let alone dated one. I would love some attention from such a boy, but since Wally, I haven't gotten any.

I am attracted to several boys in school, but they are not interested in me and I can't bring myself to go out with someone I don't feel attracted to, who might want to kiss me good night. I suddenly miss Wally and our bathroom encounters in Washington Heights.

"Please Mike," I beg, "call Wally and ask him how he's doing." I wouldn't dream of calling him myself. He says no. I bribe him promising him the use of the bedroom for three weeks in a row. Mike makes the call.

"May I speak to Wally?" I hear him say clearly.

He hangs up a few seconds later, laughing.

"What happened? Did you speak to him?"

He looks at me shaking his head in disbelief. "His father answered." Mike laughs again, "what a shmuck. You know what his dad said to me? He said, 'my son's name is *Valter* not *Vally.*' And he is not going to talk on the telephone to you Michael Schmelkes! Then the old man hangs up." Michael is hysterical. He repeats "*Valter not Vally.*"

Chapter Sixty-Two

The Dress

I have just turned eighteen but am still in high school because I am half a year behind. My mother suggests that on Friday afternoon, we go shopping for a nice new dress for me. "In fact, "she says, "we'll go to Ruth's Dresses."

There's got to be a reason for this, I think. It's not my birthday; I'm not going to anyone's wedding and I'm not even near to graduation.

"How come?" I ask suspiciously.

"You've stopped growing so you'll be able to keep it for a few years. You're already eighteen and I think it will be nice for you to have a good dress, something special."

Ruth's, the "expensive" store is a small shop, nestled between several boutiques on a pretty side street in Forest Hills.

"May I help you?" The saleslady has a French accent. She's wearing a smart black dress with a light blue silk scarf draped over one shoulder. She wants to make a statement about herself and the store: appear sophisticated and elegant. When my mother tells her why we are there, she looks at us appraisingly. "How much are you interested in spending?" My mother who only knows that Ruth's Dresses are expensive doesn't want to appear out of her element.

"It doesn't matter," she tells her indifferently. She remembers shopping at expensive stores before the war and never having to ask the price of anything. She puts on a fake rich tone of voice, "we don't care, just show us what you've got in a size ten."

The saleslady is not mollified. She hesitates, as though assessing our finances. She puts me off. I'm feeling poor. I'm much more comfortable shopping at Lerner's or Alexander's where no one cares what I want to try on. She purses her lips moving her head to one side. "Is this a dress for a

214

formal occasion? Do you want something for the evening? Or do you want something tailored?"

We have a very good idea what we want. I want something that will make me look thin and my mother wants something that is not expensive. That probably narrows the choice to about two dresses. Of course, we don't share this information with her.

"We're not sure," my mother says, unwilling to close off any options.

She persists, undaunted. "Do you want wool, silk, knit, linen?" When she sees us hesitate, she goes on arrogantly, "you have to tell me. We have many dresses in the back and I can't possibly bring out everything we have in a size ten."

Why not? I say to myself. You have no other customers in the store and you don't seem to have anything else to do. I watch them, the saleslady and my mother. They seem to be having a silent war: defending some undisclosed territory, protecting who they are from the other. I wonder. Can she see through us and realize we are poor, and that we probably will not be able to afford anything in her store anyway?

My mother regains her footing. She remembers what it was like being rich. She squares her shoulders and addresses her in an imperious tone, "show us something in wool, preferably a bright color."

She brings out several dresses. I try them on. My only criteria is "do they make me look fat?"

"How do I look?" I ask my mother.

"Hmm, maybe a little bit fat," she says looking at the price tag and realizing that this it is more than she is willing to spend.

"Take it away, I don't want it!" I peel it off and discard it, just as if it were a layer of unwanted fat.

After a half hour of trying on everything she brings out we finally find the perfect dress. It is pink wool, fitted at the waistline with a full skirt, affordable and, most important of all does not make me look fat. I love it. I inspect myself from every angle and decide that I am beautiful. I never give another thought to what it was that spurred this project although the plan has been germinating in my father's brain ever since Naomi came to Shul with her big diamond.

Chapter Sixty-Three

Dating Jewish

My father speaks to my Uncle Avrom, who speaks to a friend of his, and word is out. They are looking to make *shidduch* for me. I am the subject of discussion between my father and my uncle. I wonder how they're going to go about it, but do not ask. I continue my senior year in high school, making plans of my own. I know that I want to go to college and that it will most likely be Queens College, which is close to my house and is free to students who qualify academically.

"Alex, you have a telephone call," my mother calls to my father. "It's Avrom."

My father so rarely receives a phone call that the whole family becomes interested. We hover around him, catching only his side of the conversation, spoken in Yiddish. He nods his head in agreement with my uncle, not in the least bit mindful of the fact that the only ones who see him agreeing are my mother and I. When he gets off, his face is shiny with excitement. He beckons my mother to go into the bedroom. I put my ear up against the door, but I can't make sense of their whispered conversation.

"Uncle Avrom met a very nice young man in Shul," he tells me when he comes out. "He told him about you and now he wants to meet you. Do you want to go out with him on Sunday?"

Ohhhhh, I say to myself. Now I understand the reason for the expensive dress from Ruth's. It's not a reward for my growing up, or my good behavior; it's gift wrap for my body to package me for the marriage market. If it's someone like Richard, Naomi's fiancé, I will die. But on the other hand, I say to myself, he might be more like Wally.

"Who is this 'young man'? What does he look like and what does he do, and how old is he?" My father has never seen him or spoken to him but he

216

knows that he is a professor of French literature in one of the city colleges and that he's a little bit older than I am. "A little bit older?" I ask, skeptically. I think of Richard who was only twenty-two and looked like an old man.

I put on my new dress and sit in the living room. Joseph Winetraub, Professor Joseph Winetraub, comes to pick me up. He is thirty-three, shorter than I am, and I am only 5'2." He is very polite, shakes hands with my father and bows his head in a continental manner to my mother. I look at him and inhale sharply. He is carrying an umbrella! No one I know carries an umbrella. Well, that's not true, my mother carries one when she has to go out in the rain. Once, when caught in a downpour, I wished I had an umbrella. But today it is only drizzling. How am I going to get through this day, I wonder. And what will I do if we meet someone I know?

We go to a vegetarian restaurant on 47th Street in Manhattan, a restaurant endorsed by the Orthodox community in New York. We talk quietly, but I just can't get over how disappointed I am. Poor guy, I say to myself. His looks are not his fault, but, I tell myself, trying to console my guilty conscience, my feelings are not my fault either. He starts eating and I notice that his hands are smaller than mine, petite even.

"Are you taking French in high school?" he asks me, trying to make conversation.

"No," I answer politely, "my father thought that Spanish would be more useful to me, given the fact that there are so many Spanish speaking people in New York."

"True, true," he agrees taking a bite of his potato *latke* (pancake). I look around the restaurant and notice other religious couples talking earnestly. To me all of them appear to be mismatched. The girls are young, well dressed, nice looking, with smooth page boys and shiny hair. The men are much older, wearing suits and ties and haven't got a trace of their boyhood left. They are "men" with "girls." What makes these pretty girls so able to trade their youth for the safety of marriage, I wonder? Joseph is a nice enough man and I'm sure he realizes that we are not going to be a couple. I try to be pleasant and attentive, but I can't wait to get home and do my homework.

My parents are waiting, expectantly in the living room for me. "Well?" they inquire, "how was it?"

I answer with a Polish quotation I've heard my mother use, "*ste monki chleba niebencze,* (there will be no bread from this flour)." My father shrugs his shoulders. Much to my surprise, he doesn't seem disappointed at all, in fact, if I didn't know better, I would say he looks relieved. Maybe he realizes the folly of attempting such a match. "There will be others," he tells me, thinking I need to be reassured. "Besides," he admits, "you really have to finish high school and hopefully go to college."

My father appears to be as conflicted as I am. On one level, I feel that I must go to college, become more educated. I don't feel ready to give up my youth. On the other hand, I desperately want to get married, get out of this house and be on my own. I know that my father loves me more than anyone in this world. He has often told me that his way of expressing this love is by constantly trying to keep me safe, make me into being the best that I can be; his version of the perfect young girl. It becomes apparent to me much later, that he is terribly frightened of losing me to someone who will not be able to provide for me, who will force me to live the same insecure life that he is living. He tells me that he realizes that I am growing up and closer to woman-hood than girlhood.

In a rare moment of intimacy, he calls me into the bedroom and closes the door. We sit on the bed and I look in the mirror at our reflections. He looks small, strangely vulnerable, not the angry father I am used to. It is more uncomfortable for me to be with this strange, gentle father than the shouting man I've gotten used to. He takes my hand and looks into my eyes. I can see that he is struggling with some inner demons.

"I want you to go to college, become independent, be able to support yourself and never have to rely on anyone else," he tells me. "Women need a profession just as much as men do. Look at your cousin Elsie. Being a doctor did not stop her from getting married." I wonder, is he talking to me or trying to convince himself of the need for me to get an education? "The only difference between her and most women her age is that she can afford to buy a big, beautiful house, hire a housekeeper to clean for her and take care of her children while pursuing a highly respected profession." I agree with him. Elsie does, indeed have a rewarding life.

He reminds me. "If I had a profession I would never have had to worry about paying for food and rent." He continues, not sure of what he will say next, "but on the other hand, there comes a time when it is important for a girl to get married. You go beyond a certain age and you close off your choices. I know how men feel," he adds, "They want a pure, young pretty wife. And once you get into your twenties there are fewer choices. " I realize that he's in turmoil, sending me two messages. Get an education and get married, and that somehow he is sure that the two are mutually exclusive. I suddenly feel sorry for him. He really thinks that he can make choices for me, as if they were his for the making, or even mine for that matter?

My uncle has not given up his in his pursuit of the ideal suitor.

"Max," my father tells me several days after my date with Joseph, "is younger than Joseph and not as serious as Joseph. Uncle Avrom assured me that they have nothing in common. Would you be willing to go out with him?"

I feel sympathy for my father. I can see that he is not anxious to marry me off at this moment, but now that Uncle Avrom has been dispatched and is trying so hard, my father does not want to take his efforts for granted. And maybe "this Max" will be all that he and I hope for.

"Just go out with 'this Max,' and I will tell Uncle Avrom to stop looking," he is almost pleading with me.

"Sure, why not. But please, daddy, if this doesn't work out, let's give it a rest."

"Absolutely," my father agrees emphatically.

Max is leaning across the table towards me, at the same vegetarian restaurant I had gone to with Joseph. He is intense, his eyes are shining. "A beautiful photograph of a perfect piece of jewelry is a work of art, just like a masterpiece by a famous artist." Unlike Joseph, who was ever so courteous, educated and even deferential in his manner, Max is tall, broad, loud and cocky. To me, he appears to be flouting his ignorance.

"What are you saying?" I ask disdainfully. "That a snapshot of a necklace on a piece of velvet has as much artistic merit as a painting by Vermeer?" I have just taken a class on the Dutch masters and Vermeer's masterpieces, with their windows casting light on beautiful young girls are clear in my mind.

He says it does. I look at him and I realize that he doesn't know who Vermeer is, has probably never even been to a museum or art gallery. "The beautiful photographs in our winter catalogue have brought in more money than any paintings I have seen."

"Do you rate art by its monetary value, or by its beauty?" I ask, incredulously.

"Monetary, shmonetary, whatever you call it," he says, "money is what makes the world go round."

No you idiot, I say to myself, it's "love that makes the world go round." I say nothing and continue eating my vegetables while my soul is on fire. What a Plebe, I think. I control myself and do not say what is on the tip of my tongue. It is obvious that I am not going to marry any one of the "nice young men" my uncle fixes me up with. I think about Naomi and Richard. I'm not going to settle for a loser at the age of eighteen.

Max calls me up on Monday night and asks me out again. I tell him I am busy and that I will be busy for the next few weeks; that I am studying for college exams and won't be able to go out with him.

He gets upset, "I've never heard of a girl who has to study all day long, every day of the week." He tells his match maker, who tells my uncle, who tells my father, who tells me, that he thinks I am immature, not ready for marriage, that I am only an adolescent.

I have started dating a boy my father totally disapproves of. David is an Israeli boxer who is in this country. I have no idea why he is here, only that he is being sponsored by some rich Jewish guy, who is a boxing fan. I meet David at a school party. He came along with one of the kids. David is a hunk. He is gorgeous, and for some reason he starts lavishing all his attention on me. We dance; he gets way too close to me, but not close enough. He insists on bringing me home when I say I have to leave in time for my curfew. He comes to pick me up for a date on the following Saturday night. My father hates him, at first sight, as soon as they are introduced. When I come home later on that evening, he is in the living room waiting for me.

"I don't want you going out with that boxer again," he tells me, spitting out the word "boxer."

"Why, what's wrong with him? He's Jewish, he's even from Israel."

"I don't like him for you. I know men like this. He is interested in only one thing. Do I have to spell it out for you?"

"Yes," I say. "You do." I am furious with him for implying that all that a handsome boy could see in me was my sexual availability. "You are so afraid that I'm a tramp that you are scared to even use the word 'sex' with me." I shout at him, "just because he doesn't look like one of the creeps Uncle Avrom calls a 'fine young man,' doesn't mean that I am going to jump into bed with him. And for your information, daddy, sex is what most boys want from girls, even the religious creeps in their old man fedoras."

For a moment my father is speechless. He is shocked, astounded at my reaction. He recovers after a few seconds, "How dare you speak to me like that? I have nothing but your best interest at heart. This is not a man for you. What are you going to do? Marry a boxer?"

"I am not going to marry anyone right now. Besides, David has not asked me and I only went out on one date with him." I resent the fact that my father has set himself up as the guardian of my virginity. I continue going out with David. My father's suspicions strengthen my resolve to do as I wish. In truth, I find David boring after a few dates. All he talks about is boxing, his diet, his exercises and our dates consist of his sponsor's driver picking me up to take us to the Eastern Parkway Arena to watch David in a preliminary fight. I sit in the front row cringing at the sound of a gloved fist crushing a nose. From where I sit, I not only see blood spurt out of noses but hear bones crunch. I come to hate boxing, the punching, the screaming crowds shouting "kill him, kill him:" men staggering, panting, sweating exposing their bodies to such brutality.

I hate to admit it but my father was not wrong in his assessments of David's motives. I will never tell him he was right, he needs no encouragement from me to prove his point. After our "dates" are over, David and I sit in the back seat of the car where we make out until I am dropped off. He is so crude. The minute we get into the car he is groping and pushing himself on me. He doesn't make any attempt to talk to me, ask me how I feel, or even discuss the fight he just participated in. He never compliments me, even though I take great pains with my appearance before I go to the fight. My friends go out on dates to the Copacabana, the Latin Quarter and to the theater. He has never so much as treated me to a soda. I decide not to tell my father about my feelings for David.

He is so obsessed with the idea of sexual promiscuity on my part that he doesn't realize I've stopped seeing David. It is a Sunday morning and I am waiting on the subway platform in Forest Hills. I'm meeting a friend, spending the afternoon at the Museum of Modern Art. We're doing a paper on Picasso's "Guernica," and having an early supper after that. The trains are running slowly, typical for a Sunday morning. I walk up and down the platform, peering into the dark tunnel hoping to draw the train into the station. Suddenly, I am certain that I have spied my father out of the corner of my eye. I turn around quickly, but only see a large post. My imagination, I tell myself. I get on the train and take out a book to read. I look up for a moment and again I think I have spotted my father. I look out of the window at the black tunnel walls, refusing to let my imagination control my mind. When I get off at 53rd Street, there is no mistaking it. My father has darted behind a pole trying to appear invisible. He follows me onto the street and then I lose sight of him. What is going on? I ask myself. He scrutinizes me when I return. He is looking for something, trying to glean information. I feel as if I am being accused of a crime I haven't committed.

"Where did you go," he asks me, as if he doesn't know.

"You know where I went. I saw you. I told you I was meeting Paula at the Museum."

We continue playing cat and mouse. I can so easily put his mind at rest, if I tell him I am no longer seeing David. But would he believe me? I am not sure that he trusts me and I don't feel like defending myself for something I didn't do

Chapter Sixty-Four

Leaving Paradise

The spring semester has started. It will be my last one in Music and Art. We are the big shots, wearing our senior caps, maroon and blue, the school colors. My year book, "Con Brio" the name of graduating class is tucked under my arm. We walk around the hallways covered with the paintings of our fellow students, the art majors and we hug and cry, we don't want to graduate, but at the same time we can't wait to go to college. Music and Art has been a haven for all of us. This is the safe place to express ourselves, do what we love the most and do the best.

I sit at the piano. I am accompanying my friend Willy Schulsinger for his senior performance final. It is sometime in May and the windows are open. The fluttering breeze is making my music rustle the music on the piano stand. I'm hoping it doesn't blow off. I wonder for a minute if some eager applicant is walking underneath the window and hearing Willy's voice, just as I heard someone singing only a few years ago. Willy is wearing a navy blue suit with a red tie for the occasion. His arms are spread out, his head is tilted to one side, his voice is beautiful, full throated, deep baritone. He sings one of the German *lieder, "Ich Liebe Dich,* I Love You." I am praying that I don't make a mistake and throw him off. I listen to the singing and the words as I accompany, following him. I understand German. The song takes on extraordinary significance for me. He is singing a love song to our school; to my school, to my life. I burst out crying when he finishes. Once again, I am forced to leave a place I love. Running is what I've done all my life: away from the familiar toward the unknown, leaving the places and the people I love in order to start all over again as a new person in a strange place. I run out of the room, ashamed of my tears.

Willy tries to understand. He consoles me with a hug.

"We'll stay in touch," he tells me. "Music and Art is just a beginning of our lives."

Epilogue

After many decades of introspection, with the help of my therapist and the gift of maturity, I am able to get a better perspective on what drove my life. My father was a sad, bitter, and disenfranchised man. Having come to America and starting life over as a factory worker robbed him of his self-esteem and his standing in the Jewish community. He was tormented by inner conflicts: as a learned Talmudic scholar he expected his son to share his passion for learning holy texts. He was also aware that his lack of secular education robbed him of social standing and the ability to earn a living. He wanted both for my brother, who wanted neither.

Nothing prepared him for the reality of raising children, let alone children who had survived the terrors experienced by Michael and myself. Nevertheless my father took complete charge of us; our education, our social life, the clothes we wore, and even the books we read. My mother, who had been solely responsible for our welfare had a more gentle approach to child rearing than he had, but the years of war had drained her and she was anxious to relinquish some of her burdens.

By the time we arrived in New York, the war was coming to a close. My father's job as a leather cutter in the war industry was ending and he found it very difficult to find any employment. He tried to open a leather jacket factory and go into business for himself, but there was no call for leather jackets. Nylon was becoming available and most people preferred it to the heavy, stiff coats and jackets that were made of leather. He lost his entire investment when his business failed and he found himself unemployed and unemployable.

My father was frightened of losing me to a secular world, to sexual promiscuity, to becoming too smart to attract a husband, and to spinsterhood. He tried to control my every move in order to do whatever he thought would

223

protect me. His fears and obsessions and even his love for me were expressed through raging outbursts. They contributed to making me the frightened person, who took on his obsessions as well as his depressions. More than anything else, more than the education, the music, the diplomas, what I wanted most was the approval, admiration and respect of my father.

When my mother came to America she hardly knew the man she had married so long ago. By 1945, they had spent more time apart than they had together and she was eager to surrender the awesome duties of looking out for us to my willing father. In that process she lost much of her own sense of self, her spontaneity, sense of humor, her ability to adjust to life as it was rather than the way it should be. While I cannot forgive her for giving my things away to my cousin, I do realize that on some level she needed to restore a measure of dignity to herself. She probably felt that the only way to do that was to appear rich and successful to her older sister. She knew she was safe with me, that I would always love her no matter what she did. And she was right in that respect.

As for Michael, he did not become the dismal failure my father feared. He is a successful businessman having exceeded all expectations by building and becoming a CEO of a global enterprise as well as a published author.

I was a lucky person. Very few Jewish children survived the Holocaust and had the good fortune I have had. But the older I get, the more I realize that this period affected my entire life, and although, for years I denied that it had any relevancy to my life, I am now able to accept the fact that there is not a day that goes by, that I don't feel its terror. For me, as well as other survivors, the war did not end with the signing of the peace treaty.